AF248640

STUDIES IN SYNTAX AND SEMANTICS

FOUNDATIONS OF LANGUAGE

SUPPLEMENTARY SERIES

Editors

MORRIS HALLE, *MIT*

PETER HARTMANN, *Münster/W.*

K. KUNJUNNI RAJA, *Madras*

BENSON MATES, *Univ. of California*

J. F. STAAL, *Univ. of California*

PIETER A. VERBURG, *Groningen*

JOHN W. M. VERHAAR (Secretary), *Djakarta*

VOLUME 10

HUMANITIES PRESS / NEW YORK

STUDIES IN SYNTAX AND SEMANTICS

Edited by

F. KIEFER

D. REIDEL PUBLISHING COMPANY / DORDRECHT-HOLLAND

PREFACE

In the last decade a profound change has occurred in linguistic science. Not only have old problems been tackled from an entirely new point of view but also quite a few new fields of linguistic research have been opened. The common characteristic of the majority of the theories and methods developed recently is the search for a more adequate description of language. Adequacy does not mean simply that the theory must conform to the facts. It must also meet the general requirements of present-day theories: coherence, clear-cut notions, rigor of presentation. It has also become abundantly clear that linguistic research cannot be content with the registration and classification of linguistic phenomena. In one way or another linguistics must try to explain the deep-seated regularities in language which in general do not appear on the surface in some straightforward way. Therefore, we find the attribute 'deep' very often in contemporary linguistic literature. Linguistic theories seek an explanation for the observed facts in terms of a system of hypotheses about the functioning of language. As research proceeds these will undergo essential changes. Some of them will be waived, others complemented.

The papers of the present volume follow these general principles of linguistic theory though they may differ from each other in the way of presentation considerably. Some of the papers make use of the framework of transformational-generative grammar (e.g. Kuroda; Perlmutter), others approach the pertinent problem from a different angle (e.g. Dupraz and Rouault; Apresyan, Mel'čuk, and Žolkovski).

Some of these papers (Bierwisch and Kiefer; Brekle; Dupraz and Roualt; Fillmore; Kuroda; Perlmutter) were presented at a symposium held in Balatonszabadi (Hungary), September 7–10, 1968. The lively discussions they raised during and after the conference suggested the idea of presenting them to the public. Apart from the aforementioned papers, four others were included in the present volume. Their authors, though invited, were unable to attend the symposium (Apresyan, Mel'čuk, and Žolkovski; Bellert; Sgall; Petőfi).

Apart from the fact that all these papers represent a certain trend of modern linguistic thought, they discuss particularly timely problems. The structure of the lexicon is one of them. What types of information must be covered by an adequate description of the lexicon? How should lexical relationships be represented? What is the role of definitions in natural language? These are the central concerns of several papers (Fillmore; Apresyan, Mel'čuk, and Žolkovski; Bierwisch and Kiefer). The deep semantic structure of sentences is discussed from various points of view by another series papers (Bellert; Brekle; Dupraz and Rouault). Some intricate problems of generative grammar (presuppositions vs. selection restrictions, deep structure constraints) are tackled by Kuroda and Perlmutter. Finally, Petőfi's paper makes an attempt at the application of linguistic theory to the analysis of poetic works of art.

It is hoped that scope and variety of the contributions to this volume represents a balanced cross section of research in progress and will offer something of interest to workers in the various fields of linguistic science.

F.K.

Budapest, May 31, 1969

TABLE OF CONTENTS

YU. D. APRESYAN, I. A. MEL'ČUK AND A. K. ŽOLKOVSKY

SEMANTICS AND LEXICOGRAPHY: TOWARDS A NEW TYPE OF UNILINGUAL DICTIONARY

In this paper we shall be concerned with the lexicographic implications of the semantic model aiming at automatic synthesis of natural (Russian) texts. The general design of the model and its main components (a deep vocabulary and syntax and a system of semantic equations generating sets of synonymous Russian sentences for every input meaning) are outlined elsewhere.[1] We assume at least a superficial knowledge of the relevant details on the part of the reader and in the present publication limit ourselves to a rather sketchy outline of a special type of dictionary underlying the 'meaning-text' model in question.

The variety of the existing types of unilingual dictionaries stems from the diversity of purposes they serve. In effect, conventional explanatory dictionaries, dictionaries of borrowed and rare words, of acronyms and abbreviations, phraseological dictionaries, etc. supply information about the meaning of language units concerned; a dictionary of synonyms enables the speaker of the language to choose in a group of synonymous words the ones which most adequately convey his idea; phraseological dictionaries serve a similar purpose; ideological dictionaries place at the user's disposal sets of lexical units pertinent to a given subject of conversation, and so forth. Each such dictionary contains but a minor part of the information necessary to build an entire text from the outset, i.e. to construct standard sentences of the language proceeding from some initial meaning.

The idea of a dictionary displaying the process of text generation as an integral succession of steps has never been clearly stated by lexicographers, let alone its implementation. *The dictionary under consideration has precisely this aim in view.*

The dictionary is based on the following principle: it must be fully sufficient for a smooth, idiomatic and flexible expression of a given meaning; that is to say, it must display in an explicit and logical form whatever information may be necessary for the correct choice and usage of words and phrases to convey a given idea in a given speech context.[2]

The attempt to implement that principle most consistently has determined the essential novelty and peculiar pattern of the proposed dictionary, which does not fit into the framework of traditional lexicographic classifications. The dictionary takes its name – tolkovo-combinatornyi (lit. 'explanatory and combinatory') – from its two basic properties.

F. Kiefer (ed.), Studies in Syntax and Semantics, 1–33. © *D. Reidel, Dordrecht-Holland*

It has been labelled "combinatory" because it is primarily intended to display the combinatorial properties of words – the range of their syntactical and lexical combinability. The description of combinability with the help of a new conceptual apparatus (see below) is the chief concern of the authors.

It distinguishes the dictionary under consideration from other unilingual dictionaries.

The word "explanatory" has its usual sense, the only difference being that "explanation" is practised not only with regard to the entry words, but also with regard to word combinations and syntactic government patterns. The latter are thus semantically interpreted. The principle of overall semantic interpretation of all language facts registered in the dictionary springs from the goal set forth above: to provide for an idiomatic expression of any given meaning.

The "explanatory and combinatory" dictionary (ECD) of Modern Russian, therefore, is an essentially "active" dictionary, to use the term coined by L. V. Ščerba, or "a dictionary of synthesis" (in the terminology of computational linguistics). An idealized situation for the use of ECD might be visualized as follows: an educated foreigner, say, a scientist or a journalist, having a rudimentary knowledge of Russian but a clear understanding of the idea he wants to convey, begins by putting it in his poor Russian; he then resorts to ECD which enables him to convert the originally crude expression of the intended meaning, clumsy and unacceptable to the native speaker, into good idiomatic Russian.

The reader should keep this picture in mind in order to get a clear understanding of the dictionary structure.

The structure of the proposed dictionary is fundamentally different from the structure of current unilingual dictionaries in that its entry has a much more involved logical arrangement and contains greater linguistic information than is common in conventional dictionaries.

To arrange the whole universe of Russian words in conformity with a new and unusual system world be too tall an order. It appears reasonable therefore to begin with a tentative version of the dictionary having a relatively small number of entries (approximately two thousand). It should be emphasized that the number of entries in ECD does not give a sufficient idea of the size of its word list (i.e. the number of language units furnished with an adequate description), since in this dictionary each entry characterizes a great many words having some semantic relation to the entry word.

The majority of entry words have been selected from the abstract vocabulary commonly employed for conversation on most different subjects: politics, the humanities, science, and everyday life. Each such lexical item has rich syntactic properties, makes part of a great number of set expressions, and displays a specific semantic nature which precludes its direct interpretation. It is exactly this property of abstract words which makes them so difficult to learn and which calls for the special lexicographic approach that the authors of ECD have tried to develop.

The description of the entry structure, illustrated by a few examples, will give a clearer idea of the dictionary. The following format of the entry is envisaged (all the new terms will be explained later on):

(1) Entry word.

(2) Morphological information.

(3) Definition.

(4) Government pattern (the syntactic potentialities of the word), conditions of the compatibility of the dependent units, and examples of how the government pattern is manifested in actual phrases.

(5) Regular lexical functions.

(6) Non-regular lexical functions.

(7) The "lexical universe" of the entry word.

(8) Examples.

(9) Phraseology.

(10) Discrimination of synonyms and near-synonyms.

Let us now discuss every point successively.

As concerns *the entry word*, two things must be noted.

1. ECD treats as lexical units not only single words but also such set phrases as учебное заведение, железная дорога, давать по рукам, ломать голову, первым долгом, etc., that is, word combinations which resemble words in that they have a definition of their own and, which is more important, a peculiar combinability pattern (cf. окончить учебное заведение, выпуск учебного заведения etc., while similar combinations with заведение are impossible).

2. The traditional "homonymy-or-polysemy" problem is solved in ECD in the following way. Two graphically coincident words are considered homonyms if their definitions have no common part. Homonyms are given as separate entries with different diacritical marks: e.g. КОСА[1] (scythe), КОСА[2] (braid of hair) and КОСА[3] (spit). Two definitions having a common part are considered different meanings of a polysemantic word and are treated within the same entry. Two essentially different cases are typographically distinguished:

(1) The difference between two meanings of a word is regular, i.e. occurs in a number of words. Thus the meaning relation "place – the occupants of place" occurs in the words класс, стол, трюм etc. (cf. Класс был пуст and Класс встал). Such meanings are numbered by means of Arabic numerals.

(2) The difference between two meanings of a word is irregular, or unique e.g. the meaning relation гора – обувь occurs only in the pair подошва ≈ нижняя часть обуви [3] – подошва ≈ нижняя часть горы. Such meanings are numbered by means of Roman numerals.

As a result, the meaning structure of a polysemantic word, e.g. the word подошва, takes on the following form:

ПОДОШВА   I. 1. нижняя часть обуви
                 2. часть ступни, соответствущая подошве I.1.
             II. нижняя часть горы

(the regularity of the relation between I.1 and I.2 can be illustrated by the pairs *пояс* 'ремень' – *пояс* 'талия', *носок* [ботинка] – *носок* [ступни] cf. also *колено ноги* and *колено брюк, грудь человека* and *грудь рубашки*, etc).

Morphological information has the form of a simple code referring to a certain grammatical table, such as the well-known grammatical tables of A. A. Zaliznyak. This code points to the possibility or non-possibility and the exact procedure of generating all the word-forms of the key word.

The definition of a key word should not go beyond the current idea of its meanings inherent in the ordinary usage of the man in the street. It should not take into account the "encyclopaedic" aspects of a word's meaning present in the terminological usage of an expert; cf. the difference in the understanding and employment of the words *ягода, преступление, прибыль* etc. by an ordinary speaker (even an intellectual) and by a botanist, a lawyer, and an economist respectively.

Definitions in ECD should meet the following requirements commonly disregarded in lexicography:

(1) Definitions should not be circular, i.e. should not define A through B and B through A (as is very often the case in Ozhegov's dictionary of Russian and other current dictionaries: *большой* = 'значительный по размерам…', *значительный* = 'большой по размерам' …, etc). If this requirement is met, all the definitions will in the long run be reduced to a small number of indefinable units of meaning (elementary meanings) [4]. However they should not immediately resolve into elementary meanings but should do so through a number of intermediate stages, each stage being represented by a combination of nonprimitive meanings having specific lexical manifestations in the given language.

Thus, *покушаться (на кого-либо)* = 'пытаться убить незаконно (человека) [5], where all the three components of meaning are semantically complex words resolving in their turn into simpler components, i.e. *убить* = 'лишить жизни', *лишить* = 'каузировать утратить', *утратить* = 'перестать иметь', *перестать* = 'начать не' ('каузировать', 'иметь', 'начать' and 'не' are considered elementary meaning units).

(2) The defined word and the definition should be identical in meaning. To be more precise, if the word A in a given meaning 'X' is defined as 'YZ', then 'YZ' should be semantically substitutable for A('X') in any context, and vice versa – the meaning 'YZ' should be expressible through A('X') in any context. This condition satisfied, the definitions of any two intuitively different meanings will be formally distinct, and the definitions of any two intuitively synonymous words will be formally identical. It follows, in particular, that if A is intuitively different from B in precisely the same way, as A' from B', then their definitions will form a proportion, cf: *аккорд: нота* = *залп: выстрел* or *бороться: побеждать* = *искать: находить* = *лечить: вылечивать*, etc. It should be noted that the majority of the existing dictionaries fail to meet these simple and, in our opinion, rather reasonable requirements.

Not all the entry words are supplied with this kind of definitions. Some words stand in such meaning relations to other (key) words as are regular and can be expressed through lexical functions (see below, p. 8). In these cases a reference to the key word formulated in terms of lexical functions turns out to be sufficient, e.g. *ПОБЕДА* = S_0Perf (*побеждать*), *ПОБЕЖДАТЬ* = Real$_1$ (*бороться*), etc. Such formulas may be looked upon as definitions of a special kind. To smooth the reader's path, we include in the text of definitions various non-standard explanatory notes (given in square brackets).

The government pattern (together with examples of its speech manifestation) contains information on how the syntactic valences ('places') of the key word are expressed. The government pattern proper is a table with columns corresponding to the valences of the key word; every valence is supplied with a semantic interpretation, e.g. the first column of the word *АГРЕССИЯ* is interpreted as 'the one that commits aggression', while the second – as 'the one against whom aggression is committed'. In the lower part of the column alternative morphological types of word-forms filling the valence in question are enumerated. If the occurrence of a given morphological type is determined by certain semantic conditions, such conditions are also pointed out; thus, the first place of the word *АГРЕССИЯ* may be filled in only by the name of a state. Besides this, the column may carry an indication showing the necessity of filling the corresponding syntactic valence. Hence, the table of government contains the information about the individual properties of each valence. As to the compatibility of various ways of expressing different valences, the relevant information is presented by indicating impossible combinations. Thus, the government pattern of the word АРЕСТ I has three such indications (see p. 20):

Impossible:

(1)   1. without 2.1
(2)   2.2. $+3$
(3)   2.2, if A. is singular

which means: "the first place cannot be expressed unless the second place
is expressed in the first way; the second place cannot be expressed in the
second way in the presence of the third place or if the word *APECT* is used
in the singular".

Such a pattern of government is probably difficult to read; however, it is
not the allegedly complicated notation which is to blame, but the objective
complexity of language phenomena which have never been treated in a
sufficiently exhaustive and uniform manner. To facilitate the reader's understanding of the government pattern the latter is always supplied with examples illustrating all admissible and nonadmissible combinations of the
governed units. (It was L. V. Ščerba, who as far back as 1940 was the first
to suggest the inclusion of such non-admissible, or more exactly, non-
recommended combinations ('negative language facts') in a normative explanatory dictionary.)

By way of illustration we adduce below the government pattern of the
word ДОЛГ I.1 (моральный)

1 The subject of the duty	2 The nature of the necessity	3 The cause of the necessity	4 The interested party
1. $S_{\text{род}}$	1. V_{inf}	1. $S_{\text{род}}$ (where S belongs to a limited list)	1. *перед*$+S_{\text{твор}}$
2. $A_{\text{прит}}$	2. $S_{\text{род}}$	2. A	2. *по отношению* *к*$+S_{\text{дат}}$
		3. $S_{1\text{род}}$ 4. *как*$+S_{1\text{род}}$	

Impossible:

(1) $S_{\text{род}}+S_{\text{род}}$ in any place
(2) $2+$ any other place
(3)   3.1. $+$ something but 4.2
(4)   3.3. without 1
(5)   3.3. $+4.$
(6)   3.4. without 1.

Долг Петра, его долг; долг лечить больных, долг помощи раненым; долг дружбы [гостеприимства, приличия ...] = дружеский долг = долг друга, патриотический [интернациональный, научный, партийный, воинский] долг = долг патриота [интернационалиста, ученого, члена партии, солдата]; долг перед Родиной, долг по отношению к родителям; писательский долг Петра, мой писательский долг = долг Петра [мой долг] как писателя; долг Петра [наш долг] перед родиной, долг Петра [наш долг] по отношению к родителям; долг приличия по отношению к гостям; (мой) дружеский долг перед вами [по отношению к вам]; его долг перед обществом [по отношению к обществу] как патриота = его патриотический долг перед обществом [по отношению к обществу].

Impossible:

> *Долг помощи Петра,* *долг приличия Петра* and other combinations of the word *долг* with two governed genitives
> *Мой долг приличия;* *Долг Петра работать,* *Мой долг работать* and other combinations of the type *долг* + the infinitive + any other dependent; *долг патриота перед Родиной;* *долг как солдата.*

This is one of the most complicated examples of government patterns. It has been chosen for the sole purpose of illustrating various means of presenting government information. In other instances government patterns are much simpler; cf. the government patterns of the verb АРЕСТОВЫ-ВАТЬ I (людей).

1 the subject of the arrest	2 the one who is arrested	3 the motive of the arrest
$S_{им}$	$S_{вин}$	1. *за* + $S_{вин}$ 2. *по обвинению в* + $S_{предл}$
obligatory [6]	obligatory	

Полиция арестовывает студентов (за хранение нелегальной литературы); его арестовали (по обвинению в убийстве).

The government pattern provides for the syntactic correctness of word combinations; as far as the description of lexical combinability of the keyword is concerned, the latter is systematically taken care of by the apparatus of the so-called lexical functions.

The notion of lexical functions is the principal innovation of ECD. A standard lexical function (LF) is a meaning relation between a key word (or word combination) C_0 and other words and word combinations C_i, which meets the following three requirements:

(1) this relation occurs in a sufficiently great number of word pairs, i.e. it manifests itself through many different C_0;

(2) this relation has diverse means of expression, i.e. the number of different C_i in the language is rather great;

(3) the choice of the right C_i for the expression of a given relation with a given C_0 is determined, as a rule, by C_0 itself (sometimes under supplementary conditions).

A typical example of LF is the meaning relation between the name of a certain phenomenon and the designation of 'the biggest degree' of this phenomenon, i.e. the meaning 'very' = 'intensely' = 'in a high [the highest] degree'. This meaning is designated by the symbol Magn (Latin *magnus*); the expression Magn (*брюнетка*) is read as "Magn of *брюнетка*" and designates (in Russian) the adjective *жгучая*, i.e. Magn (*брюнетка*) = *жгучая*. Cf.:

C_0	Magn (C_0)
рыжий	*ярко, огненно —*
влияние	*сильное, большое, значительное* < *огромное*
дождь	*сильный* < *проливной*
спать	*крепко, без задних ног; сном праведника/ младенца*
поражение	*тяжелое* < *неслыханное* < *полное*
разгромить	*полностью, наголову*
вооруженный	*хорошо, прекрасно* < *до зубов*
образованный	*хорошо, прекрасно, очень; широко*
дурак	*круглый, набитый*
порядочный [*человек*]	*вполне, глубоко*

The complete theory of lexical functions is set forth in the publication mentioned in the first footnote. Here we shall limit ourselves to a list of LF with as few comments as possible, in the hope that the heart of the matter will be sufficiently brought out by means of numerous examples.

1. Syn – synonym:

Syn (*помогать*) = *содействовать*   Syn (*to help*) = *to aid*
Syn (*называть* 1) = *именовать*   Syn (*to call* 1) = *to name*.

2. Conv – conversive. A typical example of the converse term is the passive voice of a verb:

Conv (*строить*) = *строиться* [*кем*]   Conv (*to build*) = *to be built* [*by smb.*]
Conv (*содержать*) = *содержаться*   Conv (*to contain*) = *to be contained*
   [*в чем*]   [*in smth*].

In general, only such words have conversives as denote a situation with more than one participant. The replacement of the key word C_0 by its conversive leaves the situation unchanged, but requires a change in the syntactical functions of the names of its participants, or actants (with the appropriate changes in the cases and prepositions of the nouns). Compare:

А предшествует/раньше В =   *A precedes B* =
  = *В следует за/позже А*   = *B follows A*
А выиграл у В = В проиграл А   *A has won over B = B has lost to A*
Почва впитывает влагу =   *The earth seeps in the moisture* =
  = *Влага проникает в почву*   = *the moisture penetrates into the*
    earth.

А продал В С = С купил В у А   *A sold B to C = C bought B from A.*

3. Anti – antonym:

Anti (*красивый*) = *некрасивый*   Anti (*beautiful*) = *plain, ugly*
Anti (*друг*) = *враг*   Anti (*friend*) = *enemy*
Anti (*раньше*) = *позже*   Anti (*before*) = *after*
Anti (*любить*) = *ненавидеть*   Anti (*to love*) = *to hate*
Anti (*открывать*) = *закрывать*   Anti (*to open*) = *to shut.*

4. Gener – the name of the genus with respect to C_0:

Gener (*жидкость*) = *вещество*   Gener (*liquid*) = *substance*
(ср. *жидкость = жидкое вещество*)   (cf. *liquid = liquid substance*)
Gener (*синий*) = *цвет*   Gener (*blue*) = *colour*
(ср. *синий = синего цвета*)   (cf. *blue = of blue colour*)
Gener (*ползти*) = *передвигаться*   Gener (*to crawl*) = *to move*
(ср. *ползти = передвигаться*   (cf. *to crawl = to move by*
  ползком)   *crawling*)
Gener (*арест*) = *репрессии*   Gener (*arrest*) = *reprisal*
(ср. *аресты и другие репрессии*)   (cf. *arrests and other reprisal*).

5. S_0 – the noun which coincides with C_0 in meaning:

S_0 (*двигаться*) = *движение* S_0 (*to move*) = *movement*
S_0 (*молотить*) = *молотьба* S_0 (*to thresh*) = *threshing*
S_0 (*быть белым*) = *белизна* S_0 (*to be white*) = *whiteness.*

6. A_0 – the adjective with coincides with C_0 in meaning:

A_0 (*ислам*) = *исламский, мусульманский* A_0 (*Islam*) = *Islamic*

A_0 (*солнце*) = *солнечный* A_0 (*sun*) = *solar*

A_0 (*время*) = *временной* A_0 (*time*) = *temporal*.

7. Adv_0 – the adverb which coincides with C_0 in meaning:

Adv_0 (*критический*) = *критически* Adv_0 (*critical*) = *critically*

Adv_0 (*смысл*) = *по смыслу* Adv_0 (*meaning*) = *in meaning*.

8. V_0 – the verb which coincides with C_0 in meaning:

V_0 (*нападение*) = *нападать* V_0 (*attack*) = *to attack*

V_0 (*смерть*) = *умирать* V_0 (*death*) = *to die*.

Note: lexical functions 1–3 and 5–8 have variants which differ from the main type in that the coincidence of their meaning with that of C_0 is incomplete. Thus, $Syn_\supset$ denotes a quasisynonym with a broader meaning than that of C_0 [*нападение* = $Syn_\supset$ (*агрессия*)], $Syn_\subset$ denotes a quasisynonym with a narrower meaning, and $Syn_\cap$ denotes a quasisynonym, whose meaning coincides with that of C_0 only partially. The indices $\subset$, $\supset$ and $\cap$ are similarly assigned to the symbols of the other lexical functions mentioned here.

9. S_i – the generic name of the first (second, third...) participant of the situation:

S_1 (C_0) – the one who acts
      (that which acts);
S_2 (C_0) – the one who is acted upon
      (that which is acted upon) etc.

Thus,

S_1 (*нанимать на службу*) = = *работодатель* S_1 (*to employ*) = *employer*,

S_2 (*нанимать на службу*) = = *служащий* S_2 (*to employ*) = *employee*;

S_1 (*продавать*) = *продавец* S_1 (*to sell*) = *seller*,

S_2 (*продавать*) = *товар* S_2 (*to sell*) = *goods*;

S_3 (*продавать*) = *покупатель* S_3 (*to sell*) = *buyer, client, customer*

('тот, кому продают')   ('the one to whom goods are sold'),

S_4 (*продавать*) = *цена* S_4 (*to sell*) = *price*

('то, за что продают')   ('that for which the goods are sold').

10. S_{mod} – the noun denoting the mode of action:

S_{mod} (*писать* 1)= || *почерк*[7]

S_{mod} (*писать* 2, 3)=*манера* [*письма*]

S_{mod} (*держаться* 3)= || *осанка*

S_{mod} (*to write* 1)= || *handwriting*[7],

S_{mod} (*to write* 2)=*style.*

11. S_{loc} – the noun denoting the place of C_0:

S_{loc} (*стрела*)= || *колчан*

S_{loc} (*действие*)=*сцена*

S_{loc} (*arrows*)= || *quiver*

S_{loc} (*action*)=*scene.*

12. S_{instr} – the noun denoting the instrument of C_0:

S_{instr} (*общаться*)=*средство* [*общения*]

S_{instr} (*думать*)= || *ум*

S_{instr} (*убеждать*)= || *довод, аргумент*

S_{instr} (*communication*)=*means* [*of communication*],

S_{instr} (*to think*)= || *brain*

S_{instr} (*to convince*)= || *reason, argument.*

13. S_{res} – the noun denoting the result of C_0, that is, "what happened as a result of…":

S_{res} (*катастрофа*)=*последствия*

S_{res} (*охота* 1)=*охотничья добыча, трофеи*

S_{res} (*переговоры*)=*итоги*

S_{res} (*catastrophe*)=*aftermath, consequences*

S_{res} (*hunt* 1)=*bag*

S_{res} (*talks*)=*results.*

14. Sing – the word meaning 'a single item or instance of C_0':

Sing (*насилие*)=*акт*

Sing (*ярость*)=*приступ*

Sing (*violence*)=*act* (*of violence*)

Sing (*fury*)=*fit*

Sing (*advice*)=*piece* (*of advice*)

Sing (*news*)=*item* (*of news*).

15. Mult – the word denoting 'totality', 'aggregate':

Mult (*цветы*)=*букет*

Mult (*овцы*)=*стадо*

Mult (*собака*)=*свора*

Mult (*flowers*)=*bunch*

Mult (*sheep*)=*flock*

Mult (*dog*)=*pack.*

16. Cap – the name of the head (or chief):

Cap (*племя*)=*вождь*

Cap (*полк*)=*командир*

Cap (*университет*)=*ректор*

Cap (*комитет*)=*председатель*

Cap (*tribe*)=*chief*

Cap (*regiment*)=*commander*

Cap (*University*)=*Chancellor*

Cap (*committee*)=*president.*

17. Equip – the name of the staff (personnel):

Equip (*монастырь*)=*монахи*　　　Equip (*cloister*)=*monks*
Equip (*полк*)=*личный состав*　　Equip (*regiment*)=*personnel, manpower*

Equip (*орудие*)=*расчет*　　　　Equip (*gun*)=*crew.*

18. Figur – the standard figurative designation of C_0 (it is often used together with Magn):

Figur (*блокада*)=*кольцо*
Figur (*огонь*)=*шквал*
Figur (*страсть*)=*пламя*　　　Figur (*passion*)=*flame*
Figur (*ночь*)=*покров*　　　　Figur (*night*)=*cover* (cf. *under the cover of night*)
　　(ср. *под покровом ночи*)
　　　　　　　　　　　　　　Figur (*misery*)=*abyss.*

19. Centr – the name of the "central", "culminating" part of an object or process:

Centr (*слава*)=*зенит, апогей*　Centr (*glory*)=*summit*
　　　　　　　　　　　　　　Centr (*crisis*)=*peak*
Centr (*город*)=*центр*　　　　Centr (*city*)=*center*
　　　　　　　　　　　　　　Centr (*life*)=*prime.*

20. A_i – the generic attribute of the first (second, third...) participant of the situation:

A_1 (C_0) – 'such as acts',
A_2 (C_0) – 'such as is acted upon',
(A_1 and A_2 are regularly expressed by the active and passive participles respectively). Thus,

A_1 (*гореть*)=*в огне*　　　　A_1 (*to burn*)=*on fire*
A_1 (*усы*)=*с усами*　　　　A_1 (*moustach*)=*moustached*
A_1 (*знать*)=*знающий*　　　A_1 (*know*)=*aware*
A_2 (*знать*)=*известный*　　A_2 (*to know*)=*known; familiar*
A_2 (*управлять*)=*под управлением*　A_2 (*to control*)=*under control.*

21. $Able_i$ – the generic definition of the first (second, third...) potential participant of the situation:

$Able_1$ (C_0) – 'such as can act';
$Able_2$ (C_0) – 'such as can be acted upon':
$Able_1$ (*гореть*)=*горючий*　　$Able_1$ (*to burn*)=*combustible*
$Able_1$ (*происходить/иметь место*)=*потенциальный*　　$Able_1$ (*to take place/occur*)=*potential*

Able$_2$ (*есть*) = *съедобный*   Able$_2$ (*to eat*) = *edible*
                                   Able$_2$ (*to read*) = *readable; legible.*

22. Qual$_i$ – the name of the quality which usually (though not obligatorily) involves Able$_i$:

C$_0$	Qual$_1$	Able$_1$
удивлять to surprise	*необычный unusual*	*удивительный surprising*
понимать to understand	*естественный natural* [*очевидный*]	*понятный understandable* [*obvious*]

23. Magn – an attribute denoting 'very', 'to a great extent' (see examples on page 8).

24–25. Plus, Minus – attributes denoting 'more, in a greater degree', and 'less, in a smaller degree' respectively. They have no independent realizations and usually make part of a complex LF:

CausPlus (*агрессия*) = *расширять*   CausPlus (*aggression*) = *to escalate*
CausPlus (*напряжение*) = *усиливать*   CausPlus (*tension*) = *to heighten*
CausPlus (*единство*) = *крепить*   CausPlus (*unity*) = *to weld*
IncepPlus (*напряжение*) =   IncepPlus (*tension*) = *to mount*
     = *усиливаться*
IncepPlus (*движение 2*) =   IncepPlus (*movement 2*) = *to broaden*
     = *расширяться*
CausMinus (*удар*) = *смягчать*   CausMinus (*below*) = *to soften*
IncepMinus (*ценность*) =   IncepMinus (*value*) = *to shrink.*
     = *понижаться*

26. Ver – an attribute meaning 'right', 'proper':

Ver (*довод*) = *обоснованный*   Ver (*reason*) = *valid*
Ver (*гордость*) = *законная*   Ver (*pride*) = *justifiable*
Ver (*гражданин*) = *лойяльный*   Ver (*citizen*) = *loyal*
Ver (*требование*) = *законное*   Ver (*demand*) = *legitimate.*

27. Bon – an attribute meaning 'good':

Bon (*условия*) = *благоприятные*   Bon (*conditions*) = *favourable*
Bon (*помощь*) = *ценная*   Bon (*aid*) = *valuable*
Bon (*предложение 1*) = *заманчивое*   Bon (*proposal*) = *tempting*
Bon (*цель*) = *благородная*   Bon (*aim*) = *lofty.*

28. Loc – a preposition or prepositional phrase with the meaning of localization (spatial, temporal or mental):

Loc (*капитализм*) = *при* [предл. п.]   Loc (*capitalism*) = *under*
Loc (*момент*) = *в* [вин. п.]   Loc (*moment*) = *at*
Loc (*список*) = *в* [предл. п.]   Loc (*list*) = *on*.
Loc (*Кавказ*) = *на* [предл. п.]

29. Copul – a copula, a link verb meaning 'to be':

Copul (*бледный*) = *выглядеть, быть*   Copul (*pale*) = *to look, to be*
Copul (*пример*) = *служить*   Copul (*example*) = *to serve, to be*
Copul (*жертва*) = *пасть, быть*   Copul (*victim*) = *to fall*.

30. Pred – a merged expression for Copul $(C_0) + C_0$. It is marked by a specific symbol because of the important role it plays in synonymic transformations (paraphrases):

Pred (*рядом*) = *|| соседствовать*   Pred (*near*) = *|| to neighbour*
Caus Pred (*плохой*) = *|| портить,*   Caus Pred (*bad, evil*) = *|| to corrupt*
    развращать
Pred (*пьяница*) = *|| пьянствовать*   Pred (*drunkard*) = *|| to drink*.

31. $Oper_i$ – the verb connecting the name of the 1st (second, etc.) participant of the situation in the function of the subject with the name of the situation itself (C_0) in the function of the first (main) object, so that $Oper_i$ $(C_0) + (C_0)$ equals in meaning V_0 (C_0):

$Oper_1$ (*помощь*) = *оказывать* $Oper_1$ (*support*) = *to lend*
[*оказывать помощь = помогать*]   [*to lend support = to support*]
$Oper_1$ (*жертва*) = *приносить* $Oper_1$ (*sacrifice*) = *to make*
$Oper_2$ (*помощь, поддержка*) = $Oper_2$ (*aid, support*) =
    = *получать*   = *to receive*
$Oper_1$ (*поражение*) = *терпеть* $Oper_1$ (*defeat*) = *to suffer*
    $Oper_1$ (*split*) = *to undergo*
    $Oper_1$ (*recession*) = *to experience*.

32. $Func_i$ – the verb connecting the name of the situation in the function of the subject with the name of its first (second, etc.) participant in the function of the first (main) object (or with no object at all, denoting the basic action of C_0 as the subject irrespective of any other participant in the situation), so that $Func_i$ $(C_0) + C_0 = V_0$ (C_0):

$Func_0$ (*тишина*) = *стоит* $Func_0$ (*silence*) = *to reign*
$Func_1$ (*тревога*) = *гложет* (*кого-то*) $Func_1$ (*anxiety*) = *to gnaw* (*at smb.*)
$Func_2$ (*удар*) = *падает* (*на кого-то*) $Func_2$ (*blow*) = *to fall* (*on smb.*).

33. $Labor_{ij}$ – the verb connecting the name of the i-th participant of the situation C_0 in the function of the grammatical subject with the name of the j-th participant in the function of the first (main) object, while the name of the situation C_0 itself plays the part of the secondary object so that $Labor_{ij}(C_0) + C_0 = V_0(C_0)$:

$Labor_{12}$ (*аренда*) = *брать в*
$Labor_{32}$ (*аренда*) = *сдавать в*
$Labor_{12}$ (*пытка*) = *подвергать* $Labor_{12}$ (*torture*) = *to put to*
$Labor_{12}$ (*рассмотрение*) = $Labor_{12}$ (*consideration*) =
  = *подвергать*   = *to take into.*

The correlation between LF 31–33 may be exemplified by the following diagram (Y_1, Y_2 are participants in the situation; the arrows are directed from the subject to the first (main) object; for the sake of simplicity only the situation with two participants is considered):

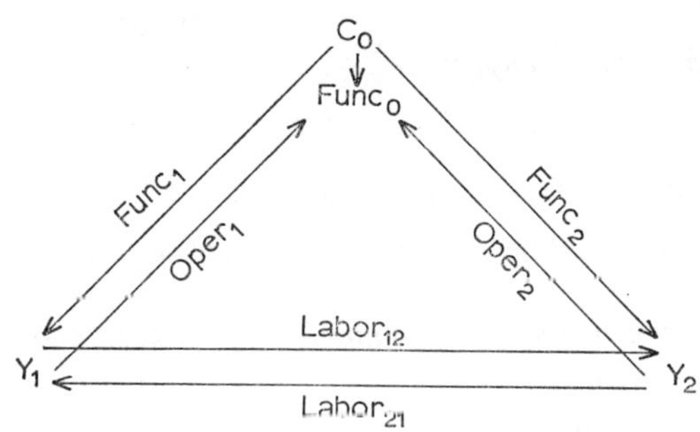

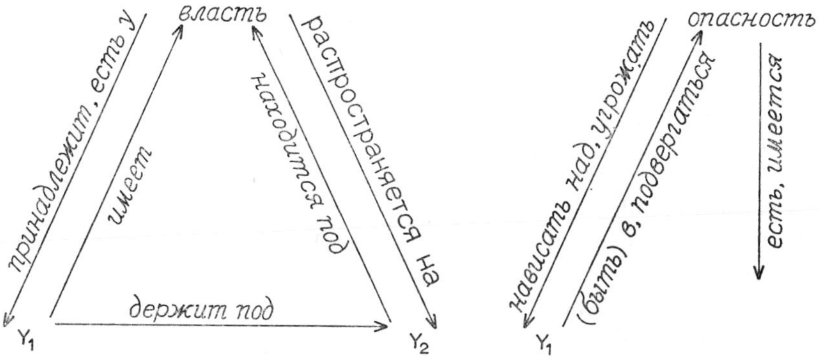

34. Caus – the verb meaning 'to act in such a way that C_0 comes into being' (= 'to create', 'to bring about'):

Caus (*кризис*) = *приводить к*   Caus (*crisis*) = *to bring about*

Caus (*ситуация*) = *порождать*   Caus (*situation*) = *to produce, to bring about*

Caus (*звук*) = *извлекать*   Caus (*sound*) = *to extract.*

Caus often makes part of complex lexical functions:

CausOper$_1$ (*отчаяние*) = = *приводить в*   CausOper$_1$ (*despair*) = = *to drive to*

CausOper$_2$ (*распоряжение*) = = *предоставлять в, отдавать в*   CausOper$_2$ (*disposal*) = *to place at*

CausFunc$_0$ (*ракета*) = = *запускать* [*ракету*]   CausFunc$_0$ (*rocket*) = *to launch.*

35. Perm – the verb meaning 'to permit', 'to make it possible to':

Perm (*падать*) = || *ронять*   Perm (*to fall*) = || *to drop*

    Perm (*terror*) = *to let loose.*

Perm (*агрессия*) = *попустительствовать*

36. Liqu – the verb meaning 'to act in such a way that C_0 ceases to take place' (= 'to liquidate', 'to destroy', 'to cause not to be'; Liqu = AntiCaus):

Liqu (*препятствия*) = *устранять*   Liqu (*obstacles*) = *to remove*

Liqu (*запрет*) = *отменять*   Liqu (*ban*) = *to lift*

Liqu (*следы*) = *стирать*   Liqu (*traces*) = *to wipe out*

Liqu (*паника*) = *прекращать*   Liqu (*panic*) = *to stop*

Liqu (*ошибка*) = *исправлять, устранять*   Liqu (*mistake*) = *to correct.*

37. Incep – the verb meaning 'to begin' (it is used only as part of complex LF's, in the same way as LF 38–41):

IncepFunc$_0$ (*война*) = *начинаться, разражаться*   IncepFunc$_0$ (*war*) = *to break out*

IncepOper$_2$ (*влияние*) = = *попадать под*   IncepOper$_2$ (*influence*) = = *to fall under*

IncepOper$_1$ (*заблуждение*) = = *впадать в*   IncepOper$_1$ (*mistake*) = = *to fall into*

IncepOper$_1$ (*трудность*) = = *сталкиваться с*   IncepOper$_1$ (*difficulty*) = = *to run into*

IncepFunc_1 (*ужас*) = *охватывать* IncepFunc_1 (*horror*) = *to take possession of.*

38. Cont – the verb meaning 'to continue':

ContOper_1 (*hold*) = *to keep* (*hold of*)

ContCaus Func_0 (*мир*) = = *поддерживать* ContCaus Func_0 (*peace*) = = *to maintain*

ContOper_1 (*молчание*) = *хранить* ContOper_1 (*silence*) = *to preserve*

ContFunc_0 (*запах*) = *держаться* ContFunc_0 (*smell*) = *to hold.*

39. Fin – the verb meaning 'to cease', 'to stop' (='to begin not to...'; Fin = AntiIncep):

FinFunc_0 (*звук*) = *замирать* FinFunc_0 (*sound*) = *to die away*

FinOper_1 (*терпение*) = *терять* FinOper_1 (*patience*) = *to lose*

FinOper_1 (*любовь*) = || *разлюбить* FinOper_1 (*love*) = *to fall out of*

FinOper_2 (*власть*) = *выходить из-под* FinOper_2 (*power*) = *to fall from under.*

40. Perf – 'the perfective' (an action or a process are carried through to their limit); its standard expression is the perfective aspect of the verb, or the Perfect tenses. (See examples below, in 41.)

41. Result – 'the resultative' (the state, or condition resulting from the completion of a certain action or process); the lexical functions Perf and Result are usually expressed by mergers, cf. the following examples:

C_0	$\text{Perf}(C_0)$	$\text{Result}(C_0)$
ложиться	*лечь*	*лежать*
to lie down	*to have lain*	(*to be*) *lying*
умирать	*умереть*	(*быть*) *мертвым*
to die	*to have died*	(*to be*) *dead*
изучать	*изучить*	*знать*
to study	*to have mastered*	*to know*

42. Fact[j] – the verb meaning 'to come true', 'to become a fact', 'to be realized, fulfilled, implemented', (C_0 is the subject; the upper index indicates the degree of 'realization' ('fulfilment', 'implementation'):

Fact (*одежда*) = *хорошо носится*   Fact (*clothes*) = *to wear well*

Fact (*мечта*) = *сбывается*   Fact (*dream*) = *to come true*

Fact (*удача*) = *не изменяет*   ContFact (*luck*) = *to stand*

AntiFact (*план*) = *проваливается*   AntiFact (*plan*) = *to collapse*
                                           AntiFact (*courage*) = *to give way.*

43. Real$_i^j$ – the verb meaning 'to realize', 'make real', 'to fulfill a certain requirement' contained in C_0' (C_0 is the main object, while the name of the i-th participant is the subject; the index j means the same as in the previous case.)

Real$_1^I$ (*программа*) = *принимать*   Real$_1^I$ (*program*) = *to adopt*;
Real$_1^{II}$ (*программа*) = *выполнять*   Real$_1^{II}$ (*program*) = *to fulfill*
Real$_1$ (*попытка*) = *преуспевать в*   Real$_1$ (*attempt*) = *to succeed in*
Real$_2^I$ (*совет*) = *выслушивать*
Real$_2^{II}$ (*совет*) = *следовать*   Real$_2^{II}$ (*advice*) = *to follow*
Real$_1^{II}$ (*голод*) = *утолять*   Real$_1^{II}$ (*hunger*) = *to satiate.*

44. Prepar – the verb meaning 'to prepare', 'to make ready for use':

Prepar (*стол*) = *накрывать на*   Prepar (*table*) = *to lay*
Prepar (*постель*) = *стелить*   Prepar (*bed*) = *to undo*
Prepar (*ружьё*) = *заряжать*   Prepar (*gun*) = *to load.*

45. Degrad – the verb meaning 'to deteriorate', 'to go bad':

Degrad (*зубы*) = *разрушаться*   Degrad (*teeth*) = *to decay*
Degrad (*дерево*) = *гнить*   Degrad (*tree*) = *to rot*
Degrad (*дом*) = *ветшать*   Degrad (*house*) = *to dilapidate*
Degrad (*одежда*) = *снашиваться*   Degrad (*clothes*) = *to wear off*
Degrad (*дисциплина*) =   Degrad (*discipline*) =
  = *расшатываться*   = *to go bad.*

46. Imper – the meaning of 'order', 'command' which is expressed in a standard (grammatical) way in the case of verbs; in other parts of speech (including a selection of verbs) it is expressed idiomatically.

Imper (*вставать* 2) = *подъём!*
Imper (*убираться* 3) =   Imper (*to go out*) = *off with you!*
  = *вон (отсюда)!*
Imper (*стрелять*) = *огонь! пли!*   Imper (*to shoot*) = *fire!*
Imper (*не шуметь*) = *тихо!*,   Imper (*silence*) = *silence!*
  тише!, тс-с-с!, тш-ш-ш!   vulg. *shut up!*
                                           Imper (*to talk*) = *go ahead!*
                                             vulg. *fire away!*

47. Son – the verb denoting the typical sound produced (emitted) by C_0:

Son (*лев*) = *рычать*   Son (*lion*) = *to roar*

Son (*осел*) = *реветь*   Son (*donkey*) = *to bray*
Son (*собака*) = *лаять*   Son (*dog*) = *to bark*
Son (*сова*) = *ухать*   Son (*owl*) = *to howl*
Son (*змея*) = *шипеть*   Son (*snake*) = *to hiss*
Son (*снег*) = *скрипеть*   Son (*snow*) = *to creak*

Apart from the standard lexical functions listed here, individual (non-standard) functions are resorted to in a number of ECD entries. Non-standard LF's are meanings which for a number of reasons (in particular, because their manifestation is not sufficiently varied) do not lend themselves to an easy inclusion in the standard list. Such meanings are denoted simply by Russian words. As a rule, they occur in combination with standard LF, e.g.

снова IncepOper$_1$ (*учеба*) = *возобновлять*,

MagnAnti легкая (*победа*) = *пиррова*

документ на право Oper$_1$ (*автомобиль*) = *водительские права*.

Information about the *lexical universe* of the key-word is an informal description of a sufficiently broad 'piece' of reality including the given situation as a constituent element. The main themes dealt with under the heading 'lexical universe' are:

1) the types of C_0; 2) the main parts, or phases of C_0; 3) typical situations occuring before or after C_0 etc. Thus, the section "Lexical universe" for the word *skis* consists of a list of the types of skis (*racing, mountain, jumping, hunting*), their main parts (*skis* proper and *bindings*), the main objects and actions necessary for the correct use (exploitation) of skis (*sticks, grease, to tar*), the main types of activities connected with skis (*a ski-trip, a ski-race...*) and so on. Even these scanty examples make it clear that the information about the lexical universe is, at least partially, of an encyclopaedic nature. We say «partially» because genuine encyclopaedic information about skis (their history, the way they are manufactured, etc.) is not supplied here: the section contains only such words and phrases as are necessary for talking on the topic, and nothing else.

For *illustrative* purposes we adduce colloquial and literary phrases which contain the key-word in combination with various values of its LF's. In contrast to the widespread lexicographic tradition (e.g. see the Academic 17-volume Dictionary) we do not draw our illustrative material from the classics (who often, for artistic purposes, diverge from the neutral standard usage), but resort instead to the ordinary speech practice of an average educated Russian-speaking person. The idea is to choose the most common cliches of Modern Russian (colloquial, newspaper, scientific).

In order to give the user a broader lexical perspective, some entries include *discrimination* of synonyms and near-synonyms, i.e. a list of words that have a meaning similar to that of the entry word, and their definitions. For the verb АРЕСТОВАТЬ 1 (deprive a person of liberty), for instance, this section includes the definitions of words and phrases having a connotation of "depriving (a person) of liberty": *задерживать* 2, *хватать* 2, *брать в плен, сажать* 3, etc. Naturally all these words and phrases have entries and definitions of their own. The duplication of these definitions in entries of other words serves to emphasize the differences and similarities of meaning.

The *Phraseology Section* fulfills essentially a reference function. The practice of compiling ECD has revealed that the better part of language information commonly treated in dictionaries as idioms is describable in terms of regular lexical functions. It has been therefore shifted to the basic section of the dictionary entry. In the phraseology section proper are now left only such idioms whose meaning is not related to that of the entry word, e.g. ДОЛГ 1 'duty': ПЕРВЫМ ДОЛГОМ 'first of all'. Expressions of this kind are treated in ECD as independent entries; they are repeatedin the Phraseology Sections of the entries of their component words solely to provide for the user an easier access to the relevant material.

The reader may get a better idea of the dictionary by looking through the appended sample entries.

APPENDIX: 10 DICTIONARY ENTRIES (7 ENTRY WORDS)

The entries as yet include no morphologic information
АРЕ́СТ 1. S_0Perf (*арестовывать* 1) [объект-лица].

1	2	3
кто арестовывает	кого арестовывают	мотивировка ареста
$S_{твор}$	1. $S_{род}$	1. *за* + $S_{вин}$
	2. *среди* + $S_{род}$	2. *по обвинению в* +
	[S – либо собират.,	$S_{предл}$
	либо во мн. ч.]	

Невозможно:

(1)   1. без 2.1
(2)   2.2 + 3
(3)   2.2, если А. – ед. 4.

Арест Рея Кинга, аресты среди студентов [среди интеллигенции], арест за контрабанду, арест по обвинению в убийстве; арест преступника силами порядка; арест Джонса за незаконный провоз оружия [по обвинению в спекуляции алмазами]; арест Ибн—Джухуля полицией нравов за спекуляцию [по обвинению в спекуляции] цепочками.

Невозможно:

* *арест полицией,*
* *арест среди студентов,*
* *аресты среди студентов за участие в демонстрации.*

Syn$_\cap$	*задержание*
Anti$_\supset$	*освобождение*
Gener	*репрессии*
S$_2$	*арестованный*
Mult	*волна ~ ов*
Func$_0$Mult	*пройти; прокатиться (по* [S$_\text{дат}$])
	| S$_\text{дат}$ – название места
Magn$_2$	*массовые, повальные ~ ы* | А. – мн. ч.
	[арестуют многих]
Ver	*законный*
AntiVer	*незаконный*
Loc	*при ~ е*
Oper$_1$	*производить ~ ы среди* [S$_\text{род, мн}$ или собират. S$_\text{род}$]
	| А. – мн. ч.
InccpOper$_1$	*начинать ~ ы* | А. – мн. ч.
FinOper$_1$	*прекращать ~ ы; приостанавливать ~ ы*
	[на время] | А. – мн. ч.
Oper$_2$	*попадать под ~ , подвергаться ~ у*
ResultOper$_2$	*быть, находиться, сидеть под ~ ом* | А. – ед. ч.
FinResultOper$_2$	*выходить, освобождаться из – под ~ а* | А. – ед. ч.
HeOper$_2$	(угрожающий + А): *избегать ~ а, ускользать*
	от ~ а
Func$_0$	идут [сов. вид – *прошли*] *~ ы* А. – мн. ч.
IncepFunc$_0$	*начинаются ~ ы* | А. – мн. ч.
ContFunc$_0$	*продолжаются ~ ы* | А. – мн. ч.
FinFunc$_0$	*прекращаются ~ ы* | А. – мн. ч.
Labor$_1$	*подвергать ~ у; брать, сажать под ~*
	| А. – ед. ч.
ImperLabor$_1$	*под ~* [S$_\text{вин}$]!
ResultLabor$_1$	(*со*)*держать под ~ ом* | А. – ед. ч.
Liqu$_1$ResultLabor$_1$	*выпускать, освобождать из — под ~ а*
	| А. – ед. ч. || *освобождать*

Caus	*приводить к ~ у* | D_1 (Caus) – предикат; *добиваться ~ а; давать указание об ~ е* | D_1 (Caus) – правомочное лицо
Perm	*санкционировать ~ , выдавать ордер на~*
Liqu	*останавливать, прекращать ~ ы, приостанавливать ~ ы* [на время] | А. – мн. ч.
Adv_2Result	*под ~ ом*
А. с содержанием на дому [т.е. запрещение покидать квартиру]	*домашний*
Документ на право А.	*ордер на~*

На следующий день всех арестованных освободили. По Кембрии прокатилась волна арестов, казней и других репрессий; массовые аресты идут также в Данирее. Остановить аресты кембрийских демократов – наш долг. – Не ходи домой, папа! Только что взяли [арестовали] Хуана! Заговор был раскрыт месяц назад, после чего были произведены аресты. При аресте он оказал сопротивление.

2. S_0Perf (*арестовывать* 2) [объект – движимая собственность]. Только ед. ч.!

1	2	3
кто арестовывает $S_{тв}$	что арестовывают $S_{род}$ обязательно	у кого арествывать —

Арест (властями) всех печатных материалов левого издательства "Палабрита роха".

Ver	*законный*
AntiVer	*незаконный*
Loc	*при ~ е*
$Oper_1$	*накладывать, налагать ~ на* [$S_{вин}$]
FinResultOper$_1$	*снимать ~ с* [$S_{род}$]
$Oper_2$	*подвергаться ~ у*
ResultOper$_2$	*быть, находиться под ~ ом*
Labor$_1$	*подвергать ~ у*
ResultLabor$_1$	*держать под ~ ом*
Adv_2Caus	*за* [$S_{вин}$]*, в связи с* [$S_{твор}$]
Adv_2Result	*под ~ ом*

На его имущество [товары] был наложен арест. В связи с напряженностью обстановки данирейские активы в Мураке будут подвергнуты аресту. Президент республики издал декрет об аресте банковских вкладов бывших правителей.

АРЕСТО́ВЫВАТЬ 1. Лишать свободы [субъект – обязательно официальные органы] в соответствии с предварительным распоряжением.

1	2	3
кто арестовывает	кого арестовывают	мотивировка ареста
$S_{им}$	$S_{вин}$	1. *за* + $S_{вин}$
		2. *по обвинению в* + $S_{предл}$
обязат.	обязат.	

NB: А. часто употребляется в неопределенно-личной конструкции.

Полиция арестовывает студентов (за хранение [по обвинению в хранении] нелегальной литературы); его арестовали.

Syn	*брать, забирать, хватать, сцапать* (прост.), *зацапать* (прост.)
Syn	*задерживать*
$Conv_2$	*попадаться 2*
$Conv_{21}$	*попадать в руки* [$S_{род}$]
Anti	*освобождать* [= $Liqu_1 Result$]
Gener	*лишать свободы; репрессировать*
Ver	*на законном основании*
AntiVer	*незаконно*
Caus	*велеть, приказывать, давать указание* | D_1(Caus) – правомочное лицо
$S_0 Perf$	*арест 1*
$S_2 Perf$	*арестованный*
LiquResult	*освобождать*

Полиция арестовала преступника прямо на борту самолета. Он был арестован при попытке перейти границу. 6 марта патриот попал в руки кондутовских сатрапов, но через три дня он был освобожден под давлением общественности.

ЗАДЕРЖИВАТЬ – лишать свободы лицо, пытающееся скрыться путем движения или маскировки [т.е. не находящееся у себя дома или в специальном убежище].

ХВАТАТЬ = АРЕСТОВЫВАТЬ 1 [пейоративно по отношению к а-
рестующим].

БРАТЬ, ЗАБИРАТЬ II = АРЕСТОВЫВАТЬ 1 [разг.; преимущественно – неопределенно-личная конструкция].

САЖАТЬ III – лишать свободы с содержанием в местах заключения
[разг.; преимущественно – неопределенно-личная конструкция, без ука-
зания "куда сажают"].

ЗАКЛЮЧАТЬ В ТЮРЬМУ – лишать свободы с содержанием в
тюрьме.

БРАТЬ В ПЛЕН – лишать свободы военнослужащих противопо-
ложной воюющей стороны в зоне военных действий.

ИНТЕРНИРОВАТЬ – лишать свободы тех граждан или транс-
портные средства одной из воюющих сторон, которые находятся на
территории интернирующей страны [противоположной или нейтраль-
ной], но не совершают враждебных или незаконных действий [дивер-
сантов и разведчиков не интернируют, а арестовывают].

2. устар. А арестовывает В у С = А лишает С права распоряжаться
В как собственностью [А – обязательно официальные органы].

1	2	3
кто арестовывает	что арестовывают	у кого арестовывают
$S_{им}$	$S_{род}$	$у + S_{род}$
обязат.	обязат.	

Власти арестовали весь тираж вечерней газеты; на таможне у NN
арестовали все бумаги.

S_0Perf   арест 2.

ПАССАЖИ́Р клиент транспорта [= лицо, которое перевозится
транспортом в соответствии со своей целью; S_2 – лицо (*перевозить;*
транспорт, поезд …)].

1	2	3
кто перевозится	кто/что везет	куда перевозится
	1. $S_{род}$	1. $до + S_{род}$
	2. $A_{прит}$	2. $Loc_{ad} + S$
—	[только название	
	лица]	

Невозможно:

     2. + 3.

NB: $до$ + $S_{род}$ обозначает конечную точку перевозки данного П., которая может и не совпадать с конечной целью самого П., – в отличие от Loc_{ad} + S, где слиты конечная точка перевозки и конечная цель П.

Пассажир дяди Мити [дядя Митя – водитель транспортного средства]; *пассажиры трамвая (такси, парохода, самолета, автобуса, лифта, дилижанса); пассажиры до Хорога, пассажиры в Чиверево.*

Невозможно:

    **пассажиры дяди Мити до Коряжска – 2,*
    **трамвайные [самолетные …] пассажиры.*

$Syn_{\subset}$	*седок*
A_0	*пассажирский*
$AntiVer_0$	|| *заяц 2; безбилетный* || *безбилетник* | в транспорте, где полагается иметь билет
$AntiVer_2$	*левый* [правила нарушает везущий, и притом за плату]
$IncepOper_2$	*брать, сажать* ~ *а; принимать* ~ *а на борт* | только если транспортное средство – корабль или летательный аппарат
$IncepFunc_2$	*садиться (на* [$S_{вин}$])
$FinFunc_2$	*сходить (с* [$S_{род}$]*), выходить*
$Func_3$	*офиц-следовать* до [$S_{род}$], *сходить в* [$S_{предл}$], *ехать до* [$S_{род}$]
$Fact_3$	*(успешно/благополучно) добираться до* [$S_{род}$], *прибывать* Loc_{ad} [S]
$Real_2$	*доставлять* ~ *а до* [$S_{род}$] Loc_{ad} [S]
Документ на право быть П.	*проездной документ*
Предназначенный для П.	*пассажирский*

    Сто пассажиров на борту
    Несут сквозь ночь турбины "ТУ" (Ю. Визбор)

Места для пассажиров с детьми и инвалидов [надпись в метро, трамваях, автобусах, троллейбусах]. – *Граждане пассажиры! Электропоезд до станции Пушкино отправляется в 18 часов 23 минуты с шестого пути* [объявление по радио на вокзале]. – *К сведению пассажиров, следующих до Хорога* [объявление по радио на вокзале или в аэропорту]. – *Пассажиров, прибывших рейсом N° 539 из Хабаровска, просят пройти в багажное отделение аэровокзала* [объявление по радио в аэропорту].

Человек, желающий *совершить поездку*/*проехать куда—либо*, может воспользоваться одним из видом *(общественного) транспорта*/средств сообщения. С целью *посадки* он является в соответствующий посадочный пункт (*на станцию, вокзал, остановку, стоянку...*), *приобретает* (если это предусмотрено *правилами* пользования данным транспортом) билет, оформляет положенным образом *провоз*/*отправку багажа*/*ручной клади* и следует *прямым сообщением* или с *пересадкой* (например, *транзитом*) – *до пункта*/*места назначения*. S_2 – нелицо (*перевозить; транспорт, поезд...*) = ГРУЗ (см.)

ПОБЕ́ДА S_0Perf (*побеждать*) = S_0 (*победить*) [= окончательный успех в борьбе].

1	2	3
кто победил	кого победил	вид борьбы
1. $S_{\text{род}}$	*над* + $S_{\text{твор}}$	1. Loc_{in} + $S_{\text{предл}}$
2. $A_{\text{прит}}$		2. A

NB: 2. + 3. без 1. нежелательно.

Победа Цезаря, его победа; победа над Гнеем Помпеем; победа в лыжной гонке, спортивная победа; победа Цезаря над Антонием, военные победы Цезаря; победа Мурака над данирейскими войсками в битве при Эль-Канистре; его победа в беге на 500 м.

Anti	*поражение* [= Conv_{213}]
Gener	*успех, достижение*
S_{res}	*плоды* ~*ы*
A_0	*победный, победоносный*
Adv_1	*с* ~*ой*; образн. *со щитом*
S_1	*победитель*
S_2	*побежденный*
Mult	*победное [триумфальное] шествие*
Magn	*убедительная, значительная, внушительная, решительная* < *крупная* < *полная, окончательнаая* < *блестящая, блистательная; с большим преимуществом, перевесом* || *триумф*
AntiMagn	*с минимальным преимуществом, перевесом; сомнительная*
Ver	*заслуженная; закономерная*
AntiVer	*незаслуженная; случайная*
Oper_1	*одерживать, завоевывать* ~*у*

IncepOper_1	*идти к ~ е*
$\text{S}_0\text{IncepOper}_1$	*путь, дорога к ~ е*
CausOper_1	*приводить к ~ е*
ResultOper_1	*торжествовать, праздновать ~ у*
Oper_1 (много + П.)	*идти от ~ ы к ~ е*
CausOper_1 (много + П.)	*вести от ~ ы к ~ е*
Недо Oper_1	*выпускать ~ у из рук, упускать ~ у*
Anti легко Oper_1	*вырывать ~ у*
Oper_3	*приносить ~ у; кончаться, оканчиваться, заканчиваться ~ ой* [$\text{S}_{\text{род}}$]
Func_1	*оставаться, быть за* [$\text{S}_{\text{тв}}$] [не присоединяет определений]; *доставаться* [$\text{S}_{\text{дат}}$]
IncepFunc_1	*склоняться на сторону* [$\text{S}_{\text{род}}$]
Недо Func_1	*ускользать от* [$\text{S}_{\text{род}}$]; *выскальзывать из рук* [$\text{S}_{\text{род}}$]
Anti легко Func_1	*доставаться, даваться* [$\text{S}_{\text{дат}}$] *дорого, дорогой ценой, недешево, нелегко, с трудом*
Caus	*приносить* | D_1 (Caus) – название ситуации, в которой победитель участвует как D_1; *обеспечивать ~ у* [$\text{S}_{\text{род}}$]
Caus_1	*бороться за ~ у; добиваться ~ ы*
$\text{Prepar}^{\text{II}}$	*ковать ~ у*
MagnAnti легкая	*пиррова* [D_1 затратил слишком много усилий, например, понес слишком большие потери]

Победу *закрепляют*, чтобы её *плоды* нельзя было *свести на нет*. В спорте победу *присуждают*.

Победа была завоевана им в упорной борьбе. В третьей партии победа осталась за ним [досталась ему].=Третья партия принесла ему победу [окончилась его победой]. Победа в бою досталась нам недешево [дорого, дорогой ценой... ценой неимоверных усилий]. Наше дело правое, победа будет за нами. – Иди и возвращайся с победой!

> *Когда...победу над врагом*
> *Россия снова торжествует...*
>
> (А. С. Пушкин)

> *Другие по живому следу*
> *Пройдут твой путь за пядью пядь,*
> *Но пораженья от победы*
> *Ты сам не должен отличать*
>
> (Б. Пастернак)

Кто привык за победу бороться,
С нами вместе пускай запоет.

(Советская песня)

Со щитом или на щите = Победа или смерть.
Невозможно:

**Победа легко осталась за ним,*
**Победа далась ему,*
**Моя помощь принесла ему победу* [надо: *...обеспечила его*
победу].

ПОБЕЖДА́ТЬ $Real_1$ (*бороться*) [=иметь успех в борьбе].

1	2	3
кто побеждает	кого побеждают	вид борьбы
$S_{им}$	$S_{вин}$	$Loc_в + S_{предл}$
обязат.		

Мы победили; NN победил MM: Кембрия победила (Мурак) в Сорока-
пятилетней войне.

Syn	*брать, одерживать верх; победить; пересили-* *вать, побороть, превозмогать; наша взяла!* [= *мы победили*]
Syn	*справляться с* [$S_{твор}$]; разг. *сладить с* [$S_{твор}$] *одолевать, осиливать*
$Conv_{132}$	*выигрывать*
$Conv_{231}$	*проигрывать*
Anti	$Oper_1 + $ *поражение*
A_0	*победный, победоносный*
$Able_1$	*победоносный*
$Magn_2 Able_1$	*всепобеждающий* [с абстрактными S]
Magn	*окончательно, полностью* || *положить, уложить* *на (обе) лопатки* [в борьбе; *перен.* о споре и т.п.], *поставить на колени* [в реальной и серь- езной борьбе]
$S_0 Perf$	*победа*
$S_1 Perf$	*победитель*
$S_2 Perf$	*побежденный*
$A_1 Perf$	*победоносный*
$A_2 Perf$	*побежденный, поверженный*

Adv$_1$Perf	*с победой*
Result	*(вос)торжествовать*
Легко П.	*легко, без труда, малой кровью*
П. (в каком-либо действии)	*пере — [перекричать, переплясать; переиграть].*

Шестая дивизия победила в бою за переправу=...выиграла бой за переправу. Хотя он и перекричал всех, он никого не переспорил=... не победил в споре. В последнем матче победиле [взяла верх] команда из Инакууру. Ура, мы победили!=Наша взяла!

СЕДО́К 1. Пассажир транспортного средства, движимого животным [=тот, кто перевозится в экипаже лошадьми, собаками, людьми и т. п. в соответствии со своей целью].

1	2	3
кто перевозится	кто/что везет	куда перевозится
	1. S$_{\text{род}}$	
	2. A$_{\text{прит}}$	
—	[только название лица]	—

Седок Петра, твой седок.

Невозможно:

**седок кареты [пролстки]*

Syn$_\supset$	*пассажир*
IncepOper$_2$	*брать, сажать ~ а*
Func$_3$	*ехать до [S$_{\text{род}}$]/Loc$_{\text{ad}}$ [S]*
Real$_2$	*довозить до [S$_{\text{род}}$]/Loc$_{\text{ad}}$ [S]*

Извозчики ссорились из-за каждого седока. Рикшам сейчас плохо: нет седоков.

2. тот, кто [=S$_1$] сидит верхом на животном.

[NB: слово СЕДОК 2 характеризует лицо только по его положению относительно животного, а в качестве движущегося предмета рассматривается исключительно животное; поэтому недопустимы фразы типа **На горизонте появился седок, *Седок мчался во весь опор и т.п.*, ср. ВСАДНИК.]

1	2
кто сидит	на ком сидит
—	S$_{\text{род}}$

Седок (крайнего) коня, седок "Урагана"

Syn	*всадник; верховой* 2
Adv_1	*верхом*
$Liqu_2Oper_1$	*сбрасывать, скидывать ~ а*
$Oper_2$	*нести ~ а* | обычно с определением

Вороной конь качнулся, подняв на стремени седока (М. Шолохов).
Увидев его лошадь без седока, они перепугались. Он выстрелил, но пуля
попала не в седока, а в лошадь.

ЧУВСТВО II. способность воспринимать.

1	2	3
кто воспринимает	воспринимаемый аспект объекта	воспринимаемый объект
1. $S_{род}$	1. $S_{род}$	
2. $A_{прит}$	2. A обязат.	—

Невозможно:

$$1.1. + 2.1.$$

Чувство пространства [опасности, времени], эстетическое [музы-
кальное] чувство (зрителей); мое эстетическое чувство; его чувство
формы.

Невозможно:

**чувство цвета живописца*

Gener	*способность [чувствовать]*
V_0	*чувствовать*
S_{instr}	*орган ~ а;* обычно *органы ~* [орган зрения – *глаза,* слуха – *уши,* обоняния – *нос,* равновесия – *вес-* *тибулярный аппарат]*
A_1	*с ~ ом [человек с ~ ом юмора, формы и т.п.]* *чуткий, восприимчивый к* [$S_{дат}$] [=$Able_1$ *(воспринимать)*]
Magn	*обостренное, развитое, врожденное, редкое;* *изощренное* [о физических чувствах]
AntiMagn	*слабое, слабо развитое, притупленное*
$Func_1$(Magn + ч.)	*быть развитым у* [$S_{род}$]

CausPlus	*развивать ~ о в* | [$S_{предл}$], *у* [$S_{род}$]; *обострять ~ о в* [$S_{предл}$], *у* [$S_{род}$] | D_1 (CausPlus) – не целесообразный деятель
IncepPlus	*обостряться, развиваться*
IncepMinus	*притупляться, слабеть*
Ver	*верное*
Bon	*изумительное, удивительное, потрясающее*
Oper$_1$	*обладать ~ ом, быть наделенным, одаренным ~ ом* | при Ч. нежелателен AntiMagn; *отличаться ~ ом* | при Ч. обязательно оценочное определение [включающее Magn, Ver, Bon]
CausOper$_1$	*наделять, одарять ~ ом* [$S_{вин}$] | D_1 (CausOper$_1$) – природа, судьба и т.п.
НедоCausOper$_1$	*обделить ~ ом* [$S_{вин}$] | D_1 (Недо CausOper$_1$) – природа, судьба и т.п.
LiquOper$_1$	*лишать ~ а* [$S_{вин}$]
FinOper$_1$	*утрачивать, терять ~ о*
ResultOper$_1$	*быть лишенным ~ а*
Func$_1$	*быть у* [$S_{род}$]; *быть присущим, свойственным* [$S_{дат}$] | при Ч. нежелателен AntiMagn
CausFunc$_1$	*воспитывать ~ о в* [$S_{предл}$], *у* [$S_{род}$]; *прививать ~ о* [$S_{дат}$]
LiquFunc$_1$	*убивать, вытравлять ~ о в* [$S_{предл}$] [также Liqu$_1$Func$_1$: *в себе*]
IncepFunc$_1$	*появляться, развиваться у* [$S_{род}$]
FinFunc$_1$	*атрофироваться, исчезать, пропадать у* [$S_{род}$]
Func$_1$	*отсутствовать у* [$S_{род}$]
Fact^I	*говорить, подсказывать* [$S_{дат}$]; *требовать от* [$S_{род}$]
AntiFact^I	*спать, дремать, молчать*
CausFact^I	*пробуждать ~ о в* [$S_{предл}$]
CausFact^I	*взывать, апеллировать к ~ у* [по поводу конкретного случая]
LiquFact^I	*заглушать ~ о в* [$S_{предл}$] | D_1 (LiquFact^I) – чувство, ощущение ощущение и т.п. [также Liqu$_1$Fact^I: *в себе*]
IncepFact^I	*просыпаться, пробуждаться в* [$S_{предл}$]
FinFact^I	*изменять* [$S_{дат}$], *покидать* [$S_{вин}$] [часто с *никогда не*]
PerfFact^I	*заговорить в* [$S_{предл}$]

Fact[II]	*не позволять* [$S_{дат}$], *заставлять* [$_{вин}S$]
AntiFact[II]	*подводить* [$S_{вин}$]
Real₁	*обнаруживать, проявлять* ~ *о*
Real₃	*удовлетворять* ~ *о* | только для эстетических, нравственных и религиозных чувств
AntiReal₃	*оскорблять* ~ *о*
AntiReal₃ (эстетическое Ч.)	|| *резать ухо, резать слух* [$S_{дат}$] | *ухо* – только ед. ч., только о диссонирующих звуках или языковых неправильностях; D_1 – не лицо; *терзать слух* [$S_{дат}$] | на D_2 воздействуют звуки; *оскорблять слух* | [также и о нравственном Ч.] | на D_2 воздействуют звуки; *резать глаз* [$S_{дат}$] | *глаз* – только ед. ч.; о зрительных диссонансах
Ч., имеющееся от рождения	*врожденное*

Его эстетическое [нравственное, религиозное] чувство было оскорблено. Чувство меры [юмора, формы] никогда ему не изменяло [его не покидало]. У отдельных руководителей это приводит к утрате чувства нового. У него было врожденное чувство цвета [формы, жанра, ритма]. Он совершенно лишен чувства времени [пространства, высоты]. Бессмысленно взывать [апеллировать] к его чувству справедливости; он давно его утратил. – Ох, уж мне этот Джонс, с его хваленым чувством справедливости! Обделенный от природы эстетическим чувством [=плохо воспринимающий прекрасное]... Мелочная опека способна начисто убить [вытравить] в человеке чувство ответственности. Люди с развитым чувством изященого [чуткие, восприимчивые к изящному] – редкость. Это замечание резануло мне слух. – Что-то в этой фразе не так: она явно режет ухо. Редактор оставит эту фразу – он не лишен чувства юмора.

> *Так век за веком – скоро ли, Господь? –*
> *Под скальпелем природы и искусства*
> *Кричит наш дух, изнемогает плоть,*
> *Рождая орган для шестого чувства*
>
> 　　　　　　　　　　(Н. Гумилев)
> 　　　　　　　　　　[Здесь *Шестое*
> 　　　　　　　　　　*чувство* – о прекрасного]
>
> *О чувство чуда! Седомое чувство!*
>
> 　　　　　　　　　　(А. Вознесенский)

Лишаться ~ = *терять сознание,* см. СОЗНАНИЕ
Приходить в ~ *о* = *приходить в сознание*

Чувство самосохранения: инстинктивное стремление обезопасить себя, см. САМОСОХРАНЕНИЕ

ЗРЕНИЕ	способность видеть [=воспринимать цвет и форму]
ОБОНЯНИЕ	способность обонять [=воспринимать запахи]
НЮХ, ЧУТЬЁ 1	обоняние у животных
СЛУХ	способность слышать [=воспринимать звуки]
ВКУС 2	способность воспринимать ВКУС 1
ОСЯЗАНИЕ	способность воспринимать механические свойства поверхностей
ИНТУИЦИЯ	чувство не явленной в фактах действительности
НЮХ 2, ЧУТЬЕ [разг.]	интуиция
ШЕСТОЕ ЧУВСТВО [образн.]	интуиция
ВКУС 3	чувство искусства [*литературный, музыкальный, эстетический вкус*]
ЭСТЕТИЧЕСКОЕ ЧУВСТВО	чувство прекрасного
ЮМОР	чувство смешного
ГЛАЗОМЕР	чувство расстояния
ОРИЕНТИРОВКА	чувство своего положения в пространстве

Soviet Academy of Sciences and Foreign Languages Institute, Moscow

REFERENCES

[1] A. K. Žolkovsky and I. A. Mel'čuk: 'O semantičeskom sinteze', in: *Problemy kibernetiki*, Vol. 19 (1967) pp. 177–238.

[2] Knowledge of grammar and, in particular, morphology is naturally presumed, and is thus beyond the scope of the dictionary proper.

[3] Meaning definitions given here and below do not claim to be complete (i.e. they are not necessarily genuine definitions): they carry only those components of meaning that are required for the purposes of illustration.

[4] These primitive units are explained by means of pictures, by a non-formal description of their usage (through examples), etc.

[5] The component 'незаконно' is indispensable because an attempt at killing in war or while on duty is not called 'покушение'.

[6] The word "obligatory" is understood in the broad sense and does not extend to a number of purely grammatical constructions (not registered in the dictionary) in which even obligatory places may be left unfilled, e.g. indefinite personal or modal constructions, etc.

[7] Two strokes denote the so-called mergers (portmanteau realizations of LF): the value of a certain lexical function covers both the meaning of C_0 and of $LF(C_0)$, therefore it cannot be combined with C_0 in a syntagm; Cf. Magn (*rain*) = *heavy* // *shower*, where *shower* = *heavy rain*.

IRENA BELLERT

ARGUMENTS AND PREDICATES IN THE LOGICO-SEMANTIC STRUCTURE OF UTTERANCES

In some of my former papers[1] I discussed certain problems connected with a possible deep structure representation – a representation which would be compatible with the fact that we never interpret utterances of natural language without understanding what expressions, or what linguistic devices, are used to identify, point to, or indicate the "objects", individuals, particulars, situations, etc. to which a given predicate is being applied. I believe that from the point of view of a linguistic description, the ontological status of the "objects" or situations being indicated is of no relevance, and cannot even be taken into consideration by a linguist without his running the risk of pursuing a poor philosophy, which would be an outgrowth of certain influences exerted by various philosophical attitudes on natural languages.

A linguist may, however, try to make it clear (what is intuitively clear to all users of natural languages) what linguistic devices serve to indicate or identify "things", particulars or situations, and which serve to say something about them. The "essence of things" may very well remain unveiled to a linguist, for he must assume a deep structure description that will represent in the same manner an utterance, for instance, "Mary was a student of mathematics", no matter whether such an utterance occurs in everyday discourse or in the context of a novel. Thus whenever I use here the terms individual, particular, or I speak simply of an "object", it is only a purported object that is meant.

Any utterance used in normal conditions of communication expresses to a certain extent a complete thought[2], says something definite, and thus resembles a logical statement (logical sentence) or proposition, rather than a propositional form with free variables. It will be argued in this paper that in the deep structure representation of an utterance, there must occur at least one predicate and one argument bound by a quantifying linguistic operator, and the value of the argument always corresponds to the purported object to which that predicate is being applied.

By now it has become quite obvious to most linguists that, for the reasons set forth most clearly by transformationalists, surface structures of utterances are not a sufficient basis for the semantic interpretation which would be compatible with the native speaker's intuitions. Accordingly an abstract deep structure representation has to be assumed in any linguistic description supposed to correlate meanings with sounds. Moreover, it has become clear

F. Kiefer (ed.), Studies in Syntax and Semantics, 34–54. © D. Reidel, Dordrecht-Holland

to many a linguist that the deep structure representations so far proposed are not deep enough for this purpose. However, the problem of how deep structures should be represented remains open for linguists, even for those who have been known as adherents of the generative transformational grammar (as it appears from the preprints of E. Bach, G. Lakoff, P. M. Postal, C. J. Fillmore, J. D. McCawley, and others).

Without committing myself to any claims concerning the status of a possible deep structure representation, and the theory in which my proposals could be incorporated, I will discuss here certain aspects of such a representation which would be compatible with the semantic interpretation of utterances from the standpoint of the identifying and predicating function of linguistic devices.

Accordingly, I will refer here to an abstract structure, which I call the logico-semantic structure (LS structure)[3], in terms of which it will be possible to distinguish those linguistic devices which have an identifying function and those which have a predicating function. The former will be represented in the LS structure by quantified expressions of the argument type, the latter will be represented as predicates (called logical predicates, if confusion may arise as to whether we refer to deep or surface structure).

It was long ago when Charles Sanders Peirce stated that "designations" (that is, indices of a certain type) "are absolutely indispensable both to communication and to thought. No assertion has any meaning unless there is some designation".[4] The correctness and importance of this statement seems intuitively obvious. I believe that in fact it concerns not only declarative utterances, but all types of utterances produced in the normal process of communication. Accordingly, it seems necessary to assume such a representation of the LS structure that its expressions may unambiguously represent arguments and predicates in relation to their formal exponents or other signals on the surface of utterances. This is of course a basic requirement, for certain lexical items of the same form now function as arguments, now as predicates in several natural languages, yet the overall structure of utterances and other signals on the surface make it possible for competent speakers to distinguish between the identifying and the predicating function.

In the present paper, I will use examples in English, but the general idea may hold for other natural languages, in spite of very different surface structures of utterances in various languages.

As I have already mentioned, it does not seem necessary for a linguist to commit himself to an attempt at solving philosophical or ontological problems connected with the existence, fictitious existence, nonexistence – or in general the mode of existence of the individuals, particulars, "objects", situations, etc. being referred to by means of such or other expressions. The deep structure representation should account for the speaker's or hearer's competance to realize or understand what "identifiers" and what predicates are present or implied by a given utterance adequately interpreted (and this can be confirmed by empirical tests) – independently of whether such identifiers point to real, existing "objects" or not; thus independently of whether, an argument, for instance, the index "Mary", functions as an identifier of a living creature we can see and touch, or as an identifier of an imagined or assumed personage which occurs in the context of a reported dream, a novel, a myth or a hypothetical theory. In most cases it is the knowledge of the context, the type of discourse (everyday, literary, scientific, etc.) which tells us whether the speaker or author believes, imagines or assumes that there is such an "object", but this has no bearing on the identifying function of such or other indices. In many cases, the question concerning the mode of existence of such or other "objects" may be resolved, if at all, only by our general knowledge of the world.

One of the basic assumptions accepted here therefore is that ontological considerations – which would lead linguists to resume the endless philosophical discussion concerning the existence of abstract entities, such as universals – are simply out of place in the description of natural language, as the latter prove to be sufficiently good tools for the normal process of communication of thousands of native speakers, who to be sure do not need to solve for this purpose the question of the existence of universals, or even to realize that such a problem arises.

In the simplest cases, the arguments and predicates have the corresponding formal exponents expressed explicitly on the surface of the utterance, in other cases, they are in some way formally signaled and implied by the utterance. If we analyse utterances such as

(1)   John has got married
(2)   This young boy has got married

we easily distinguish the argument – which in this case corresponds to the linguistic indices[5] – "John" and "This young boy", and the logical predicate which corresponds to "has got married". It is clear that in each case when the speaker or author uses the proper name "John" or the nominal phrase "this young boy" in such utterances, it is with the intention of pointing to or identifying a certain individual (existing or assumed as in a novel) to which he applies the predicate "has got married". Arguments, clearly, do not always coincide with the expressions which stand in the position of grammatical subject, as in our two examples. In the utterance

(3)   A bad accident happened to John

the argument corresponds to the linguistic index "John", which stands in the position of prepositional object.

In the present paper we will discuss arguments only in simple utterances. We will call simple utterances those which express one elementary proposition, that is, a proposition which would be represented by one n-place predicate with n arguments, inserted in a modal frame.[6] We will distinguish three types of such arguments: (1) those which serve to identify uniquely, that is, to indicate one and only one "object" to which a logical predicate applies (linguistic indices), (2) those which serve to indicate all the "objects" to which a given logical predicate applies, and (3) those which serve to indicate a number of "objects" to which a given logical predicate applies. Arguments of type 1 will be represented with the aid of a variable bound by the iota operator, those of type 2, by the use of a variable bound by the all-operator, and finally those of type 3 will be represented with the aid of a variable bound by any other quantifying linguistic operator. Thus in all cases an argument in the LS structure representation of a simple utterance will consist of: a quantifying linguistic operator, a variable (an unknown the interpretation of which is: extralinguistic "object"), and a function which corresponds to a name or a description. Such a description, as part of the argument, is used only to form an expression with an identifying function; its function is not purely descriptive as in the case of a logical predicate, but it provides, so to say, an "instruction" for identification. Accordingly, linguistic expressions, independently of whether they are nouns, adjectives, certain verbal forms, nominal groups or clauses, can be used as descriptions which in some utterances correspond to arguments in their LS structure, in others to logical predicates. The function of a description used in an utterance depends on whether in interpreting its occurrence we have to make use of a quantifying operator in the LS structure, or not. If we have to interpret it as a quantified expression, this means that the given description corresponds to a part of the argument, otherwise it corresponds to a logical predicate.

I. LINGUISTIC INDICES AS ARGUMENTS OF TYPE 1

Arguments of type 1, which I called logical subjects[7] in my former papers, will be used in the LS structure representation of sentences of particular reference, that is, sentences by means of which the utterer identifies uniquely at least one "object", and ascribes it a predicate (cf. examples 1, 2 and 3). It seems plausible to assume that for each sentence of particular reference (I consider English sentences), it is possible to find a paraphrase in which there will occur as many linguistic indices as the number of individuals or particulars which are supposed to be uniquely identifiable any time such a sentence is uttered in the normal process of communication (not when it is presented as an example).

If we agree that two utterances have the same interpretation, at least for one of their readings, that is, if we accept them as paraphrases, then independently of the fact that their surface structures may considerably differ, they should be assigned the same LS structure representation (for the readings under consideration). The surface structure of an utterance in which linguistic indices are explicitly expressed is clearly much closer to its LS structure, and hence more convenient as a basis for postulating a possible LS structure representation, than those of its paraphrases in which linguistic indices do not occur, although they are somehow implied, if the utterances are recognized as paraphrases. The fact that a speaker who has the competence of a given language recognizes two utterances as paraphrases (as equivalent in a certain respect) should be taken as an empirically given condition which has to be satisfied by a theory assumed to account for the interrelation between sounds and meanings – a theory which should somehow reflect language competence in its evident respects. Thus a theory which does not satisfy such a condition would prove to be on a lower level of descriptive adequacy[8] than one which does.

Arguments of type 1 correspond to those linguistic indices that do not occur within another linguistic index or within another quantified expression (other quantified expressions will be discussed below). Linguistic indices have a common semantic interpretation, which is independent of their syntactic position in the sentence. The common interpretation of any linguistic index φ can be expressed as: "that one and only 'object' which is referred to as φ by the speaker at the time of producing the given utterance". Accordingly, the common semantic interpretation of arguments of type 1 is the same as that of a linguistic index, the only difference between the two consisting in the role required of an argument in the LS structure of an utterance, an argument to which a logical predicate is applied and with which it makes up a proposition, whereas a linguistic index may also play a different role in the LS structure, for instance, it can be used only as a part of an argument (cf. the index "Mary" which occurs within the index "the man who is sitting next to Mary"). Notice that a simple utterance in the sense of the term accepted here is in fact simple only with respect to its logical predicate. Its arguments, however, may be quite complex.

It seems clear that in order to understand a logical predicate, that is, that expression whose function in the LS structure is to describe or classify a given particular (or particulars) indicated by an index (or indices), it is sufficient to know the language being used, while the knowledge of the speaker, the context, the time or the situation is unnecessary. On the other hand, the knowledge of language is only a necessary condition for the identification of the particular referred to by means of an index. With the exception of very rare cases (which almost never occur in the normal process of communication), our identification of the particulars referred to comes out as a result not only of our knowledge of the language being used, and thus not only of our understanding of the "instruction" contained in the linguistic index in question, but – in accordance with the common semantic interpretation of linguistic indices – it is realized through the identification of the speaker, the time (or place in a written text) of the given utterance, that is, generally speaking through the identification of the *situational context*.

In spite of such complex conditions required for identification, we have to admit that they are satisfied in the normal process of communication, for although each linguistic index is undoubtedly ambiguous, we always interpret linguistic indices contained in utterances normally used in a unique manner. If such is not the case, then we treat the given utterance as ambiguous or inappropriately used, and we are not in a position to understand fully the message conveyed. It might also be the case that the speaker or author wants to express himself ambiguously, and intentionally produces an utterance which deviates from the norm, for which the conditions for identification are not satisfied, the apparent linguistic index being thus deprived of its ordinary function.

In general, however, the addresser of the utterance "John has got married" (used in normal conditions as an intended message, not as an example) intends to identify one and only individual (whom the addressee is supposed to identify in accordance with the situational context), in order to apply to it the predicate "has got married". If the conditions for identification are not satisfied by the situational context, then the addressee, who will not be able to understand the message, may react by asking "Which John? Your son or your nephew?" Such a question asks for a more detailed "instruction" contained in the index.

From the point of view of a linguistic description, however, of significance is only the interpretation of the "instruction" contained in a linguistic index, *plus the indication* that such instructions are to be interpreted as uniquely determining a certain individual or particular. In other words, we should require of a deep structure representation that a distinction be made between identifiers and logical predicates. If the contextual situation is not a linguistic context, then the verification of the fact whether a given index fulfils its identifying function uniquely or not, is not a linguistic problem. It is no more a linguistic problem than the problem of whether a given synthetic utterance is true or false. This problem does belong, however, to the semantic description of a coherent text or discourse, that is, in the case when the contextual situation is linguistic.

Notice that the addresser adjusts the "instructions" for identification contained in linguistic indices with respect to the contextual situation understood widely enough to comprise the degree of knowledge about the world which he assumes about his listener or reader. The use of one or another predicate can also have a bearing on the possibility of limiting such "instructions". Thus, for instance, if among the nearest friends of the addresser and the addressee there are two men whose name is John, one of them being a student, the other a worker, then the addresser need not give a more detailed "instruction" in order to identify the former John, when he says: "John has flunked his exam". The contextual situation is such that the index "John" can perform its identifying function.

On the basis of the above reasoning which supports the proposed common semantic interpretation of linguistic indices used in utterances (see page 38), it seems correct to assume that an adequate representation of a linguistic index in the LS structure will be the unit function prefixed by the iota operator [9]

$$(4) \qquad (\imath x)\, \varphi(x)$$

By definition, φ is a unit function if two conditions are satisfied for the use of φ, one which guarantees the existence, and the other the uniqueness of the object thus described:

$$(5a) \qquad (\exists x)\, \varphi(x)$$

$$(5b) \qquad (\forall x, y)\, [\varphi(x) \wedge \varphi(y)] \to (x = y)$$

The expression (4) in a formalized theory is interpreted as: "that one and only object which is φ". In the case of natural language, as I have argued, it is indispensable to include in the semantic interpretation of linguistic indices such parameters as the addresser (for instance, the interpretation of the pronoun "I"), the addressee, the time, and in general what I have called the contextual situation. Accordingly, our interpretation of the expression (4) is not: "that one and only object which is φ", but "that one and only 'object' (purported object) which is referred to as φ by the speaker at the time of producing the given utterance". Although a linguistic index, as such, does not satisfy the condition of uniqueness (5b), it does satisfy such a condition whenever used in a given utterance by a given speaker or author. And this is precisely what is of relevance to the semantic interpretation: the way we do interpret utterances of natural language – the proof being given empirically.

We will now discuss condition (5a) concerning the existence of a given individual or particular which is referred to by means of a linguistic index. Our interpretation of the condition expressed by (5a) has also to be modified according to the rules which govern the semantic interpretation of utterances in natural language. By now it seems clear to many a linguist that a full semantic interpretation of any utterance requires the specification of what is often called "pragmatical elements", "modalities" or "modal frames".[10] In short, the proposition or propositions expressed by each utterance are never – so to say – hung in the air, but are interpreted as if they were preceded by a statement about the attitude of the speaker towards the event, situation or state of affairs described. Such statements, roughly speaking, may be, for instance: "I believe that S", "I want to know if S", "I doubt whether S", "I assume that S", "I assert that S" etc. The same holds true for the proposition expressed by condition (5a) which says "There is an x which is φ". According to our argumentation, such a proposition, which only thus may be one of the conditions of the appropriate use of a linguistic index[11], should not be represented as occurring within an assertoric modal frame, but in the frame: "I believe (or: I assume) that there is an x which is φ". No speaker will use appropriately the utterance: "The present king of France is bald" (to use the famous example), if he does not believe, pretend to believe[12] or assume (as in a novel or in a hypothetical theory) that there is an individual which is the present king of France. Such an interpretation holds true even if the speaker is misinformed as to the present regime in France, or if he is making a joke (which would in fact consist in identifying de Gaulle by means of the index "the present king of France"). The same holds true of the appropriate use of any other linguistic indices.

There remains one more remark to be made about such pseudoexistential statements as those represented by condition (5a). The copula "is" in terms of which we interpret (5a) should be understood as – so to speak – tenseless, for in fact its tense is also dependent on the tense of the verb used as a logical predicate.[13]

As we see, the apparently existential statements by which we interpret condition (5a) have a very specific sense which is devoid of any implications with respect to the ontological status of the individuals or particulars concerned. Thus our interpretation of condition (5a) could as well be paraphrased by "I believe (or: I assume) that φ is applicable to an 'object'".

II. ARGUMENTS OF TYPE 2

At present we shall discuss those arguments which serve to indicate all the individuals or particulars to which a given logical predicate applies. Their explicit exponents on the surface are usually nominal phrases preceded by "all", "every", "each". However, it is not always the case that such nominal phrases are interpreted as arguments of type 2 (cf. "all Europe", "every second student", "each day", etc). Consider the following examples which show an analogy between arguments of type 1 and those of type 2.

(8)   John is gay
(9)   My father is gay
(10)   My parents are gay
(11)   All members of my family are gay
(12)   All the inhabitants of this town are gay
(13)   All the Italians are gay
(14)   All the inhabitants of the moon are gay

Independently of other problems connected with the proper LS structure representation of utterances such as (10, 11, 12, 13, 14) and others in which a logical predicate applies to each individual of a set determined by a given description, we have to admit that from the point of view of the difference between the identifying and the descriptive function of linguistic devices, all the nominal phrases in our examples serve to identify either a single individual (8, 9) or a number of individuals (10, 11, 12, 13, 14), and thus serve to indicate the values of the argument which is used with the predicate "gay". All of them may then be represented as arguments in the LS structure.

Notice incidentally that there is a difference between utterances such as (10) and, for instance, "My parents bought a new house", in which the description "my parents" should be represented as a linguistic index (argument of type 1), which has a unique value and by means of which we identify one and only "object" (a group of individuals as a whole) to which the given predicate applies. The predicate is not here distributive as in the case of (10), where it applies to each individual referred to by the description "my parents".

Now if we compare

(15)   The girl sitting on this sofa is pretty

with

(16)   All the girls sitting on this sofa are pretty

it seems clear that the difference between the two lies in that the nominal phrase in (15) serves to indicate or identify one individual, whereas the nominal phrase in (16) serves to indicate or identify a number of individuals, both nominal phrases being used as "instructions" for identification. Accordingly, we have to admit that such "instructions" are used appropriately only if the speaker believes or assumes that there is a girl sitting on the sofa in question (for (15)), and there are girls sitting on that sofa (for (16)). Consequently, by a very general assumption that people use their utterances appropriately, the hearer may infer such pseudo-existential propositions preceded by the modal frame "The speaker believes or assumes that...".[14]

One might object to this interpretation of all-statements and try, by analogy to logical statements with a general quantifier, to interpret them as implicational statements: "For any x, if x is φ then x is ψ". Under such an interpretation (16) would be a paraphrase of:

> (17)   If anything is a girl sitting on this sofa it is pretty
> If anybody is a girl sitting on this sofa she is pretty
> Anybody who is a girl sitting on this sofa is pretty.

Even if we ignore the awkwardness of utterances such as (17), we cannot accept such utterances as paraphrases of (16) for two reasons. First, (17) could, then, be equally taken as a paraphrase of (15) as well as that of (16), as there is no mention with respect to the plurality of the individuals referred to. Second, the speaker implies by (16) his belief that there are individuals who are girls sitting on the sofa in question, whereas no such implication holds for (17). To give a better example, if someone says:

> (18)   All the inhabitants of the moon must feel cold

the hearer's reaction might be expressed by: "What are you talking about? There are no inhabitants on the moon." On the other hand, no such reaction would follow upon hearing the utterance:

> (19)   If anything is an inhabitant of the moon it must feel cold

The response might be: "Right you are, but fortunately there are no inhabitants on the moon."

Another argument supporting our interpretation may be provided by the following test. If we produce the utterance:

> (20)   I doubt whether there are inhabitants on the moon, but all inhabitants of the moon must feel cold

it leaves the impression of a certain awkwardness, which is a result of the inconsistency between the expressed doubt and the implied belief concerning the same proposition. On the other hand, the utterance

> (21)   I doubt whether there are inhabitants on the moon, but if anything is an inhabitant of the moon it must feel cold

does not seem awkward.

Evidently there are different implicational rules concerning the if…then-sentences, and they depend on the tense used in the if-clause. If we denote the if-clause by S, the hearer may infer, for instance, that the speaker believes that S, or believes that it is not the case that S, or believes that it is probable that S, etc.

In any case, is seems clear for the reasons given above that (19) is not a paraphrase of (18), nor (17) is a paraphrase of (16). In spite of the fact that implicational statements can be considered as truthfunctionally equivalent to the corresponding all-statements (and this is the basis of the logical equivalence), yet they cannot be represented by the same LS structure, for obviously the latter convey additional semantic information.

Accordingly, instead of making use of a general quantifier, we will introduce an operator which will be called all-operator. The all-operator will be assumed as an argument-forming operator, not a statement-forming operator (as in the case of a general quantifier in logic). In other words, it will not be an operator which makes a statement when added to a propositional form, but an operator which makes an argument when added to a function. It will thus have the category of the iota operator which is used to make an expression of the category of an argument (for the expression $(\imath x)\,\varphi(x)$ is interpreted as "that one and only object which is φ", and not as "there is one and only object which is φ").

We thus assume that the all-operator belongs to a specific class of modifiers which are called here quantifying linguistic operators. Such operators will always be prefixed to an x (variable) in the LS structure representation. A logical statement which is prefixed by a general quantifier with limited range

$$(22) \qquad \forall_{\varphi(x)}\,\psi(x)$$

is an abbreviation for the implicational statement

$$(23) \qquad (\forall x)\,[\varphi(x) \to \psi(x)]$$

We will, however, use a different expression, provisionally denoted by (All x) $\varphi(x)$, which will not be interpreted as a statement equivalent to an implicational statement, but – by analogy to the expression bound by the iota operator – it will be interpreted as an expression of the argument type: "all the x's which are φ". According to our interpretation, the corresponding implicational statement is only one of the conclusions following from the appropriate use of all-statements.

Thus by analogy to the iota operator, we can also define here two conditions for the use of the all-operator on the basis of the empirically given conditions of the appropriate use of the discussed all-statements, which may be schematized by $\psi\,[(\text{All }x)\,\varphi(x)]$. The two conditions are as follows:

(a)   There is more than one x which is φ,
(b)   For any x, if x is φ, x is ψ.

(a) will represent the corresponding purported belief of the speaker who is uttering an all-statement, while (b) will represent the corresponding assertion or claim of the speaker. In fact, in any case, by saying, for instance, "All the inhabitants of the town X are French citizens", the speaker implies his belief that there is more than one inhabitant of the town X, and his assertion that if any individual is an inhabitant of the town X, he is a French citizen. Thus (a) and (b), if inserted in the respective modal frames, may be accepted as the necessary conditions for the appropriate use of the utterance in question. We may accordingly establish a general quasi-implication (see note 14) which will account for such conclusions in all cases of the use of all-statements.

Notice that if an all-statement is converted into a corresponding question, negation, etc., then the first conclusion which expresses the speaker's belief will remain the same, whereas the second one will appear, respectively, in different modal frames: "I want to know whether it is the case that...", "I deny that...", etc.

It may be worth while to emphasize that a predicate applies always to the value of the argument, which we identify with the purported object, no matter whether it is an argument of type 1, which has a unique value and thus indicates a unique object, or it is an argument of type 2, for which the value is identified with the set of objects which belong to the class φ.

III. ARGUMENTS OF TYPE 3

We will now discuss other expressions which function as arguments, that is, indicate the purported objects to which a logical predicate applies. Similarly as arguments of type 1 and 2, those of type 3 may also be represented in the LS structure as expressions prefixed by a quantifying linguistic operator. While arguments of type 1 and 2 are bound by the iota operator and the all-operator, respectively, those we are discussing now will be bound by other quantifying operators, which will have to be defined in a formalized language (perhaps in an extended and modified language of predicate calculus) which we need for our purposes. Their explicit exponents on the surface are usually all such expressions which refer to the quantity of individuals or particulars indicated by a given nominal phrase (*an* inhabitant of Warsaw, *four* students, *most* young boys, *few* people, *some of* your books, etc.), that is, numerals, indefinite article, indefinite pronouns or adjectives.

The common characteristic of such arguments and those of type 1 and type 2 is that all serve to identify or indicate the extralinguistic individuals or particulars to which a logical predicate is applied, although the argument of type 1 is used to identify a unique individual or particular, that of type 2 is employed to indicate all the particulars determined by a given description, and that of type 3 is used to indicate only a certain number of such particulars, not in a unique way.[15] Moreover, the use of arguments of type 3 also implies the belief or assumption of the speaker that there are individuals or particulars which are such and such, or, in other words, that the given indefinite description is applicable to some individuals or particulars. Thus if we say:

(22)   Three inhabitants of the moon died
(23)   Most inhabitants of the moon are sick
(24)   Many inhabitants of the moon will be making trips to the earth,

the hearer may react by saying:

(25)   What are you talking about? Do you believe there were inhabitants on the moon? (in response to 22)
(26)   Do you really believe there are inhabitants on the moon? (in response to 23)
(27)   Do you really believe there will be inhabitants on the moon? (in response to 24)

The situation is exactly the same as when we use arguments of type 1 and 2.

The important fact concerning quantifying operators is that they never occur with logical predicates. If such expressions, which have been mentioned above as formal exponents of indefinite quantifying operators, do occur on the surface before an expression that corresponds to the logical predicate in the LS structure of an utterance, they have no quantifying function, and as a matter of fact such utterances are usually paraphrasable into others in which there is no quantifying operator before the expression corresponding to the logical predicate.

We do not have utterances, such as,

  *John is one student of mathematics
  *My children are many students
  *These students are several intelligent boys

On the other hand, the utterance

(28)   John is a student of mathematics

is paraphrasable into

(29)   John studies mathematics

for the indefinite article "a" is not used in (28) as a device with a quantifying function. It has no semantic function at all. The use of "a" in this case is subject to the rules of surface grammar; for if a logical predicate is applied to a unique individual pointed to by a linguistic index (in this case "John"), there is no need of using another quantifying operator which would be redundant in expressing the singleness of that unique individual.

We use, however, quantifying operators at both sides of the copula "is" only in what I call identification statements[16]

(30)   This person standing in the doorway is my husband
(31)   These people are my parents
(32)   This one is professor X

It would be incorrect to interpret the utterance (28) as an identification statement. The argument that (28) cannot be interpreted as an identification statement runs as follows. If we invert the order of any identification statement, we obtain a paraphrase which differs from it only stylistically or pragmatically (we would use it in different situational contexts, the cognitive meaning remaining the same). On the other hand, we cannot invert the order in utterances such as (28) with the same result. If we invert the order in (28), we obtain an unacceptable sentence which, therefore, cannot be said to be its paraphrase (*A student of mathematics is John).

An utterance, in which an indefinite determiner occurs before the nominal phrase at the left side of the copula "is" and an index occurs at the right side, can only be interpreted (it makes sense only) as an identification statement:

(33)   One of the professors standing here is Bertrand Russell

By uttering (33) we intend to identify one of the individuals referred to by "the professors standing here" with one and only individual referred to by means of the index "Bertrand Russell". Under such an interpretation, however, we may also invert the order in (33), as normally in identification statements:

(34)   Bertrand Russell is one of the professors standing here.

The difference between (33) and (34) is again only pragmatical.

IV. CONCLUDING REMARKS

Summing up, we may say that the LS structure of a simple utterance (an utterance which expresses an elementary proposition containing one logical predicate) could be represented, basically[17], as an n-argument logical predicate with *n* arguments, each of which being bound by a quantifying operator (either an iota operator, or an all-operator, or an indefinite operator). If I have put emphasis on the common semantic function of all these operators, it is by no means that I want to disregard the essential differences between such operators, the differences which are especially obvious when we consider the interrelation between the different types of quantifying operators and negation. I have discussed some aspects of such interrelation in my former paper ('On the Semantic Interpretation of Subject-Predicate Relations...', *op. cit.*), where I pointed out the essential differences between the interpretation of the expressions which can be represented with the aid of the iota operator, and those for the representation of which I proposed the referential operator (see below).

It is worthwhile to observe that the presence of an indefinite determiner on the surface of an utterance does not always indicate that a quantifying operator should occur in the LS structure representation, for in certain cases, expressions which in most utterances correspond to quantifying operators, may be used by virtue of surface grammar rules, and have no semantic function characteristic of a quantifying operator (cf. the example "John is a student"). Moreover, in other cases, indefinite articles in certain structures can assume a different semantic interpretation, and their use on the surface contributes only to signal a more complex LS structure, or such that cannot be set into direct correspondence with the surface elements. Consider the utterance

(35)   It is a beautiful girl who is entering the room

which is a paraphrase of

(36)   The one who is entering the room is a beautiful girl

where "a beautiful girl" functions as a logical predicate applied to the individual referred to by the index "the one who is entering the room". The only possible negation of (35) is:

(37)   The one who is entering the room is not a beautiful girl

Consider also other utterances with the generic use of the article "a":

(38)   A mouse is a small rodent mammal

or utterances of the type:

(39)   An average Frenchman has one child

In (38), the interpretation of the phrase "a mouse" is close to that of "all mice", and an all-operator would be more correct here, although the problem is not at all clear. In (39), the phrase "an average Frenchman" is obviously an abbreviation by which we understand a very complex statement concerning the ratio between the number of all French children and all Frenchmen. Accordingly such a phrase does not refer to any particular individual at all. Similarly, in the utterance

(40)   Every second woman in this town is a spinster

"every" does not have the same interpretation than in its other uses.

In the cases of the use of the article "a" as a quantifying operator, there is a problem of distinguishing between those occurrences of "a" which are paraphrasable by "a certain" ("the one I am referring to"), and those which may roughly be paraphrasable by "one" ("a single"). In the first case, I suggested the use of what I called "referential operator".[18] The use of such an operator was defined in such a manner that its interpretation would be: "that one and only 'object' to which the speaker is referring to at a given time and which is φ". Notice that the function of φ is to indicate the class to which the given individual belongs, not to identify it uniquely, as such is the case when an indefinite description is used.

In the second case, when the article "a" should be interpreted only as a signal of "singleness", it could be represented by the same type of quantifying operator as that representing all other numerals, the difference consisting only in the number of individuals or particulars being indicated. For instance, the utterances

(41)   I need a pencil
(42)   I need three pencils

differ only in the number of particulars referred to by the phrase "pencil".

In concluding I would like to sketch only some ideas concerning a possible interpretation of complex utterances, which express more than one elementary proposition (which fall outside the scope of the present paper). The arguments which would occur in the LS structure representation of such utterances may also be of a higher type. The x's prefixed by quantifying operators in the LS structure representation of simple utterances represent individuals or particulars referred to by means of the names and descriptions, whereas the X's of higher type would represent situations, states of affairs, events, etc. referred to by given propositions (expressed by clauses or their abbreviations, even by abstract names). The quantifying operators prefixed to X's of higher type would then refer to the number of situations, etc. which are such and such. Notice that in such a case, quantifying operators may

often be expressed on the surface interchangeably with time expressions
(always, sometimes, twice, etc.)

It may be worth pointing out here that all abstract names are abbreviations
usually for propositions, and thus many utterances which resemble simple
utterances on the surface should be represented in the LS structure as complex ones. Thus a quantifying operator before an abstract name is misleading.

(43)   John saw a murder

is roughly a paraphrase of

(44)   John saw a situation: somebody murdered somebody

where the two place predicate "saw" has as its arguments the index "John"
and a higher type argument which is quantified by the operator "a".
On the other hand

(45)   John saw the murder of Robert Kennedy

is paraphrasable as

(46)   John saw the situation: somebody murdered Robert Kennedy

where the two place predicate "saw" is applied to the unique individual
referred to by the index "John", and the unique situation referred to be the
given proposition.

What has been said so far does not exclude such an interpretation of
utterances in which a logical predicate applies to another predicate. In such
a case it will be necessary to use some modified language of second order
predicates. This does not disprove however, the general conception, for even
in such a case, the predicate used as an argument of higher order must also
be quantified in the sense of the term as used in this paper.

For if we speak about properties or relations, then the property or relation
indicated by the argument is either any given relation (we can speak, for
instance, about the equivalence relation in general, that is, about any equivalence relation, and describe its properties), or about a particular or unique
relation (say, a relation between two specific individuals), or about some of
the relations which are such and such. In any case, however, when such or
other predicate is applied to an argument, it appears that whatever the latter
is supposed to represent ("object", situation or relation), it is interpretable

as somehow quantified, otherwise the utterance would not express any proposition, but in a way would be analogous to a propositional form.

Thus from the proposed standpoint of the semantic rules of interpretation, we would ignore the problem concerning the "essence of the matter", we would not try to resolve any questions as to *what* is the "object" represented by an argument, but only the question of *how* it is described, and what makes such or other linguistic devices arguments. Consequently, we should attempt at clarifying what makes an argument different from a logical predicate *from a linguistic point of view*, not from a philosophical standpoint. A possible answer which seems tempting is that quantifying operators make this difference.

Finally, I would like to add that the present paper is intended as only a preliminary, intuitive version. Obviously there remains lots to be said more conclusively on the topic. In particular, the complex problem concerning indefinite descriptions which – depending on the structure in which they occur – may be treated as arguments of type 3, predicates, or abbreviations for propositions, has not been given enough attention here, chiefly because my provisional solutions do not seem, as yet, ready for presentation. I believe, however, that even in the present form, the paper may prove to be worth submitting to readers for the purpose of eliciting a discussion on the subject on which so little can authoratively be said for the moment.[19]

Warsaw University

REFERENCES

[1] I. Bellert, 'On the Problem of the Semantic Interpretation of Subject and Predicate in Sentences of Particular Reference', paper delivered at the International Congress of Linguists, Bucharest, September 1967 (to appear in the Proceedings of the Congress); 'On the Semantic Interpretation of Subject-Predicate Relations in Sentences of Particular Reference', (a largely extended version of the former paper) to appear in *Recent Developments in Linguistics* (eds. M. Bierwisch and K. E. Heidolph), Mouton, The Hague; 'On a Condition of the Coherence of Texts', paper delivered at the International Congress of Semiotics, Warsaw, August 1968 (to appear in the Proceedings of the Congress).

[2] It might be argued that a complete thought is usually expressed in a larger portion of a text, thus for a written text it would be at least a paragraph, if not the whole piece of work. However, if we interpret sentence by sentence in a coherent text, or in a lecture, it appears then possible to interpret adequately all the linguistic indices (which refer to the previous context), and then each sentence adds a new complete thought to what has been said before.

[3] As the term "deep structure" has become by now ambiguous, for several linguists use it in very different senses, I introduced the term logico-semantic structure (see, I. Bellert, *op. cit.*), by which I mean an abstract deep structure which is to be in full agreement with the semantic interpretation of syntactic relations. The formal representation of the LS structure is being sought for in terms of the language of predicate calculus, which, however, has to be modified in several respects to fit the interpretation of natural language utterances. I attempt at establishing such a description of the LS structures of utterances which makes it possible to formulate rules referred to as quasi-implications (see note

14) and derive the corresponding conclusions which are implied by the use of utterances.

[4] *Collected Papers of Charles Sanders Peirce*, Vol. VIII (ed. Arthur Burks), p. 24.

[5] I defined a linguistic index in my paper, 'On the Semantic Interpretation of Subject-Predicate Relations...', *op. cit.* Roughly speaking, a linguistic index in English is

(1) a simple designation (proper name, personal or demonstrative pronoun),

(2) a nominal phrase preceded by a definite determiner,

(3) an expression constructed with the aid of linguistic indices according to the following pattern: definite determiner, nominal phrase, restrictive relative pronoun..., where in the place of dots there may occur a number (at least one) of linguistic indices within the subordinate construction. This is a rule-of-thumb definition which only roughly corresponds to linguistic indices, as it is too wide, for it covers for instance, also generic descriptions.

[6] By "modal frame" I mean that component in the description of an utterance which expresses the attitude of the speaker towards the proposition expressed. The term "modal", which is ambiguous, should be understood only in the sense indicated here, not in the sense used in logic.

[7] I dropped altogether the confusing term "logical subject" and replaced it by "argument".

[8] The problem of descriptive adequacy, and the conditions given empirically which a descriptively adequate theory of language should meet, was raised by Chomsky and discussed in several papers by Chomsky and others (the problem is fully presented in N. Chomsky, *Current Issues in Linguistic Theory*, Mouton, The Hague, 1964). As regards his examples, Chomsky presents among others those which prove that a descriptively adequate theory provides a proper basis for ambiguity concerning homonymous sentences. Probably no linguist would disagree that the differentiation of two different but homophonous signals belongs to the empirically given conditions which should be met by a descriptively adequate grammar. However, another question immediately suggests itself here, as to why, by the very same reasons, the grammar should not meet a parallel empirically given condition, namely, that of providing a common basis for two different but synonymous signals, and thus succeed in expressing the basis for the synonymy. For a detailed discussion of this matter, the reader may be referred to my review of Chomsky's 'Topics in the Theory of Generative Grammar', to appear in the journal *Linguistics*, ed. by Mouton, The Hague.

[9] The iota operator was first used by Peano, then by Russell, Reichenbach, Mostowski and several others. Alonzo Church calls it a description operator (*Introduction to Mathematical Logic*, Vol. I, Princeton University Press, 1956).

[10] No one of these terms is free of ambiguity. The term "pragmatical element" or "pragmatical relation" was used by Hans Reichenbach and Charles W. Morris, the term "modalities" is used by a French linguist, Antoine Culioli, and the term "modal frames" is employed by Polish linguists, Andrzej Bogusławski, Anna Wierzbicka.

[11] Briefly, a speaker is said to use an utterance appropriately, if he uses it consistently with the rules of language, and with his purported beliefs, that is, simply, if he makes a correct use of the utterance according with what he intends to say.

[12] From the point of view of the semantic interpretation which is concerned with the information conveyed by utterances as such, not with the states of minds of the speakers, it makes no difference whether the speaker actually believes or only pretends to believe that such and such is the case. We are always concerned here only with the speaker's purported belief.

[13] Thus, for instance, if someone says:

    (a)   Mary's house had two floors
    (b)   Mary's house has two floors
    (c)   Mary's house will have two floors

he implies his belief or assumption that there was an "object" referred to as "Mary's house" (for (a)), that there is such an "object" (for (b)), and finally that there will be such an "object" (for (c)). This is implied merely by the use of the index "Mary's house" and the corresponding tense of the verb. Obviously, in most cases, we may draw additional conclusions based on our knowledge of the world. For instance, upon hearing: "Mary's husband will enter the room in a minute", we understand in accordance with the implied belief of the speaker, that it is not only the case that there will be such an individual, but our knowledge of the world tells us that if there will be someone referred to as Mary's husband, who will enter the room in a minute, then there must be someone who is Mary's husband at the very moment. But such conclusions do not follow from linguistic rules, and we need not discuss them here.

[14] The problem concerning inferences, which I have dealt with in my former papers ('On the Semantic Interpretation...', *op. cit.*, 'On a Condition of the Coherence of Texts', *op. cit.*), will not be discussed here. This problem, however, clearly belongs to the semantics of natural languages, and has recently been given some attention, independently, by a number of linguists dealing with semantics (although it has been treated in slightly different terms). My approach to this problem may briefly be sketched in the following way.

In natural language there are various devices which allow the hearer to draw certain conclusions from utterances. We may distinguish those conclusions which are drawn on the grounds of what I called quasi-implications, and for which it is sufficient to know the language, the knowledge of the world being irrelevant. Such quasi-implications reflect, then, what a competent speaker implicitly knows about his language. For each language, we may specify such quasi-implications which concern lexical items (and which should thus belong to the description of the lexicon) and those which concern specific structures (for instance, the structures of if...then-statements, definite descriptions, etc.). Some quasi-implications seem to have, a more universal validity. Consider, for instance, the following quasi-implicational statement:

For any linguistic index φ, the speaker uses appropriately φ only if he believes (pretends to believe) or assumes that there is an "object" which is φ (or: that φ is applicable to a purported object). Since the consequent of this statement can be assumed to express one of the necessary conditions for the antecedent, we may consider the whole as a quasi-implication. In the case of any utterance which contains a linguistic index we can accept a statement corresponding to the antecedent as holding true, by a very general assumption that people use their utterances appropriately, such an assumption being indispensable for any consistent semantic interpretation. We, therefore, can always infer the corresponding consequent as a conclusion.

Quasi-implications are so defined that they have a very wide scope of application, and the conclusions are derivable not only from declarative utterances, but also from questions, commands, etc. Thus the inference rules concern all types of utterances. In my latest work I accept a radical approach, and assume that the semantic interpretation of an utterance may be identified with the set of conclusions (consequences) derivable from it (On the Use of Linguistic Quantifying Operators in the Logico-Semantic Structure of Utterances, paper submitted for the Conference on Computational Linguistics, Stockholm, 1969).

[15] We are discussing here simple utterances only. A complex utterance, for instance, one with a non-restrictive relative clause, would not be interpreted as an elementary proposition with one logical predicate, but would correspond to two elementary propositions each of which would contain a logical predicate, for in such a case two statements are asserted about the same individual or particular.

[16] By identification statements, I mean such utterances by which an individual or particular to be identified by one linguistic index is said to be the same as that to be identified by another index. In other words, identification statements convey the following information: Two linguistic indices φ and ψ refer to the same "object". We use such utterances when we suppose that the hearer knows that one of the indices applies to a given "object", but does not know that the other one applies to it, too.

[17] Obviously, I am speaking only of the basic, overall LS structure representation of simple utterances, with concern to one of its essential aspects, the identifying and the descriptive function of its elements – without going into other considerations concerning other aspects of the proposed representation which are of relevance to the present topic.

For instance, the problem of how to represent formally the modal frame, which constitutes a component of the proposed LS structure representation, is not discussed here.

[18] I. Bellert, 'On the Semantic Interpretation of Subject-Predicate Relations...', *op. cit.*

[19] I wish to express my indebtedness to Dr Z. Saloni for a helpful discussion on some issues presented here. Finally I would like to excuse myself for the rather loose way I am using certain terms which are well defined in logic (argument, value, etc.). I hope, however, that the reader will get from my rough presentation the underlying linguistic concepts which I attempted to submit for discussion.

MANFRED BIERWISCH AND FERENC KIEFER

REMARKS ON DEFINITIONS IN NATURAL LANGUAGE

1. INTRODUCTION

At first glance the problem of definitions in natural language seems to be a more or less marginal question. This is, however, far from being true. While discussing definitions we shall be forced to touch upon some fairly intricate and central problems of linguistic theory. Though even the formal properties of definitional sentences are far from being clear, the more difficult problems arise with respect to their semantic interpretation, their role in introducing new terms into a given language, and their relation to non-definitional generic sentences. Questions of this type may shed new light on certain properties of lexical readings and lexical systems of natural languages in general and on the relation between analytic and empirical generic sentences based on these properties in particular. We cannot answer these questions within the limits of the present article. We only intend to explore some hitherto poorly considered problems of linguistic theory and to stipulate some concepts that might be useful for further and more detailed investigations.

The framework of the following considerations is that of generative grammar (Chomsky, 1965), and with respect to semantic interpretation the theory propounded by Fodor and Katz (1963), Katz and Postal (1964), and Katz (1966, 1967), though with certain modifications as to the form of semantic representations (Bierwisch, 1969a, 1969b). According to this proposal the basic semantic elements (features, markers, components) are considered to be predicate constants in the sense of symbolic logic, the referential indices – needed in syntax for independent reasons – as individual variables functioning as arguments for these predicates.

2. ON THE SYNTACTIC FORM AND THE SEMANTIC INTERPRETATION OF DEFINITIONS

It is readily seen that there is a great variety of forms which a definition may assume. It may appear as a simple or complex sentence, as an embedded clause or some appositive expression, etc. Here are some examples:

(1)   (a) A paradigm is a set of substitutable forms.

             (b) A set of substitutable forms is called a paradigm.

F. Kiefer (ed.), Studies in Syntax and Semantics, 55–79. © D. Reidel, Dordrecht-Holland

      (c) By a paradigm we understand a set of substitutable forms.

      (d) ... a paradigm, which is a set of substitutable forms, ...

      (e) ... a paradigm, i.e. a set of substitutable forms, ...

      (f) ... a paradigm, a set of substitutable forms, ...

      (g) ... a set of substitutable forms or (for short) a paradigm ...

(2)   (a) To langwile means to listen to an official talk.

      (b) Langwiling is listening to an official talk.

      (c) He langwiled, i.e. he listened to an official talk.

      (d) He listens to an official talk, or langwiles.

      (e) Someone langwiles if he listens to an official talk (and only then).

Some of these examples are different surface forms derived from identical deep structures. Thus, for instance, definitional relative clauses as (1d) and appositions as (1f) are derived from embedded structures underlying copula sentences of the form (1a). Other examples have obviously different deep structures. It is evident, however, that in all cases under (1) *paradigm* and in those under (2) the verb *langwile* is the term to be defined.

The examples (1)–(2) demonstrate neither the necessary nor the sufficient conditions for an expression to be a definition in English. On the one hand, other forms are possible; on the other, not all expressions of the exemplified types are necessarily definitions. Thus, for instance, (1a) may be used under suitable conditions as a generic statement. (We shall return to this problem in Sections 6 and 7.) This amounts to saying that definitional sentences cannot be identified on the basis of their syntactic form alone. We do not intend to give here a formal specification of all and only the definitional expressions in a certain natural language. For the ease of presentation we restrict our further discussion to definitional copula sentences such as (1a), i.e. sentences with the structure NP_1 *is* NP_2, where NP_1 is the definiendum and NP_2 the definiens. In the present context this restriction does not mean loss of generality, since the problems connected with definitional verbs or expressions as *be, be called, understand by, mean, i.e., or* are mostly syntactic in nature and do not affect our general conclusions.

We do not want to specify the internal structure of NP_1 and NP_2 either. In particular, we will not consider the problems connected with the use of articles, partly because the syntactic behavior of articles is anything but clear (for some discussion see Perlmutter, 1969) and also because our considerations should not be restricted to English. Namely, we can assume with good reason that the structure NP_1 *is* NP_2 is universal (if, of course, NP_1 and NP_2 are represented at a sufficiently abstract level), while the use of articles is highly language-specific.

With respect to the copula *is* we assume that it represents a simple connective without time specification, although it goes without saying that definitions in natural language are not restricted to present tense statements. Consider, for example, the following sentences

(3)   Nominalism was a philosophical trend in the early Middle Ages that...
The Royal Chamber was the highest administrative body before 1765...
Remember: a paradigm was a...

In order to account for (3) further specifications are required that need not concern us in the present context.

After these rather cursory remarks on the syntactic form of definitions let us now turn to some aspects of the semantic interpretation of definitions.

Let us consider the following sentence

(4)   [A rhomb]$_{NP_1}$ is [an oblique equilateral four-sided rectilineal figure whose opposite sides are parallel]$_{NP_2}$.

Assume that (4) is a definition. (4) has, then, the following function. Whatever NP_1 may be, the definition indicates an equivalence in some sense between NP_1 and NP_2. In order to clarify the exact nature of this equivalence, we must discuss some questions concerning the notion 'language' which we relegate to the following section. For the present purpose it will suffice to say that in (4) NP_1 is equivalent to NP_2 if (4) is intended to be a definition. In general NP_1 is an abbreviation for NP_2, and (4) may be interpreted as an instruction to the effect that the term *rhomb* is substitutable for the underlying structure of the expression *oblique equilateral four-sided rectilineal figure whose opposite sides are parallel* in every sentence of a given language, say, L. If *rhomb* was previously contained in the lexicon of L, then (4) is simply a statement of the equivalence of NP_1 and NP_2.

We may refer to this particular type of definition as *analytic definition*. This is, by the way, the type of definition that lexicographers are mostly concerned with.[1] It is, however, not our main concern in this paper. The definition we are interested in extends L into another language, say, L'. This happens if NP_1 contains something that is unknown in L. We will call this an *introduction definition*.[2] As a first approximation one might say that NP_1 contains not more than a determiner and a noun. The noun, then, may occur among the dictionary entries of L but with a different meaning. The mechanism of assigning new meanings to already existing words is an extremely complicated process. It stands to reason that, when a new meaning is introduced, the original meaning of some of the already existing words will play somehow a decisive role in the choice of the item for that new meaning. Sometimes it is the function of the designatum, sometimes its shape and in other cases some other property that prompts us to chose the designans from the items in the lexicon. The precise nature of this mechanism is anything but clear at present.

On the other hand, definitions like (4) may also introduce completely new items, i.e. items that were not previously contained in the lexicon of L. Notice, however, that in this case, too, the term to be defined cannot be completely new with respect to L. It must conform to a certain degree to the phonemic structure of L, in other words, it must be, roughly speaking, pronounceable in L.

In either case we may say that the definiendum, the noun in NP_1, is given in the form of a phonemic matrix, which is in accordance with the phonological rules of L, and nothing else, i.e. without any semantic specification. It is now a minor issue whether the item represented by this phonemic matrix occurs already among the dictionary entries of L or not.

We might further idealize the issue by stipulating this as a general representation for any new NP_1, even if it may have a more complicated structure than suggested by our examples (1)–(2). We may have, for instance, as definienda *Abelian group, distinctive feature, generative grammar, United Kingdom, German Democratic Republic*, etc. Though all these expressions do have an internal syntactic structure, it would seem that the only way to introduce them is by means of definitions.[3]

There are some reasons suggesting that we may represent expressions in the same way as single words. This is, however, a much more intricate problem, which we must leave out of consideration for the moment.

We may now turn to the semantic interpretation of definitions. Once again, we restrict ourselves to the simplest case, i.e. where the definiendum NP_1 consists of the term to be defined, functioning as head noun, and a determiner.

Discussing the interpretation of cases such as (4) we assume that *is* and all elements occurring in NP_2 are part of the language L, i.e. they may assumed to be known to the speaker-listener with all their syntactic and semantic properties. Under these conditions, the semantic interpretation of NP_2 according to the accepted theory is straightforward. Every lexical entry, viz. *oblique, equilateral, four, sided, figure*, etc., is associated with a combination of elementary predicates with suitable variables for arguments or referential indices, and these complexes are then combined with each other according to the internal syntactic deep structure of NP_2 and the general principles of combination leading to the semantic interpretation or reading of NP_2. (See, for some details of the semantic representation by means of predicate calculus, Bierwisch 1969a, b.) Since the details are of no importance here we may abbreviate this reading by $R(x)$, where the argument x represents the individuals referred to by this particular occurrence of NP_2.

Now the critical problem is that of interpreting NP_1. We shall symbolize the missing reading of NP_1 by M and render the semantic interpretation of (4) in the following form:

(5)   If $M(x)$ then $R(x)$,

where we consider *if ... then* as the approximative reading for *is*. (5) amounts to saying that every time an object is referred to by the hitherto unknown NP_1 it has the properties R, i.e. it might be referred to by NP_2 as well. In other words, (5) is an instruction to enter the item *rhomb* into the dictionary and to associate with it the reading R.

It seems now especially important to precisely determine the status of the symbol M in (5). Formally it functions as a predicate of the same type as the complex predicate of the definiendum, i.e. R in the present case. M, however, must be taken as a semantically unanalyzed entity. Would not this be the case, then the reading of NP_1 would already be known and (4) would not be a definition in the intended sense (i.e. it would be an analytic definition at the best). On the other hand, M cannot be something like a variable over predicates but must rather be determined as the missing reading of a particular expression, viz. *rhomb* in (4). These considerations may lead us to the following hypothesis. We shall consider M a universal constant with the following interpretation: associate the phonemic matrix of this formative with the reading of the definiens. Or, alternatively we may interpret M in a still more general fashion: M is the reading to be associated to the formative in question. In other words, the meaning of the definiendum is the address for the corresponding phonemic matrix.

On this interpretation of definitions it is apparent that the new items are, if necessary, distinguished from each other by means of their respective phonemic matrices, and the universal constant representing their reading constitutes the basis for their semantic interpretation. This universal constant functions formally as a predicate associated with the same argument or referential index as the reading of the defining expression.

Of course, this is not everything that can be said about the interpretation of definitions. We shall pick up some loose ends in the subsequent sections.

3. LEXICAL RELATEDNESS OF GRAMMARS

In order to clarify the specific status of definitions with respect to other linguistic expressions, it might be useful to consider briefly their treatment in formal languages. Given a formal language L, then, in general, a definition is given as an expression in a metalanguage of L, which has the general shape '"X" $=_{def}$ "Y"' with 'X' as the definiendum and 'Y' as the definiens. Here 'Y' must be already an expression of L and 'X' contains a new term to be introduced into L, thus yielding an extended system L'. In this sense, a definition is a metalinguistic operation transforming L into L'. It indicates that in each expression of L' 'X' may be substituted by 'Y', reducing thus the expressions of L' to those of L.

A second possibility is to consider an expression 'X $\equiv$ Y', which corresponds in an obvious way to the above form of definitions, to be part of the object language L' itself. In this case the expression in question is not a metalinguistic statement, but simply a postulate or an analytic statement of L'. Since on the basis of this statement the same substitution of 'Y' for 'X' in the expressions of L' is admitted, its effect is identical to that of the definition conceived as a metalinguistic expression.

It can easily be seen that these two possibilities of treating definitions correspond to the two major functions of definitions in natural language mentioned above: 'X $\equiv$ Y' is the analogue of analytic definitions, '"X" $=_{def}$ "Y"' is the analogue of introductory definitions. It must be noted, however, that the difference between these two possibilities is not, in general, formally expressed in natural language. Since the metalanguage, in which an introductory definition is formulated, might very well be the same as the language to which the terms of the definition belong, the analytic and the introductory status of a definitional expression are necessarily distinct only with respect to their semantic interpretation in the manner discussed above. We will now consider in some detail the function of introductory definitions and the relationship that it brings about between L and L'.

Let G_1 be the grammar of a particular language L_1. Assume furthermore that another grammar G_2 differs from G_1 only in that its dictionary contains a small number of entries not belonging to the dictionary of G_1.[4] Obviously, the language L_2 specified by G_2 contains a (potentially infinite) set of sentences not belonging to L_1, viz. all those in which one of the dictionary entries $E_1, E_2, ..., E_n$ occurs, which belong to G_2 but not to G_1. Hence from a strictly formal point of view G_1 and G_2 are grammars of different languages. We would not say, on the other hand, that two speakers of English, whose linguistic competence differs only in the fact that one has acquired, for example, the word *corrosion*, whereas the other has not, speak two different languages. They are rather, in a fairly plausible sense, speakers of the same language. The point at issue here is the question: 'What do we mean by *the same language*?' This question might be left open for many purposes of linguistic analysis. But it is by no means a marginal one for the linguistic theory in general, and for the topic of the present paper in particular. To provide a partial answer to it, we will introduce the following notions.

(6)   Grammar G_2 *directly succeeds* grammar G_1 iff G_2 is identical to G_1 except that there is a dictionary entry E such that E belongs to the dictionary of G_2 and E does not belong to the dictionary of G_1.

(7)   A sequence of grammars G_1, G_2 ..., G_n is a (*dictionary based*) *succession* of grammars iff G_i directly *succeeds* G_{i-1} $(1 < i \leqslant n)$. In this case G_n succeeds G_1.

It is obvious that language acquisition consists in part – but by no means only – in running through dictionary based successions of grammars. Language acquisition comprises, of course, completely different processes as well, which modify the systems of syntactic, phonological, and perhaps semantic rules. Notice that there are only finite successions of grammars, since the dictionary of any grammar consists always of a finite, though perhaps rather large set of entries.[5] A dictionary based succession of grammars can be taken now as a first step towards an explication of the notion 'the same language': it is a sufficient condition for the languages L_1, L_2, ..., L_n to be variants of the same language L, if the corresponding grammars G_1 through G_n form a succession of grammars. Such an approach brings up the relativity of the notion 'same language', as it is by no means clear whether we are to admit successions of grammars of arbitrary length constituting one language, or not. Thus we would not hesitate to consider L_i and L_j as variants of the same language if they differ only by a few dozen of dictionary entries. The question is less obvious, if they differ by many thousands of entries. It is evident, however, that any restriction on the length of successions of grammars must be motivated by independent considerations, to which then the notion of sameness of language is related. We need not pursue this question here any further.

The existence of a succession of grammars is, however, not a necessary condition for two languages L_i and L_j to be variants of the same language in some reasonable sense. Assume that there are e.g. two dictionary entries E_i and E_j, such that G_i contains E_i but not E_j, and G_j contains E_j but not E_i, and that G_i and G_j are otherwise identical. In general we would, consider L_i and L_j as variants of the same language, even though they are not connected by a sucession of grammars. L_i and L_j can be related, however, in an obvious way by a grammar G_k identical to G_i (and G_j), except that it does not contain E_i (and E_j). We may say now that two languages L_i and L_j are variants of the same language L if there is a grammer G_k such that G_i and G_j are related to G_k by different successions of grammars. Notice that this comprises also the case of succession between G_i and G_j, G_k then being simply identical to G_j. We will generalize these notions by the following definitions:

(8)   Let $F_1 = G_1, ..., G_n$ and $F_2 = G'_1, ..., G'_m$ be two successions of grammars. F_1 and F_2 are *related successions of grammars* if there is a succession $G_1, ..., G_k (k \leqslant n)$ of F_1 identical to the succession $G'_1, ..., G'_k (k \leqslant m)$ of F_2.

(9) G_i *alternates with* G_j if G_i and G_j are members of the related successions of grammars F_1 and F_2, respectively, and G_i is not identical to any G_p of F_2 and G_j is not identical to any G_q of F_1.

(10)   A set of related successions of grammars is a (*dictionary based*) *family of grammars.*

A family of grammars can be represented as a directed tree whose nodes are labelled by the related grammars. A succession of grammars is a branch of the tree, nodes on the same branch are succeeding grammars, nodes on different branches are alternating grammars. Given the above-mentioned additional restrictions on the admitted length of successions of grammars, we might say that the elements of such a family of grammars specify the variants of a language L.

It goes without saying that the notions defined in (6)–(10) provide the framework for only a partial answer to the problem of sameness of language. It is based on the idealization that changes in the dictionary are essentially independent of all other parts of the grammar[6] and it relies exclusively on differences in the set of dictionary entries. It is obvious that corresponding notions with respect to modifications in other parts of the grammar are called for in order to be able to formulate precisely the notions of sameness, difference, and change of language, and that these additional notions would be interrelated with the already defined ones in a fairly complex way. However, we need not consider for the present purpose these by far more complicated problems. It is rather clear that the notion of dictionary based families of grammars enables us already to deal with a fairly large set of non-trivial problems, since the dictionary is clearly the least stable part of the grammar, and since even in the most homogencous speech community there may always be differences in the dictionaries of two arbitrarily selected speakers.

Let us consider now how two directly succeeding grammars G_1 and G_2 are related. According to definition (6) G_2 is an extension of G_1. There are, in principle, two essentially different ways on which an extension of G_1 can emerge.

(a) A speaker who has already acquired G_1 encounters in an arbitrary context a dictionary entry E which is not part of his grammar; he tries to determine the reading associated with E from the (linguistic and non-linguistic) context in which he experiences occurrences of E; he may try to apply E in his own speach, registering corrections or success of its use; finally he incorporates E into his grammar which is extended thereby to G_2. We might call this the *implicit* acquisition of E.

(b) A speaker whose language is based on G_1 is provided with a definitional expression whose definiendum NP_1 contains a dictionary entry E which is not part of G_1. As the result of the understanding the definition, the speaker/hearer incorporates E with the appropriate reading provided by the NP_2 of the definition into his dictionary, thus extending G_1 to G_2. This process could be called the *explicit* acquisition of E.

The two possibilities sketched under (a) and (b) may interact, e.g. if a speaker/hearer has already determined the reading of E to a certain extent on the basis of intuitive experience and then encounters an explicit definition of E. Though this might in fact be a fairly frequent way of extending dictionaries, we need not deal here with these mixed processes. In general, then, (a) and (b) are two different processes connecting directly succeeding grammars. In other words, intuitive processes of the type (a) and/or definitions of the appropriate type connect neighboring nodes in a tree representing a dictionary based family of grammars. The process we are interested in here is, of course, that of extension by means of definition.

Notice that there are many different realizations of the abstract process of extending a grammar on the basis of a definition. The definition might be explicitely stated as such, e.g. in a scientific paper or discussion, or in language teaching; it might be given in by passing during a conversation. Creating a new term by means of a definition and acquiring a new term by means of understanding a definition are completely analoguous processes insofar a grammar G_1 is extended by means of the same definition into G_2.[7] Thus, what we are dealing with in considering the status of introductory definitions is not a problem of performance. It is rather a true phenomenon of competence, i.e. of the domain specified by the question: According to which rules are the sound-meaning correspondences constructed in a given language? There is, however, an additional aspect not present in the phenomena of competence in general. Whereas usually one need not bother about the effect of a given sentence belonging to the language under consideration, because this effect cannot have any bearing on the problems of competence, exactly this influence on the underlying competence is the crucial point in introductory definitions. Thus, the effect of the sentence cannot simply be relegated to the theory of performance in the case of introductory definitions. In other words, introductory definitions are not only specified in their form by the underlying competence, they affect this competence itself as well.[8] This aspect seems to us of considerable interest for the general linguistic theory, since according to this point of view, which considers certain mechanisms involved in extending the competence specifying a language L_i as being part of L_i itself, a precise understanding of the formal nature of definitions might yield some insights into that part of language acquisition that makes use of verbal definitions. Though this aspect of language acquisition should not be overestimated, it is certainly not a marginal one – at least with respect to the important task of dictionary acquisition. Because of the relevance of this aspect of definitions for the present discussion, we will consider it in some more detail.

4. LEXICAL ASPECTS AND OSTENSIVE DEFINITIONS

Notice first that there are, corresponding to introductory definitions, particular questions asking for the meaning of a particular lexical entry. Let us call such a question a *lexical question*. Examples of lexical questions might be:

(11)   Daddy, what is a tarantula?
(12)   What is a perfect number?
(13)   What is a rhomb?

Lexical questions might connect in an obvious way implicite and explicite acquisition of a lexical entry. Obviously the reading of a lexical question must contain the universal element M introduced in Section 2 as the reading of the term to be defined in an introductory definition. More precisely, the underlying structure of questions like (13) will be something like (14) with M as the reading of NP_1:

(14) $[Q[\text{rhomb}]_{NP_1}$ is $[\text{WH something}]_{NP_2}]_S$.

This analysis accounts automatically for the fact that a question like (13) implies the presupposition 'an x called "rhomb" is something'. In other words, that is, to ask 'what is a rhomb?' presupposes that one has encountered the term 'rhomb', that this term means something, and that this something is unknown. (For the notion of the presupposition of a question see Katz and Postal (1964).) The lexical questions (11), (12), and (13) might be answered by (15), (16), and (4) respectively:

(15)   A tarantula is a big poisonous spider.

(16)   A perfect number is a natural number that equals the sum of its proper divisors.

If we assume, then, that L_i is the language of the speaker who utters (11), (15) functions as an introductory definition extending L_i into L_{i+1}. This presupposes, of course, that all lexical elements occurring in the NP_2 of (15) are already part of G_i.[9] In the following discussion we will assume that this condition on NP_2 is met.

Having introduced the notion of lexical questions we must notice next that an introductory definition is an appropriate, but by no means the only possible natural answer to a lexical question. Thus (11) might as well be answered for example by one of the following sentences:

(17)   Look here, this is a tarantula.

(18)   A tarantula is a beast very similar to the big spider we saw in the zoo last week.

(17) requires, of course, an additional gesture towards an appropriate object or picture. Though sentences like (17) and (18) provide at least relevant parts of the information requested by (11), it is obvious that they do this in a manner completely different from that of sentences like (15). Sentences of the type (17), if used as an answer to an (overt or implicit) lexical question, are frequently called ostensive definitions.

They do not specify the meaning of the term in question, they rather illustrate the meaning by applying the term to an appropriate example. It goes without saying that, in general, one cannot infer the relevant predicates which make up the meaning of the questioned term from one example, but only from a set of examples and counterexamples. We are not concerned here with the fairly complicated processes that eventually lead to the abstraction of the meaning of a term used in a sufficient set of examples and counterexamples of the form (17). It is clear, however, that sentences of this kind are by no means definitions in the sense discussed in Section 2. From these they differ also formally in that the term to be defined does not function as the subject of the sentence. In ostensive definitions the NP with the reading M functions as a predicate NP whose semantic content is to be inferred from the putatively relevant properties of the object referred to by the subject NP 'this', 'that', etc.

Between the two extreme types of appropriate answers to a lexical question – ostensive definitions relying on extralinguistic information only and definitional sentences relying on no extralinguistic information – there are several mixed cases. (18) is one of them. It differs from (17) in that the term to be defined does not appear as subject *NP* and by providing the linguistic information represented by 'beast' and 'very similar to a big spider'. It is similar to an ostensive definition insofar as it relies on an exemplifying instance, viz. the object 'we saw in the zoo last week'. There are several intricate problems with respect to such 'mixed definitions', e.g. the status of phrases like 'similar to' in the definiens, which invoke factual knowledge, relying at the same time on certain abstract operations, i.e. on the construction of the relevant similarity. We need not go into the problems connected to this and other cases of 'mixed definitions'. For the present purpose it is sufficient to realize that a lexical question can appropriately be answered by sentences which make use of extralinguistic, factual information in various degrees. What they have in common is essentially the fact that they contain a constituent whose reading is the universal dummy element M.[10] After this provisional clarification of the wide variety of sentences introducing a new term into a given grammar G, we will return to some particular problems of introductory definitions, which are based on linguistic information only.

5. PARTIAL AND COMPLETE DEFINITIONS

According to the foregoing discussion a sentence that is an introductory definition with respect to some language L_i is always an analytic statement in L_{i+1}. It is not equally obvious which analytic sentences of some L_i might function as an introductory definition with respect to the corresponding L_{i-1}. Thus whereas e.g.

(19)   A rhomb is a four-sided figure.

might be an analytic sentence in L_i, we would not, however, consider it as an introductory definition with respect to L_{i-1} whose dictionary does not contain the word 'rhomb'. Nevertheless, (19) could be taken as an appropriate answer to the lexical question (13) 'What is a rhomb' and hence it might lead to an extension of G_{i-1} by introducing 'rhomb' into its dictionary with the reading of 'four-sided figure' assigned to it. The resulting grammar is, of course, not identical to G_i, if we assume that G_i contains the term 'rhomb' with the reading represented by the defining NP_2 of (4) above. Because of this pecularity of sentences like (19), viz. that they do not completely specify the reading of the term that they can be used to introduce, we may call them 'partial definitions', as opposed to 'complete definitions' which provide the fully specified reading of the term to be defined. It is obvious that the distinction between partial and complete definitions is related to the grammar

G_i that already contains the term to be defined. In other words, if (19) functions as an introductory definition with respect to some language L_{i-1}, then it might be a partial definition with respect to a certain L_i (e.g. that language which contains 'rhomb' with the reading specified in (4)), but a complete definition with respect to another language L_i' (viz. that which has incorporated 'rhomb' on the basis of (19)). These notions can provisionally be made more precise in the following way:

(20)   Let a sentence S with the structure NP_1 *is* NP_2 be an introductory definition with respect to L_i and an analytic sentence with respect to L_{i+1}.

       (i) S is a *complete definition* with respect to L_{i+1}, if and only if the reading of NP_1 is identical to the reading of NP_2 in L_{i+1}.

      (ii) S is a *partial definition* with respect to L_{i+1}, if the reading of NP_1 contains semantic specifications not contained in NP_2 in L_{i+1}.

It follows from the previous discussion that only a complete definition relates a pair of grammars G_i and G_{i+1} in the sense presupposed in the definition (6) of succeeding grammars. A partial definition relates G_i to an intermediate grammar G_i', whose relation to G_{i+1} will be taken up in the next section.[11] It is important to note, however, that partial and complete definitions cannot be distinguished of the basis of L_i alone. In other words, insofar an introductory definition is taken as a sentence of the language that is to be extended by means of it, the partial/complete distinction does not exist. It is for this reason that we have stipulated the interpretation 'if... then...' for the copula of definitional sentences in (5) above; as there is, in general, no overt indication for the completeness of a definition, i.e. for the equivalence of the reading of NP_1 and NP_2 with respect to L_{i+1} an introductory definition in L_i must be interpreted in the weaker sense of an implicational rule.

Given the distinction between complete and partial definitions, we will turn to certain related problems. Consider first introductory definitions of the following kind:

(21)   A rhomb is a four-sided figure of a certain type.

(22)   A tarantula is a spider of a certain kind.

Obviously, (21) is not a complete definition with respect to a language L_{i+1} according to which (4) would be complete. It is, however, not partial in the same sense in which (19) is partial, given the same conditions. (21) explicitly indicates that rhombs are only a species of the class of four-sided figures, while (19) leaves this restriction open. Hence, although (21) is incomplete insofar it does not specify the difference of rhombs with respect to other types of four-sided figures, it makes explicit that the class of rhombs and the class of four-sided figures are not identical: it provides, so to speak, a variable for the differentiating properties. The same considerations apply to (22) with respect to (15). We might consider introductory definitions of this kind as *explicitely partial*. There is, however, a further observation to be made here: it might very well be the case that a sentence like (21), taken as an analytic definition in L_{i+1}, has the same reading for NP_1 'rhomb' and NP_2 'four-sided figure of a certain type'. This situation automatically arises if the speaker of L_{i+1} has incorporated the term 'rhomb' into his dictionary without being able to find out its specific difference with respect to other four-sided figures. (This is obviously a fairly common situation in natural language: we have always a great number of dictionary items at our disposal whose readings are not fully specified within our linguistic competence.) Assume that such a situation holds with respect to 'rhomb' in L_{i+1}; then (21) possibly qualifies as a complete definition with respect to L_{i+1} according to (20i). This apparently paradoxical result suggests that we should define partial and complete definitions not with respect to an arbitrary language L_{i+1} that differs from L_i only by the occurrence of the term in question in the dictionary of L_{i+1}, but rather with respect to a particular language L^* that contains the term to be defined with all and only the relevant semantic specifications. This, however, raises many intricate questions.

First of all, it is by no means clear, whether for every dictionary entry E there is always a fixed L^* that uniquely meets the relevant condition. Secondly, it seems to be obvious that such an L^* cannot be characterized with respect to single lexical entries, but only for somehow coherent sets of entries. Thus the L^* with respect to which the completeness of 'rhomb' might be determined, must also provide the basis for complete definitions of 'square', 'oblong', 'parallelogram', etc. On the other hand, it seems to be equally obvious that one should not postulate one single L^* with respect to which the completeness of definitions for arbitrary entries can be specified. Thus, given an L^* providing the desired basis for a complete definition of 'rhomb', this L^* need not at the same time account for a complete definition of 'tarantula' or 'spider'.[12] Thirdly, it is not clear whether there is a general characterization of the relevant properties of the different languages L^* and a particular place of their pertinent grammars within a succession of grammars. We are not able to deal with these problems within the limits of the present paper. We cannot even provide the framework within which they might correctly be formulated. We can only discuss some questions that are closely connected to problems of this kind.

6. REDUNDANT DEFINITIONS, LINGUISTIC AND ENCYCLOPEDIC KNOWLEDGE

Let us assume that (15) 'A tarantula is a big poisonous spider' is an introductory definition with respect to some language L_i. Obviously, (15) is a partial definition with respect to some language L^*, even if it were a complete definition with respect to L_{i+1}. Let us ignore, for the moment this hypothetical L^* and consider the following sentence, taken as an introductory definition with respect to L_i:

(23)   A tarantula is a big poisonous spider living in Mediterranean countries.

Let us inspect now the following two situations:

(a) Both (15) and (23) are true generic sentences in L_{i+1} and (15) is a complete definition with respect to L_{i+1}. In this case (23) is not a definition in the usual sense. It is rather a generic sentence that is equivalent to the conjunction of (15) and one of the following (non-definitional) generic sentences:

(24)   (a) Tarantulae are living in Mediterranean countries.

(b) The tarantula is living in Mediterranean countries.

We will call a sentence composed of a (complete) definition and a generic sentence a *redundant definition*.[13]

(b) Both (15) and (23) are true generic sentences of a language L'_{i+1}, but (23) is the complete definition linking L_i to L'_{i+1}. In this case (15) is only a partial definition with respect to L'_{i+1}, and it would be a complete definition with respect to some 'intermediate' language L'_i. (This L'_i is identical to the L_{i+1} under (a).)

According to these assumptions, we have the following situation: L_i is connected by the introductory definition (15) to $L_{i+1} = L'_i$, and by the introductory definition (23) to L'_{i+1}. We might ask now, in what sense $L_{i+1} (= L'_i)$ is connected to L'_{i+1}, i.e. whether a generic sentence contributes to the meaning of its subject[14], and what such an interpretation of the status of generic sentences would mean. A similar question concerns the status of redundant definitions, i.e. the role of (23) with respect to L_{i+1}. These questions are tied up with far-reaching problems of the organization of lexical readings and systems of lexical readings.

Let us tentatively assume that the semantic characterization of any lexical entry E can be divided into two parts, which we will call the core, $C(E)$ and the periphery $P(E)$ of E, respectively. The *core* of a lexical reading comprises all and only those semantic specifications that determine, roughly speaking, its place within the system of dictionary entries, i.e. delimit it from other (non-synonymous) entries. The *periphery* consists of those semantic specifications that contribute to the meaning of a lexical entry without distinguishing it from other dictionary entries, i.e. of specifications which could be removed from the reading without changing its relation to other lexical readings within the same grammar. To give an oversimplified example let us assume that $C(spoon)$ represents the core of 'spoon', containing such semantic components as *Physical Object, Artifact, Used for eating liquid food*, etc. and distinguishing 'spoon' from other dictionary entries, in particular 'fork', 'knife', 'instrument', 'tool', etc. A change in the semantic specifications contained in $C(spoon)$ would affect the relative position of 'spoon' to the other pertinent elements of the dictionary, i.e. it would alter the classification of potential objects induced by the dictionary in question. Assume, on the other hand, that the periphery $P(spoon)$ of spoon in the dictionary in question contains specifications such as *Consisting of solid material, Having a certain average size, Not used in Asiatic cultures*, etc. A change in $P(spoon)$ would not affect the relative position of 'spoon' within the dictionary and the categorization of objects associated with it.

There are several problems connected with the proposed division of lexical readings. First of all, it is obvious that every lexical entry E must have a nonempty $C(E)$, whereas its periphery $P(E)$ might be empty: an entry without a $C(E)$ would not have any determinable position within the dictionary at all, an entry without a $P(E)$ would be specified with respect to this position exclusively.

A second problem concerns the distinction between $C(E)$ and $P(E)$. Obviously, certain elements that are part of $P(E)$ in one grammar might be part of $C(E)$ in another one.[15] In other words, the division of the reading $R(E)$ into $C(E)$ and $P(E)$ is dependent on the grammar to which E belongs. This problem is connected with the following question: what would be the effect of transferring a part of $P(E)$ into $C(E)$? According to the observation that the division of $R(E)$ into $C(E)$ and $P(E)$ depends on the dictionary as a whole, a change of the type in question is not a matter of a single entry E. In other words, a change in the delimitation between core and periphery in one entry E will cause a corresponding change in the core of certain other entries of the same dictionary. We cannot pursue here the complicated problems involved in modifications of this type. We may point out only one fairly obvious and simple case. Given the core $C(E)$ of an entry E and a (possibly complex) semantic specification F that is transferred from the periphery $P(E)$, such that the new resulting core $C'(E)$ is the logical conjunction $C(E) \wedge F$, then E enters by this transfer a set of species concepts, of which it was formerly the *genus proximum*. If the dictionary does not contain other species concepts subordinate to the *genus proximum* specified by $C(E)$, then the transfer of F into the core of E introduces the place for a set of potential entries of this type, which could minimally be occupied by an entry whose core would be $C(E) \wedge \sim F$. In our above example the introduction of the content of 'living in Mediterranean countries' into $C(taran-tula)$ of L_{i+1} would provide the possibility of a differentiation of big poisonous spiders into those living in Mediterranean countries and those living elsewhere.[16] Hence L'_{i+1} might contain a set of dictionary entries whose readings could be paraphrased as 'big poisonous spiders living in X', where X is a variable over geographic specifications, while L_{i+1} cannot contain such entries in its dictionary.

A third, still more complicated problem concerns the conditions that a semantic specification F must meet in order to be transferable from $P(E)$ to $C(E)$. The problem might be illustrated by a comparison of the following examples:

(25)   (a) tarantula living in the Mediterranean countries
        (b) triangle the sum of whose angles is 180°.

We have considered above a language L_i not containing 'tarantula', a language L_{i+1} containing 'tarantula' with a reading whose core does not contain the semantic content of the phrase 'living in the Mediterranean countries', and a hypothetical language L'_{i+1} with an entry 'tarantula' whose core is equivalent to the complete reading of (25a). Though L_{i+1} is probably closer to average English, L'_{i+1} is surely a possible language. (Its relevant properties have been mentioned in the previous paragraph.) Consider now a language M_i not containing the term 'triangle' and connected to M_{i+1} by the following introductory definition:

(26)   A triangle is a plane figure bounded by three straight lines.

There is no language M'_{i+1} corresponding to M_{i+1} on the basis of (25b) in the sense in which L'_{i+1} corresponds to L_{i+1} on the basis of (25a). In other words, the semantic content of the phrase 'the sum of whose angles is 180°' cannot be incorporated into $C(triangle)$, since it could in no way change the relation of 'triangle' to other actual (or even potential) dictionary entries as e.g. 'figure', 'square', 'rhomb', etc.[17] Although the content of the phrase in question is – according to (26) – not part of the reading of 'triangle' in M_{i+1}, it can be deduced from it on *a priori* grounds, and hence it cannot distinguish different potential kinds of triangles, unlike the phrase 'living in Mediterranean countries', which is not deducible from the reading of 'tarantula' in L_{i+1} and might very well distinguish different kinds of objects. We are touching here on the much disputed problem of *a priori,* analytic, synthetic, and empirical truth. Though this problem obviously has important bearing on a more detailed analysis of the conditions for incorporating parts of $P(E)$ into $C(E)$, we cannot go into it here.[18] We must be content to point out that there are deep-seated systematic restrictions for a semantic element F to enter into the core $C(E)$ of an entry E, though F might very well be part of $P(E)$ of the same entry. These restrictions depend on systematic properties of the whole dictionary, which are partly conventional, i.e. different for various languages, partly universal constraints for any possible dictionary.[19]

It goes without saying that the proposed distinction between core and periphery needs a much more detailed and less vague treatment than could be given here, and that our examples are extremely oversimplified and perhaps misleading in some respect. It seems clear to us, however, that a distinction of the type proposed here is indispensible for many reasons. It is of particular importance for the difficult problem of the relation between linguistic and encyclopedic knowledge. The status of lexical knowledge in the narrower sense vs. factual knowledge has been discussed several times, but, to our mind, in a fairly inconclusive way. It can hardly be doubted, on the one hand, that theoretical means are required that allow us to differentiate between encyclopedic knowledge and strictly linguistic knowledge, though in many cases the borderline between both types of knowledge is anything but obvious. On the other hand, linguistic and encyclopedic knowledge cannot be of a completely different, unrelated kind for several reasons. An adequate linguistic theory must provide a principled basis for both similarity and difference between linguistic and encyclopedic knowledge; it must account for the fact that at least a large part of our encyclopedic knowledge is closely connected to what we know about objects, facts, properties, etc. on the basis of the purely linguistic information stored in the pertinent vocabulary. It seems reasonable to propose now that the distinction between $C(E)$ and $P(E)$ corresponds essentially to that between linguistic and encyclopedic knowledge. In other words, the periphery of an entry E of the language L contains what might be called the non-linguistic knowledge about the objects, facts, or properties of the speaker of L, conceptualized by the reading of E in the dictionary of L. The core of E, on the other hand, contains the linguistic knowledge associated with E in the sense that the core includes all and only those specifications that specify the delimitation of E within the dictionary of L. From this explication of the linguistic/encyclopedic distinction it would follow that this distinction depends in the same way on the dictionary as a whole as does the core/periphery distinction. This is the desired result, since there is no language-independent borderline between linguistic and encyclopedic knowledge in general.[20] A further plausible corollary of the proposed explication is the fact that only certain classes of dictionary entries have relevant encyclopedic knowledge associated with them, while others consist of only linguistic knowledge. Thus, whereas entries such as 'give', 'long', 'friend' in general have no particular encyclopedic knowledge associated with them, i.e. they have an empty periphery, entries like 'electronic', 'generate', 'tarantula', 'galaxis' have peripheries of different types and varying shapes.

Notice finally that the distinction of core and periphery must not be confused with that between inherent semantic markers and selectional restrictions in the sense of Fodor and Katz (1963). Similarly, it is different from the distinction of semantic markers and distinguishers proposed in Fodor and Katz (1963).[21]

To return now to the question raised above with respect to examples (15), (23), and (24) and the relation between L_i, L_{i+1}, and L'_{i+1} established by them, we can account for the relevant problems in terms of core and periphery. First of all, we may characterize non-redundant, or proper definitions as those definitional sentences whose definiens provide only specifications pertaining to the core of the term to be defined, as opposed to redundant definitions, whose definiens contain specifications pertaining to the periphery of the definiendum. A more precise formulation of this distinction requires also reformulation of the partial/complete distinction given in (20) above. We may summarize the pertinent discussion in the following way:

(27)   Let a sentence S with the structure NP_1 *ls* NP_2 be an introductory definition connecting L_i with L_{i+1}.

      (i) S is a *proper definition* with respect to L_{i+1}, iff the reading of NP_2 contains only semantic specifications contained in the core of the reading of NP_1 in L_{i+1}.

      (ii) S is a *redundant definition* with respect to L_{i+1}, iff the reading of NP_2 contains semantic specifications not contained in the core of the reading of NP_1 in L_{i+1}.

      (iii) S is a *complete definition* with respect to L_{i+1}, iff the reading of NP_2 contains all specifications occurring in the core of the reading of NP_1 in L_{i+1}.

      (iv) S is a *partial definition* with respect to L_{i+1}, iff the reading of NP_2 contains some, but not all specifications occurring in the core of the reading of NP_1 in L_{i+1}.

According to this classification, there are four possible types of definitions: *complete proper*, *partial proper*, *complete redundant*, and *partial redundant*. It seems that these are not merely theoretical possibilities, but actually occurring cases. Given the relation between L_i, L_{i+1}, and L'_{i+1} with respect to the reading of 'tarantula' as assumed above, (15) would be a proper complete definition with respect to L_{i+1}, and a proper partial definition with respect to L'_{i+1}. (23) would be a complete redundant definition with respect to L_{i+1} and a proper complete definition with respect to L'_{i+1}. (28) would be an example of a partial redundant definition with respect to L_{i+1}:

(28)   A tarantula is a big spider living in Mediterranean countries.

7. GENERIC SENTENCES AND COMPLETING DEFINITIONS

According to the above distinction of core and periphery a lexical reading may contain semantic information not required to specify the proper relation of a lexical entry within the system of the dictionary entries of a given language. This in a sense extralinguistic knowledge can be incorporated into the grammar either on the basis of a redundant definition or by means of non-definitional generic sentences.[22] Thus we might assume that the reading of 'tarantula' in L_{i+1} might be extended by a periphery based on one of the sentences in (24). It is by now clear that a distinction must be made between introducing new specifications into the periphery of an entry and completing its core, if this is only partially specified. We have not dealt so far with what might be called *completing definitions*, i.e. definitional sentences that do not introduce a new entry, but specify further semantic information of the core of an already introduced entry. It seems that in general a completing definition of this type is formally distinct from a nondefinitional generic sentence. Thus (29) might be a completing definition corresponding to the generic sentences (24):

(29)   A tarantula is a spider living in Mediterranean countries.

The formal differences require, however, further investigation. They are to a large extent language-specific – involving particular properties of the determiner system – whereas the different status of non-definitional sentences and completing definitions does not depend on language-specific formal properties. It depends on the overall structure of the dictionary which imposes the partition of the reading of the entry in question into core and periphery. It follows from this consideration that, in fact, the languages L_{i+1} and L'_{i+1} are not connected by the generic definitions (24), but rather by a completing definition of the type (29), while the generic sentences (24) would only extend the periphery of 'tarantula' in L_{i+1} without changing it into L'_{i+1}.

It seems worthwhile to point out some consequences with respect to the role of non-definitional generic sentences that follow from the previous considerations. According to these considerations the semantic content of the predicate phrase of a generic sentence will possibly be incorporated into the periphery of the reading of its subject. (But see note 14.) This has the by no means trivial consequence that not only introductory definitions, whose influence on the structure of the underlying competence has been pointed out above, but also generic sentences in general might change certain aspects of the structure of the presupposed competence. There are two differences to be noted here. First of all, introductory definitions affect the linguistic competence in the narrower sense, insofar as they contribute to the core of the system of dictionary entries, while generic sentences in general contribute to the periphery of the system, i.e. to encyclopedic knowledge. Secondly, an introductory definition, if taken appropriately by the speaker-hearer, obligatorily changes the grammar in question. A generic sentence, on the other hand, affects the structure of competence only under certain conditions. These conditions are not inherently linguistic: whether the relevant specifications are incorporated into the periphery of the given grammar depends on the nature of the discourse in question, the character of the specifications in questions and on non-linguistic knowledge in general.

Given these restrictions on the possible incorporation of the semantic content of generic sentences into the underlying grammar, the resulting effect seems fairly plausible. Notice first of all that a large class of generic sentences are not *ad hoc* statements, describing a particular situation, relevant only in the actual context, but rather expressions of general claims relevant for the situationally invariant knowledge underlying concrete verbalizations. As this general knowledge must be associated with the relevant linguistic knowledge in the narrower sense, it seems quite natural to integrate it into the periphery of the linguistic knowledge in the sense described above. Secondly it is important that semantic specifications based on non-definitional sentences are not automatically included into the underlying grammar – as is the case with information based on an accepted definition. It rather requires additional motivation or justification. Such motivations may be of different nature. They might consist in *a priori* reasoning, or in accepted empirical beliefs based on experience or simply on confidence. This leads to a third point. Generic sentences obviously play a different role in different types of discourse. They have certainly considerable relevance in rational talk, in scientific or prescientific discourse, i.e. in discourse concerned rather with changing certain aspects of general knowledge than with reacting on actual situations. It is characteristic that such discourse involves a stepwise enrichment or change of the underlying permanent knowledge, insofar as it presupposes, in principle, the content of earlier sentences for the interpretation of subsequent ones. This is, of course, an idealization, but it points in a still to be explored direction. It seems to us that considerations of this type might also shed some light on the complex problem of the character and development of systems of theory-bound terms. This problem concerns by no means only scientific terminologies in the narrower sense, but to a large extent also prescientific conceptual systems. Such systems can be created for arbitrary purposes by an interplay of definitional and generic sentences. And even if such systems are created *ad hoc* and dropped after the pertinent discourse has been finished, it constitutes the particular competence underlying the discourse in question.

We conclude our highly preliminary inspection of a set of problems connected with the status of definitional sentences in natural languages with the remark that with certain modifications the introduced notions do not only apply to lexical readings and introductory definitions of generic terms, but also to individual concepts and to the pertinent proper names. The main difference consists in the different role of core and periphery in the case of proper names. It seems reasonable to assume that the core of proper names is almost empty, containing only such specifications as 'Human', 'Male', 'Geographic Area', etc. But we will not go any further into the difficult peculiarities of the status of proper names and the sentences introducing them into a given grammar.

German Academy of Sciences, Berlin
Hungarian Academy of Sciences, Budapest

BIBLIOGRAPHY

Bierwisch, M.: 1969a, 'On Certain Problems of Semantic Representations', *Foundations of Language* **5**, 153–84.

Bierwisch, M.: 1969b, 'On Classifying Semantic Features', in *Semantics: An Interdisciplinary Reader in Philosophy, Linguistics, Psychology, and Anthropology* (ed. by Jakobovits and Steinberg), The University of Illinois Press.

Carnap, R.: 1955, 'Meaning and Synonymy in Natural Language', *Philosophical Studies* **6**, 33–47.

Chomsky, N.: 1965, *Aspects of the Theory of Syntax*, The M.I.T. Press, Cambridge, Mass.

Kamlah, W. and Lorenzen, P.: 1967, *Logische Propädeutik, Vorschule des vernünftigen Redens*, Bibliographisches Institut.

Katz, J. J.: 1966, *The Philosophy of Language*, Harper and Row, New York.

Katz, J. J.: 1967, 'Recent Issues in Semantic Theory', *Foundations of Language* **3**, 124–94.

Katz, J. J. and Fodor, J. A.: 1964, 'The Structure of a Semantic Theory', *Language* **39**, 170–211.

Katz, J. J. and Postal, P.: 1964, *An Integrated Theory of Linguistic Descriptions*, The M.I.T. Press, Cambridge, Mass.

Perlmutter, D.: 1969, 'On Articles in English', in *Progress in Linguistics* (ed. by Bierwisch and Heidolph), Mouton and Co., The Hague.

Robinson, R.: 1950, *Definition*, Oxford, Clarendon Press.

REFERENCES

[1] This is not meant to suggest that analytic definitions take always the form of definitions by analysis, i.e. by the analysis of the definiendum. Lexicographers very often make use of the methods of synonyms or other methods as well. The important point is that whatever method is used the definition is not intended to be a means of teaching to somebody a new word but to characterize a particular lexical item of a given language.

[2] Introductory definitions thus cover the notion of stipulative definitions as well as definitions establishing an already existing usage of a given item with the intention to teach this usage to somebody to whom it is yet unknown. (See Robinson (1950) for some informal discussion.) Ordinary language is more concerned with the latter case, while in scientific discourse it is the former one that prevails. "A stipulative definition stipulates that, whatever the word may mean in other communications or even in earlier parts of this communication, it is for the rest of this communication to be taken as having *no meaning whatever* except the one now stipulated. Any previous meanings are thereby abolished for the remainder of this communication" (Robinson, *op. cit.*, p. 60). On the contrary, other forms of introductory definitions report in a more or less complete and adequate way (see, for some special cases Sections 4, 5, 6 and 7) the common usage of some language community. Thus, there is an important difference between stipulative and non-stipulative introductory definitions. While we can assign a truth-value to non-stipulative introductory definitions (is this the common usage of this term or not?), this is certainly not the case with stipulative definitions. Thus while the latter are rather free and hence arbitrary, not so the former. This important difference will, however, not be our concern in what follows. (See, however, note 7.)

[3] This may, perhaps, have some bearing on the problem of word formation. In many cases at least, not only new words but also new expressions are introduced by means of definitions. Since all attempts to derive syntactically expressions like those adduced above have failed so far, it seems reasonable to describe them by means of some definitional patterns. This, however, lies well beyond the scope of the present paper.

[4] Let us consider for the sake of simplicity different readings of the same phonemic matrix as constituting separate dictionary entries. Thus G_1 and G_2 do not necessarily differ in the phonemic matrices occurring in their respective dictionaries, but only in the readings assigned to them. This assumption is a considerable simplification that will be reconsidered later on. For the present purpose it is not relevant whether G_2 differs from G_1 only in the readings of its dictionary entries, or in the corresponding phonemic matrices as well.

[5] The possible successions of grammars might further be restricted if we assume that there should be a certain lower limit for the necessary number of dictionary entries in the grammar of a natural language. Though formally there might be grammars with only two distinct dictionary entries, we would not consider such a grammar as specifying a natural language. It is however a rather dubious question how something like a dictionary minimum should be specified. We need not quarrel about this question in the present context.

[6] This is certainly an oversimplification, since changes in the dictionary may very well lead to modifications in the system of phonological and morphological and even in the syntactic rules. Thus the incorporation of a larger number of foreign words, for instance, can lead to a change in the set of underlying phonemic segments and/or the permissible morpheme structures, and this in turn to a modification of certain phonological rules. We may, however, ignore such consequences of changes in the dictionary entries for the present purpose.

[7] There are, of course, also important differences between creating and acquiring a term by definition: creating a certain term involves the necessity to choose its particular phonemic and syntactic structure, the possibility to utilize an already existing form and the relationship of the new reading to those already assigned to the form in the dictionary. These aspects, which we briefly mentioned above, and the principles possibly governing them, are beyond the scope of this paper. Notice, however, that the asymmetry between creating and acquiring a term by definition corresponds in a sense to that between producing an

appropriate sentence and understanding it. The problems involved in these asymmetries do not belong to linguistics proper.

[8] It is, incidentally, by no means clear whether this is true with respect to definitions only. We will discuss below some problems which suggest an extension of this aspect to other phenomena as well.

[9] If this condition were not met, (15) would prompt an additional lexical question, e.g.

(15′)   And what is a spider, daddy?

which in turn might lead to answers like

(15″)   A spider is a small animal with eight long, thin legs.

In this case (15″) would extend L_i into a different language L'_{i+1} which then would be extended by (15) into a new L'_{i+2}. In a similar way (16) might be followed by

(16′)   And what is a natural number?

(16″)   A natural number is an arbitrary element that can be constructed by counting upward from one.

In general, there is always a chain of lexical questions and introductory definitions, such that each definition contains only elements that have been introduced previously.

[10] It is certainly this property which has led to the fact that ostensive definitions are grouped with true definitions under one heading, although they have completely different properties in all other respects. – It might be noted, incidentally, that a sentence like (17) is an ostensive definition only if it belongs to a language whose dictionary does not contain the predicate noun, just as a sentence like (15) is an introductory definition only with respect to a language whose grammar does not contain the head of the subject *NP*. It is important to realize that, once again, we are not dealing with distinctions belonging to the domain of performance: whether the predicate noun of an ostensive definition is part of the dictionary of a language or not is a proper fact of competence.

[11] It might be noted that only what we have called complete definitions are accepted as definitions in general in the pertinent literature, while partial definitions in the sense of (20ii) would figure as implicative meaning postulates in the framework of Carnap (1955) or predicator rules in the terminology of Kamlah and Lorenzen (1967).

[12] Notice that these problems, though they are of primary importance for technical vocabularies of particular domains, are by no means restricted to scientific terminologies, as possibly suggested by some of our examples. The same questions arise with respect to everyday vocabulary such as 'spider', 'blood', 'crown', etc., and in general with respect to an arbitrary dictionary entry. The difference consists only in the expected divergence among the pertinent grammars G* within a dictionary based family of grammars.

[13] We will see below that there is also the possibility of combining a partial definition with a generic sentence. The resulting sentence might be called a *redundant partial definition*. – Notice that the phrase 'living in the Mediterranean countries' in (23) under the conditions discussed under (a) is derived from an appositive relative clause, while the same phrase under the conditions discussed under (b) below is a reduced restrictive relative clause.

[14] The restriction of the problem to subjects of generic sentences is nothing but a *façon de parler*. In fact the question might be raised with respect to every constituent of a generic sentence.

[15] The semantic content of 'living in Mediterranean countries' provides an instances of this situation within our above hypothetical example. it is part of $P(tarantula)$ in L_{i+1}, but part of $C(tarantula)$ in L'_{i+1}.

[16] We are introducing here the notion of semantically possible dictionary entries. A possible entry in this sense may, but need not be realized in the dictionary in question. Thus while the content of 'big poisonous spider living on the Pacific Islands' is the reading of a possible entry in the dictionary of L'_{i+1}, this need not be realized by a particular phonemic matrix. Notice that the notion of possible dictionary entry of L must sharply

be distinguished from the notion of concept expressible in L. Because of the syntactic organization of L there is an infinite number of expressible concepts which are not readings of possible dictionary entries of L. The concept of possible dictionary entries involves intricate problems which must be left open here.

[17] This is true, of course, only if we do not delete the content of 'plane' from $C(triangle)$, thereby turning to non-Euclidean geometry.

[18] For an interesting treatment of the distinction of *a priori* vs. empiric truth see Chapter VI of Kamlah and Lorenzen (1967). There an account of the problem of analyticity is given which goes beyond the conventionalist and the empiricist position taken by Carnap and Quine, respectively.

[19] Thus a universal restriction, based on what Kamlah and Lorenzen (1967) call 'ideative norms', would prevent the meaning of 'the sum of whose angles is 180°' from being incorporated into $C(triangle)$. It would be a conventional restriction, on the other hand, if the semantic content of 'red' could not be incorporated into e.g. $C(blood)$. This restriction would result from the fact, that a term for blood of other color than red would not be admitted for empirical (or even arbitrary) reasons. – It might be noted, by the way, that a careful investigation of these restrictions might lead to the specification of some of the relevant properties of a language L* mentioned above.

[20] There remain, however, important problems still unsolved here. According to the core/periphery distinction introduced informally, certain specifications that are of an *a priori* character (cf. the discussion of (25b) above) are part of the periphery. (They are probably to be restricted, however, to what Kamlah and Lorenzen (1967) would classify as synthetic *a priori* truth). Since no clear characterization of the notion of encyclopedic knowledge has yet been given, we cannot decide whether the proposed explication in terms of core and periphery implies a modification of the original concept or not.

[21] For a general criticism of the latter distinction see Bierwisch (1969a).

[22] We are again ignoring the possibility that an extension of a reading might be brought about on the basis of not explicitly verbalized experiences, just as the acquisition of a lexical entry might proceed implicitly in the manner sketched in Section 3 above.

GENERATIVE SEMANTICS VS. DEEP SYNTAX

0.1. In this paper I propose that the base component of a generative-transformational grammar be constructed by using purely semantic concepts. This postulate clearly implies a neat difference between the theoretical structure of the grammatical model to be outlined here and the mainly syntactically motivated grammatical model as proposed by Chomsky, Postal, Katz and others.

0.2. The reason why this alternative to the structure of the Chomskyan model is proposed, is not to be sought within the purely syntactical domain of grammar. On the contrary, it is assumed that the syntax of a language described according to the principles laid down e.g. in Chomsky's *Aspects* can be said to be adequately described insofar as the generative and transformational processes leading to well-formed syntactic surface-structures are concerned.[1]

0.3. It is rather the semantic side of languages, or – to be more exact – the semantic structure of sentences which I think cannot be optimally be accounted for by a grammatical model with a strictly syntactically motivated base or deep structure component. The main justification for this view derives from the necessity that in a Chomskyan type of grammar semantics comes into the picture solely in the form of an interpretive component; i.e., it is assumed – e.g. by Katz – that syntactic configurations that are admittedly constructed without any view to semantic criteria are nevertheless taken as the interpretive basis for semantic relations constituting the semantic structure of a sentence.[2]

0.4. The inherent theoretical weakness of this approach shall be discussed presently; I regard Bertrand Russell's objection to such a position as still valid: "I found that, just as there are formalists in arithmetic, who are content to lay down rules for doing sums without reflecting that numbers have to be used in counting, so there are formalists in the wider field of language in general who think that truth [or, in our case, the semantic structure of language = logos semantikós] is a matter of following certain rules and not of correspondence with fact."[3]

F. Kiefer (ed.), Studies in Syntax and Semantics, 80–90. © *D. Reidel, Dordrecht-Holland*

0.5. In the second section of this paper a rather sketchy attempt will be made to bring together the notion 'generative semantics' with Chomsky's generative syntax. According to this view, the structures generated by each component would then be related by means of a set of mapping rules and thus preserve the constructional unity of the grammatical model into which these two 'base components' are to be integrated.

0.6. The last part of this contribution will contain some ideas on how to construct a semantically motivated base component together with some indications concerning the elements out of which the semantic representations of sentences and other compounded or simple linguistic expressions may be constructed.[4]

1.1. In recent times several weaknesses of a generative-transformational model of grammar with a syntactically motivated base component have been pointed out by various writers.[5] I shall be referring only to those problems which concern the relationships between syntactic deep structures of sentences and their semantic interpretation.

As has been already pointed out by McCawley (1968, 557) "...there is a wide range of 'aspects of syntactic description' which could reasonably be proposed as the input to 'rules of semantic interpretation', and there is indeed nothing a priori to prevent one from taking 'rule of semantic interpretation' in so broad a sense as to include the inverses of all transformations and thus take 'deep structure' to be identical to 'surface structure'."

A slight extension of this argument may perhaps clarify further the point I want to make here: syntactic structures as appear in Chomsky's base component can be generated according to relatively arbitrary principles; i.e., there may be several ways to arrive at well-formed surface structures of sentences. The relations or nodes inherent in some syntactic deep structure are, by assumption, non-semantic; at the same time Chomsky claims that the deep structure of a sentence is *that* aspect of the syntactic description "that uniquely determines its semantic interpretation..." (Chomsky 1966, 7). It is not clear how admittedly non-semantic grammatical (or syntactic) deep structures could determine "uniquely" the semantic structure of a sentence.[6]

1.2. Starting from Chomsky's just-quoted premiss, it would seem to be impossible to account for the long-known differences between the semantic structures of sentences containing stative/actional verbs or transitive verbs accompanied by affected/effected objects:

(1)	puer aegrotat	(stative verb, equivalent to 'puer aegrotus est')
(2)	puer currit	(actional verb)
(3)	librum lego	(affected object)
(4)	literam scribo	(effected object)

The various semantic relations in which the verbs of sentences (1)–(4) are involved cannot be represented overtly if one starts with their respective syntactic description which is fundamentally the same for all four examples (of course, in (1) and (2) the VP-symbol has to be rewritten as V, whereas in (3) and (4) VP is replaced by V + NP). But from their syntactic description alone we cannot account for the fact that in (1) there is an affective relation between the contents of verb and noun, whereas in (2) we may assume a causal relation between the contents of noun and verb. In a similar way the verbs in (3) and (4) are related to their objects differently.[7]

Within Chomsky's grammatical model information about these or similar semantic concepts could probably be drawn from the subcategorizational apparatus appended to the terminal symbols of deep structures, but then the interrelations of this semantic information with the syntactic structure of a given expression is again unclear.

1.3.   Another serious criticism of the suitability of syntactic deep structures for the semantic representation of sentences has been raised by Jacques Lerot (1968b):

1.5. ... Mit Hilfe der Tiefenstruktur [i.e. a deep structure à la Chomsky] müßte man beweisen können, daß die Sätze

| (9) | Hans liebt die Arbeit |
| (10) | Hans arbeitet gern |

bedeutungsähnlich sind. Nach den Auffassungen Chomskys, wie sie in *Aspects* dargelegt sind, ist diese Möglichkeit von vornherein versperrt, denn die Verzweigungsregeln ('branching rules') generieren Kategorialsymbole wie N (Nomen), V (Verb), Adverbial usw., sodaß den Sätzen (9) und (10) bereits verschiedene Tiefenstrukturen unterliegen, bevor [sic] die ersten Subkategorisierungsregeln angewendet werden... Weder Subkategorisierungsregeln noch Lexikonregeln sind imstande, die Tiefenstrukturen beider Sätze [einander] näherzubringen. Es handelt sich hier um ein sehr wichtiges Problem, das unbedingt zu lösen ist, wenn die Tiefenstruktur die semantische Interpretation von Sätzen einwandfrei bestimmen soll.

The gist of Lerot's argument may be paraphrased as follows: since a Chomskyan base component generates categorial symbols of the type N, V, Adv, etc., which are nothing else than symbols for the traditional word-classes, it is impossible to establish some sort of synonymity relation between (9) and (10).[8] It is exactly with respect to word-classes that these sentences differ from one another; nevertheless, it seems that they can be said to express the same 'proposition' (in Russell's sense).

In order to overcome this 'impasse' the categorial symbols introduced in a deep structure component should be independent from the notion 'word-class'; i.e., these categorial symbols should be considered as representations of real semantic classes or properties which cut across the areas covered by traditional word-classes.[9] This amounts to the postulate that, e.g., the expressions (9) and (10) should be assigned the same semantic deep structure. This can be achieved by choosing suitable types of predicates (in the logical sense)[10] and by relating them in such a way that a common semantic deep structure for (9) and (10) arises.

It would be then the task of special transformation rules to produce different syntactic representations at the surface level, as, e.g., in (9) and (10); another surface variant would be: 'Hans liebt es zu arbeiten'.

1.4. All the foregoing arguments, sketchy and incomplete as they are, lead to a revised conception of a generative grammar containing a base component that generates directly univocal semantic structures of sentences, i.e., propositions or propositional concepts.[11] A very similar idea has been quite recently expressed by McCawley: "...that the rules for combining material into sentences are really rules for combining semantic material, and that the dictionary is part of a single system of rules ('transformations') for associating semantic representations with surface structures" (1968, 586).

2.0. In the following lines I shall try to show how possibly most of the undoubtedly valuable results of a primarily syntactically motivated generative grammar could be preserved as part of a complete grammatical description of some given language.

2.1. In order to make this possible – and in order to avoid at the same time the aforementioned difficulties that arise if syntax is taken as *the* basis for semantic representations – I propose as a theoretically possible alternative to assume two generative components within a grammatical model: a semantic *and* a syntactic base component.

2.2. These two base components can be viewed as interpreted 'calculi' in the Carnapian sense[12], provided that the range of significance for all symbols occurring in the expressions generated within the two 'calculi' is stated.[13] Suitable formation rules have to be chosen in order to ascertain that in both components only well-formed expressions are generated. We thus arrive at syntactical representations (in the logical sense) for the objects and their interrelations of both the semantic and syntactic (in the linguistic sense) levels of a grammatical model.

2.2.1. The semantic base component would then ideally consist of a finite inventory of symbols representing fundamental semantic categories (variables of suitable sorts plus certain constants) together with a set of formation rules that lead to well-formed representations of sentential semantic structures. The lexicon which specifies possible semantic values of variables may be a subcomponent of the semantic base component. The question at what stage of the generative and transformational processes going on in the model lexical elements (with their respective semantic, syntactic and phonetic features) should be inserted, is left open for the time being.

2.2.2. The second base component would generate syntactic structures and contain furthermore transformational rules whose task it would be to combine primary structures to complex ones and to ascertain the well-formedness of linear surface expressions.

2.3. In order not to isolate the expressions generated in the two base components a set of mapping rules has to be constructed which establish well-defined mapping or correspondence relations[14] between semantic and syntactic primary expressions. As was shown above (1.2.), it cannot be assumed that the correspondence relations between semantic and syntactic expressions are of a homomorphous nature; it seems rather that between most semantic and syntactic expressions many-one correspondence relations will have to be established.[15]

Under 2.2.2. it has been assumed that the occurrence of transformational rules is restricted to the syntactic component. This would mean that they operate solely on strings of symbols that are generated by the syntactic component, which, on the other side are always linked with their respective semantic structures. This highly tentative assumption would have the advantage that most of the hitherto developed transformational regularities could probably be incorporated in the grammatical model proposed here. It is evident that the workability of this proposal must be subject to extensive empirical investigation.

3.1. As far as I can see, it was Petr Sgall who, in recent times, was the first to explicitly propose that the basis of a generative grammar should be constructed out of a set of semantic concepts, and that by a set of formation rules the symbols representing these concepts should be combined to yield expressions which, in their turn, represent the semantic structure of sentences.

In a mimeographed conference paper issued during the Magdeburg symposium *Zeichen und System der Sprache* (1964) Sgall gave the following sketch of a generative model with a semantically motivated base component:

A) Die erste Komponente besteht aus einer Menge von Regeln, mittels derer die Repräsentation des Satzes auf der Ebene der Satzsemantik generiert wird. ...

B) Als zweite Komponente folgen dann Regeln, die die erwähnte [satzsemantische] Formel in eine andere verwandeln, die als Repräsentation der Satzgliederstruktur des Satzes interpretiert werden kann....

C) Weiter folgen noch einige Komponenten, nämlich Mengen von Regeln, die die B-terminale Kette in eine Kette von Morphemen verwandeln, diese dann in eine Kette von Phonemen und endlich in eine von Sprachlauten....[16]

If we take into consideration the criticisms launched against the Chomskyan model of a transformational grammar (e.g. by Weinreich, Lerot, and McCawley) the concluding remark in Sgall's 1964-paper concerning the adequacy of a semantically motivated generative grammar seems still to be valid: "Wir glauben, daß das vorgeschlagene System einem Modell des Sprechenden und deshalb auch einem Übersetzungsalgorithmus (der Synthese) näher steht als die Transformationsgrammatik...".

3.2. Of the many problems concerning the construction of a semantic generative component two questions shall be touched upon:

(1) What is the theoretical status that can be most suitably assigned to the expressions generated in the semantic component?

(2) How can these expressions be represented in a formal way?

3.2.1. In most treatises on generative grammar it is normal to assume that the generative and transformational processes going on in the base component of some grammar lead directly to the derivation of expressions that represent actual sentences. This approach implies that in the course of deriving sentences from some initial symbol – say S – all the factors involving assertion, quantification, negation, interrogation, tense, mood, aspect and probably several others have to be dealt with simultaneously. Instead, I propose to introduce the notion 'propositional concept' as that construction that represents the relational nucleus of a sentence when stripped of the above-mentioned factors. The notion 'propositional concept' is not new.[17] Every actual sentence asserts that a certain state of affairs exists:

(1)   some man sings arias
(2)   man sing(ing) aria

(1) and (2) exhibit exactly the difference between an actualized declarative sentence and a propositional concept; the latter does not assert anything, but just represents an abstract state of affairs as a possible, not as an asserted configuration of certain predicates. This means also that a propositional concept is neutral with respect to truth or falsehood; this distinction applies only to declarative sentences.[18]

3.2.2. We now assume that the deep structure component of one grammatical model will first generate semantic representations of propositional concepts, such as *baby crying, someone teaching grammar to someone at school*, etc. These structures will then have to be specialized by adding modal constituents such as assertion, quantification, etc.[19]

3.2.3. The generation of semantic representations of propositional concepts does not only have the advantage of representing explicitly the semantic nuclei of sentences; the semantic structures of propositional concepts may also serve as a basis for the derivation of semantic structures of compounds and all sorts of morphological derivatives[20], *and*, – what could prove to be helpful for the development of the field of generative *lexical* semantics – the semantic structures of propositional concepts may also serve as a starting-point for a theoretically satisfying description of the semantic structures of lexical elements. Anyhow, there is no sharp line between linguistic expressions that are normally considered to fall into the domain of word-formation and those expressions which are treated as simple lexical entries.

3.3.1. The methodical and theoretical instruments for the derivation of the semantic structure of lexical elements (morphologically simple or complex) from propositional concepts of variable complexity can be supplied by a special branch of symbolic logic, namely, 'combinatory logic'.[21] It can be assumed that the semantic structure of propositional concepts can be represented by using the notation of some predicate calculus (with this assumption we are entering the discussion of the second above mentioned question: 'How can propositional concepts be represented in a formal way?').

A notational system – or the syntactic inventory – of a predicate calculus for the representation of a set of propositional concepts may contain one- or many-place predicate variables and predicate constants of different sorts[22] which are connected by a finite set of relational categories – partly of a logical, partly of an ontological nature (e.g. '$\wedge$', '$\vee$', '$\subset$', '$\supset$', etc.; causal, affecting, local, directional, temporal, instrumental and similar relations). A set of formation rules will guarantee the well-formedness of expressions consisting of the symbols just mentioned.[23]

3.3.2. If we try to apply some of the principles of combinatory logic – as they are e.g. given in Feys and Fitch (1969, 74f.) – to the problem of deriving the semantic structure of words (be they monemic or morphologically compounded) from propositional concepts, we can correlate the notion 'propositional concept' with the notion 'associated form of a function' (as used by Feys and Fitch 1969, 05.3 and 40.2). Given some propositional concept, e.g.

of the form

(a)   AFF (F, w)

(where AFF stands for 'affecting'; the formula (a) may also be paraphrased by 'object w having contingently the property F' or 'a state-denoting property F applying to some object w').

This form of a propositional concept can be considered as the associated form of a function, e.g.

(b) $\lambda w\,[\text{AFF}\,(F, w)]$ [24]

Applied to linguistic matters this may mean that compounds like *madman, blue-bird; driftwood, sounding-board* etc. can be derived by the application of the λ-operator to propositional concepts like 'being mad affecting man', etc.

It is the task of special rules to guarantee the correct application of the λ-operator to some variable contained in the formula of a propositional concept.[25]

Another function of formula (a) may be

(c) $\lambda F\,[\text{AFF}\,(F, w)]$

(c) may represent the semantic structure of such compounds as *earthquake, heartburning, soundchange, population growth,* etc. In the case of (c) the λ-operator applies to the predicate variable F; the linguistic result is that state- or process-denoting lexical elements appear as second elements (determinata) of compounds.[26]

3.3.3. Similar views concerning the derivability of the semantic structure of lexical elements from sentences or sentence-like constructions are expressed in Weinreich (1966, 446) (quoted from McCawley's review, 585f.; McCawley explicitly subscribes to this idea):

... he [Weinreich] points out that a single word may have the same meaning as an expression of arbitrary syntactic complexity, ... He eventually concludes that 'every relation that may hold between components of a sentence also occurs among the components of meaning of a dictionary entry. This is as much as to say that the semantic part of a dictionary is a sentence – more specifically, a deep-structure sentence...'. These observations contain the germ of the idea (subsequently adopted by Lakoff, Ross, Bach, Gruber, and myself, among others) ... that the dictionary is part of a single system of rules ('transformations') for associating semantic representations with surface structures.

It is the aim of the foregoing remarks to point out along which lines future research work in semantics could be directed.

Universität Tübingen, Seminar für Englische Philologie

BIBLIOGRAPHY

Bolzano, B. (1837), *Wissenschaftslehre*.

Brekle, H. E. (1968), 'Bemerkungen zur generativen Satzsemantik', Drittes linguistisches Kolloquium über generative Grammatik. Burg Stettenfels bei Untergruppenbach (Heilbronn) 1.–4.10. 68. Universität Stuttgart. Lehrstuhl für Linguistik. Papier Nr. 8. December 1968, 13–20.

– (1969), Review of Katz (1966), *Anglia* **87**, 236–43.

– (forthcoming), *Generative Satzsemantik und transformationelle Syntax im System der englischen Nominalkomposition* (Tübingen Habilitationsschrift).

Carnap, R. (1956), *Meaning and Necessity. A Study in Semantics and Modal Logic*, Chicago UP.

– (1958), *Introduction to Symbolic Logic and Its Applications*, New York.

Chafe, W. L. (1968), 'Idiomaticity as an Anomaly in the Chomskyan Paradigm', *Foundations of Language* **4**, 109–27.

Chomsky, N. (1965), *Aspects of the Theory of Syntax*, Cambridge, Mass.

– (1966), 'Topics in the Theory of Generative Grammar', in *Current Trends in Linguistics*, Vol. 3: *Theoretical Foundations* (ed. by Th. A. Sebeok), The Hague, 1–60.

Coseriu, E. (1962), 'Logicismo y antilogicismo en la gramática', in *Teoría del lenguaje y lingüística general*, Madrid, 235–60.

Feys, R. and Fitch, F. B. (1969), *Dictionary of Symbols of Mathematical Logic*, Amsterdam.

Fillmore, Ch. J. (1968), 'The Case for Case', in *Universals in Linguistic Theory* (ed. by Bach and Harms), New York.

Hasenjaeger, G. (1962), *Einführung in die Grundbegriffe und Probleme der modernen Logik*, Freiburg i. Br.

Heringer, H.-J. (forthcoming), *Neuhochdeutsche Syntax* (Heidelberg Habilitationsschrift).

Hincha, G. and Richter, H. (1967), 'Grundzüge eines 'Syllogon'-Modells zur Beschreibung syntaktischer Elementarstrukturen', *Folia Linguistica* **I**, 3/4 (publ. 1969), 135–45.

Joannis Saresberiensis Episcopi carnotensis Metalogicon libri IV (ed. by C. J. Webb), Oxford 1929.

Katz, J. J. (1966), *The Philosophy of Language*, New York.

Klaus, G. (Ed.) (1967), *Wörterbuch der Kybernetik*, Berlin.

Langer, S. K. (1927), 'A Logical Study of Verbs', *Journal of Philosophy* **24**, 120–9.

Lerot, J. (1968a), 'Zur Grundlegung einer formalen Wissenschaft der linguistischen Bedeutungen (Noetik)', Universität Stuttgart. Lehrstuhl für Linguistik. Papier Nr. 4, May 1968.

– (1968b), 'Zur Integration der Semantik in die Transformationsgrammatik', 3. linguistisches Kolloquium über generative Grammatik. Burg Stettenfels 1.–4.10. 68. Universität Stuttgart. Lehrstuhl für Linguistik. Papier Nr. 8. December 1968, 117–131.

McCawley, J. D. (1968), 'Review of *Current Trends in Linguistics*, Vol. 3: *Theoretical Foundations* (ed. by Th. A. Sebeok)', *Lg.* **44**, 556–93.

Russell, B. (1959), *My Philosophical Development*, London.

Sgall, P. (1964), 'Zum Verhältnis von Grammatik und Semantik im generativen System' *Zeichen und System der Sprache*, Vol. 3 (ed. by G. E. Meier), Berlin, 225–39.

– (1967), 'Zur Eingliederung der Semantik in die Sprachbeschreibung', *Folia Linguistica* **I**, 1/2, 18–22.

Weinreich, U. (1966), 'Explorations in Semantic Theory', in *Current Trends in Linguistics*, Vol. 3: *Theoretical Foundations* (ed. by Th. A. Sebeok), The Hague, 395–477.

REFERENCES

[1] This does not mean that a syntax of the Chomskyan type is to be considered the only or most adequate one; cf. as a contrast the syntactical principles as set forth in H. J. Heringer's Heidelberg thesis *Neuhochdeutsche Syntax* (forthcoming).

[2] Cf. e.g. Katz (1966, 156–75) and my review of Katz's book in *Anglia*. Within the scope of this contribution I shall not explicitly discuss the validity of Katz's views on semantics; instead reference is made to several publications dealing explicitly with Katz's semantic theory: e.g. Sgall (1964, 1967), Weinreich (1966), Chafe (1968), and McCawley (1968).

[3] Russell (1959, 132). In a similar vein Weinreich (1966, 410) criticizes Katz's 'theory of semantics': "What is particularly ironic is that an enterprise in semantics inspired by the most sophisticated syntactic research ever undertaken should end up with a fundamentally asyntactic theory of meaning…".

[4] For fuller information about such an alternative proposal the reader is referred to my paper 'Bemerkungen zur generativen Satzsemantik' (December 1968) and to my thesis *Generative Satzsemantik und transformationelle Syntax im System der englischen Nominal-komposition* (forthcoming).

[5] In this respect McCawley's extensive review (*Lg.* **44**, 556–93) of Chomsky's 'Topics in the Theory of Generative Grammar' (= Chomsky 1966) deserves special attention together with his pertinent remarks on Weinreich's 'Explorations in Semantic Theory' (=Weinreich 1966). Cf. also Chafe (1968), Lerot (1968a, 1968b).

[6] Cf. McCawley (1968, 558): "As far as I can tell, Chomsky's 'grammatical relations' are as much semantic as syntactic…".

[7] For a detailed treatment of semantic relations of the sort just mentioned, cf. Brekle (forthcoming, 3.6.ff).

[8] Cf. Weinreich (1966, 398–9): "…Semantic theories can and should be so formulated as to guarantee that deep structures (including their lexical components) are specified as unambiguous in the first place and proceed from there to account for the interpretation of a complex expression from the known meanings of its components."

[9] Cf. Lerot (1968b): "2.1. Die Wortartzugehörigkeit ist kein semantisches Merkmal."

[10] Cf. for this problem Brekle (forthcoming, 4.2.1): 'Symbolinventar und Formations-regeln der satzsemantischen Komponente'.

[11] See for this notion below 3.2.1.

[12] Carnap (1958), 101: "One who constructs a syntactical system usually has in mind from the outset some interpretation of this system. (This interpretation need not itself have a prior representation as a semantical system…). While this intended interpretation can receive no explicit indication in the syntactical rules – since these rules must be strictly formal – the author's intention respecting interpretation naturally affects his choice of the formation and transformation rules of the syntactical system. E.g. he chooses primitive signs in such a way that certain concepts (perhaps of some given unsystematized theory) can be expressed."

[13] Cf. for a method how this can be done Carnap (1956, 4f. *et passim*): 'Rules of designation for individual constants, predicates'.

[14] See Klaus (1967) under the articles *Abbildung, Bild, Codierung, Homomorphie, Operator, Transformation*.

[15] The mapping or correspondence relations proposed here as a link between the primary expressions of a semantic and a syntactic component have nothing to do with the relations as implied in Katz's notion of 'projection rules'. With this notion Katz seeks to establish a one-one correspondence – we deny the feasibility of such a proposal – between syntactic and semantic structures. Cf. Katz (1966, 165): "…The number of projection rules required is, consequently, dictated by the number of grammatical relations defined in the theory of the syntactic component".

[16] 'Zum Verhältnis von Grammatik und Semantik im generativen System', pp. 1–2. Similar views are expressed in Lerot (1968a, 2.0., 2.1., 3.3. *et passim*).

[17] Cf. e.g. Langer (1927, 120–9) where the philosophical relevance of this notion is discussed. Bernard Bolzano's notion 'Satz an sich' (Wissenschaftslehre §§ 19, 48) can be considered to be at least partly identical with the notion 'propositional concept'. Cf. also a very recent contribution where a notion similar to 'propositional concept' seems to play a role: Hincha and Richter (1967, 139): "Mit der Einführung dieses Formalismus [a set of predicates, logical connectives, operators, etc.] ist die Unterscheidung von eigentlichen

Aussagen, die wahr oder falsch sein können, und bloßen *Aussagefunktionen* verbunden. Bei Verwendung von Individuenvariablen in einer Aussagefunktion geht der Wahrheitswert des Ausdrucks und damit sein Aussagecharakter verloren sofern nicht eine sog. *Quantifikation* oder *Bindung der Variablen* vorgenommen wird".

[18] Cf. Coseriu (1962, 238f.): "…el lenguaje como tal es simplemente *logos semántico*: expresión significativa, en la que no hay verdad ni falsedad, pues éstas se dan sólo en la afirmación y negación, en el *logos apofántico*". This conception was already present in scholastic philosophy; cf. John of Salisbury's *Metalogicon*, I, c.15, 844c: "Grammatica enim absurdam habet incompetentem iuncturam dictionum; sed ad examinandi ueri iudicium non aspirat". Insofar as a propositional concept does not denote some definite spatio-temporal state of affairs, we can regard propositional concepts as universals (in the medieval sense); cf. *Metalogicon* II, c.20, 881a: "Nominantur singularia, sed universalia significantur".

[19] Essentially the same procedure was proposed by Fillmore (1968, 23): "In the basic structure of sentences we find the 'proposition', which is a tenseless set of relationships involving verbs and nouns (and embedded sentences, if there are any), separated from what might be called the 'modality' constituent. This latter will include such modalities on the sentence-as-a-whole as negation, tense, mood and aspect".

[20] For the application of this idea reference is made to Brekle (forthcoming), Ch. 4: 'Grammatisches Modell der Nominalkomposition des Englischen'; Ch. 5: 'Beschreibung der nach Kap. 4 erzeugbaren nominalen Kompositionstypen des Englischen'.

[21] Cf. e.g. Feys and Fitch (1969, §§ 40ff.) and Carnap (1958, § 33). The λ-operator.

[22] Cf. for a sketch of a sortal logic Hasenjaeger (1962, 59f., 112f.). In order to guarantee the applicability of this predicate calculus within the domain of linguistics it is necessary to assign to the different predicate symbols certain semantically relevant ranges of values (e.g. the range of things, states, processes, actions, etc.).

[23] A set of types of propositional concepts as they are outlined here can be found in Brekle (forthcoming) where they are taken as a basis for deriving semantic structures of types of nominal compounds in modern English.

[24] For the principles governing the use of the λ-operator cf. e.g. Carnap (1958, § 33); Carnap (1956: 3, 9, 39, *et passim*); Feys and Fitch (1969, 06.2., 32.25., 40.02. *et passim*).

[25] Cf. for a set of such rules which govern processes similar to those implied in the grammatical notions 'topic' and 'comment' Brekle (forthcoming, 3.5. and 4.2.1.3).

[26] Cf. Brekle (forthcoming, Ch. 5) for a treatment of English nominal compounds according to such methods.

M. DUPRAZ ET J. ROUAULT

LEXIS – AFFIRMATION – NÉGATION:
ÉTUDE FONDÉE SUR LES CLASSES

0. INTRODUCTION

Notre but est de formaliser une partie (la plus vaste possible, évidemment...) de la sémantique de certaines langues naturelles afin de pouvoir rendre plus efficaces les programmes de traduction automatique. Un premier document (Baille et Rouault, 1966) indiquait l'état d'esprit dans lequel nous comptions travailler et certains outils qui nous paraissaient intéressants. Ce document était muet sur le schéma général d'organisation du système et c'est une réponse partielle à cette question qu'essaie d'apporter le présent travail (Dupraz et Rouault, 1968).

Ce travail est né de notre rencontre avec Monsieur le Professeur Culioli; nous ayant exposé ses idées sur le problème de la sémantique (Culioli, 1969), Monsieur Culioli nous demanda d'étudier les relations logiques qui lient la lexis, l'affirmation et la négation. Outre l'intérêt propre de cette étude, le système de Monsieur Culioli nous fournit un cadre pour organiser nos propres travaux et pour essayer, au moins formellement, de scinder le problème de la Sémantique en des parties plus réduites, et donc plus faciles à étudier.

Le système de Monsieur Culioli s'est montré d'une telle richesse qu'il nous a paru nécessaire de poser correctement le problème du point de vue mathématique avant de passer au niveau logique. Pour cela le langage des classes (incluant classes distributives, c'est-à-dire ensembles, classes collectives (Clay, 1965; Sobocinski, 1949/1950) et classes d'équivalence) s'est révélé un outil bien adapté. Il nous a permis d'exprimer les différents concepts linguistiques que l'on rencontre après la "notion" qui, elle, est exprimée dans un langage formalisé L. Au stade suivant les univers deviendront des systèmes logiques fondés sur le langage L; les relations données ici entre les différents univers fourniront des relations entre ces systèmes logiques. Il en résulte que le langage des classes n'est qu'un auxiliaire destiné à poser le problème. Ce travail est donc un point de départ; nous espérons ne pas y avoir trop trahi les concepts introduits par Monsieur Culioli. Il convient cependant de noter qu'il existe une différence importante entre nos deux points de vue: alors que Monsieur Culioli laisse jusqu'au niveau de l'affirmation la possibilité à certains arguments d'être soit le complément de rang 0, soit le complément de rang 1 d'un prédicat, nous avons imposé dès le départ qu'un argument donné

F. Kiefer (ed.), Studies in Syntax and Semantics, 91–108. © *D. Reidel, Dordrecht-Holland*

soit le complément de rang 0 et qu'un autre soit le complément de rang 1 (nous avons donc "ordonné" les arguments figurant dans une lexis – cf. II.2).

Nous devons signaler que nous n'espérons pas que les différents systèmes logiques résultant des univers donnés ici permettent de résoudre toutes les ambiguités d'une phrase ou d'un texte; Cette formalisation logique nous conduit cependant à envisager une "valuation" des formules, valuation nous permettant de lever de nouvelles ambiguités.

1. UNIVERS DE DÉPART

1.1. On suppose défini un alphabet comportant au moins des prédicats, des constantes individuelles, des variables individuelles, et des connectives logiques de propositions (V, $\wedge$, $\overline{}$, $\Rightarrow$, ...). Cet alphabet permettra suivant des règles qu'il nous faudra préciser (mais que nous ne pouvons pas connaître actuellement), de construire un langage formel **L**.

Parallèlement à cet alphabet nous utiliserons le langage de la théorie des ensembles où les opérations seront notées: U, $\cap$, $\complement$, $\in$ et $\subset$.

1.2. Dans le langage **L** (où, par définition, il n'y a ni axiomes, ni règles d'inférence) on note les prédicats p, q, ...; dans ce qui suit nous supposons, que les prédicats sont à deux places d'argument. Les notions introduites se généralisent facilement lorsque le prédicat est à un nombre quelconque de places. Cependant, on peut remarquer que, dans la langue, les prédicats sont au plus à trois places; les arguments que l'on pourrait rencontrer en dehors de ceux-ci sont d'un autre type (lieu, temps, ...) et ils nous conduiront, en particulier, à des problèmes de substitution d'une lexis dans une autre. Nous nous intéressons ici uniquement à la construction d'une lexis, et, nous remettons à plus tard la définition des différents types d'opérations que l'on pourrait faire sur les concepts introduits, et en particulier sur les lexis.

1.3. A partir du prédicat p et des deux connectives V et $\overline{}$, on peut définir dans **L** la formule suivante:

$$n(p) = pv \overline{} p$$

appelée *notion de p*.

Nous insistons sur le fait que $n(p)$ est une formule d'un langage et non un théorème d'une théorie mathématique. Ceci a la conséquence suivante: si p et q désignent deux prédicats différents, les formules: $n(p) = pv \overline{} p$ et $n(q) = qv \overline{} q$ sont distinctes. (Si l'on était dans une théorie de logique classique, où le "tiers exclus" est un axiome, ces deux formules seraient des tautologies, et, par conséquent, équivalentes.)

1.4. *On suppose donnés deux univers:*

a) L'univers V des notions: si p est un prédicat quelconque alors $n(p) \in V$.

b) L'univers U de toutes les constantes et variables pouvant intervenir comme arguments de n'importe quel prédicat, à n'importe quelle place.

1.5. *On définit alors un autre univers $\mathscr{U}$ par:*

$$\mathscr{U} = V \times U \times U$$

soit encore par:

$$(1) \qquad \mathscr{U} = \{\langle n(p), \mu_0, \mu_1 \rangle / (n(p) \in V) \wedge (\mu_0 \in U) \cup (\mu_1 \in U)\}.$$

Remarque: dans les triplets $\langle \alpha, \beta, \gamma \rangle$, α se rapporte au prédicat, β au complément de rang 0 et γ au complément de rang 1. Cette convention est valable pour tout ce qui suit.

A ce stade, nous pourrions avoir par exemple:

$$\langle n(\text{manger}), \text{cheval}, \text{herbe} \rangle$$
$$\langle n(\text{manger}), \text{herbe}, \text{souris} \rangle$$
$$\langle n(\text{manger}), \text{souris}, \text{cheval} \rangle$$
$$\langle n(\text{boire}), \text{table}, \text{cheval} \rangle$$
$$\langle n(\text{boire}), \text{chien}, \text{chaise} \rangle$$
$$\langle n(\text{monter}), \text{table}, \text{chaise} \rangle.$$

D'autre part β et γ peuvent être des expressions complexes, par exemple dans le triplet:

$$\langle n(\text{manger}), \text{beau cheval}, \text{herbe verte} \rangle.$$

α est, en général, une notion d'un prédicat quelconque:

$$\langle n(\text{être lent}), \text{escargot} \rangle \text{ (cas d'un prédicat à un seul argument)}.$$

2. LES LEXIS

On considère ici une suite d'ensembles qui font passer de $\mathscr{U}$ à des expressions pré-assertées.

2.1. *Premier stade: équivalence de prédicats et choix d'une notion*

Nous entrons ici dans le niveau logique: nous supposons construit un système logique qui va nous permettre de dire si deux notions sont, ou non, équivalentes. Comme il s'agit d'équivalence fondée sur une logique, nous parlerons de L-équivalence.

D'autre part, le monde qui nous entoure nous impose certaines contraintes sur les prédicats, donc aussi sur les notions. Ces contraintes peuvent-entraîner des équivalences ne résultant pas du système logique (ce ne sont donc pas des L-équivalences) mais des faits de la connaissance encyclopédique, ...; nous parlerons alors de F-équivalence.

Remarquons que la L-équivalence est un concept plus fort que la F-équivalence; la classe $\|n(p)\|_L$ des notions L-équivalentes à une notion donnée $n(p)$ est incluse dans la classe $\|n(p)\|_F$ de F-équivalence de cette même notion.

Par exemple, dans la même classe d'équivalence, on trouve "être sur", "se trouver sur", "il y a ... sur", ... La distinction entre L-équivalence et F-équivalence provient uniquement de la définition, et donc de la puissance, du système logique supposé construit. Si celui-ci n'est pas assez puissant pour recouvrir toute la réalité, on fera appel à la notion supplémentaire de F-équivalence; le cas idéal étant celui où ces deux notions sont confondues.

Nous sommes ainsi amenés, une notion $n(p)$ étant donnée, à séparer $\mathscr{U}$ (défini par (1)) en deux sous-ensembles disjoints et complémentaires: d'une part l'ensemble des triplets comprenant comme premier élément tous les éléments de V non F-équivalents à $n(p)$, d'autre part l'ensemble des triplets dont le premier élément parcourt la classe de F-équivalence de $n(p)$. A l'intérieur de ce dernier ensemble, nous distinguons l'ensemble des triplets comportant comme premier élément tous les éléments de V L-équivalents à $n(p)$.

De façon précise nous distinguons trois ensembles dont les deux premiers sont déterminés par:

La classe de F-équivalence de $n(p)$:

$$\lambda\big(n(p)\big) = \|n(p)\|_F \times U \times U.$$

La classe de L-équivalence de $n(p)$:

$$\lambda'\big(n(p)\big) = \|n(p)\|_L \times U \times U.$$

Le troisième ensemble étant:

$$\mathsf{C}_{\mathscr{U}}\lambda\big(n(p)\big) = \mathsf{C}_V\big(\|n(p)\|_F\big) \times U \times U.$$

Par exemple si $q = $ "être sur":

$$\langle\, n\,(\text{se trouver sur}),\, \mu_0,\, \mu_1 \rangle \in \lambda\,\big(n(\text{être sur})\big),$$

suivant le système logique construit au départ, ce triplet appartiendra ou non à $\lambda'\,(n(\text{être sur}))$.

$$\langle n\,(\text{manger}),\, \mu_0,\, \mu_1 \rangle \in \mathsf{C}_{\mathscr{U}}\,\lambda\,\big(n(\text{être sur})\big).$$

Ceci peut être illustré par le schéma suivant:

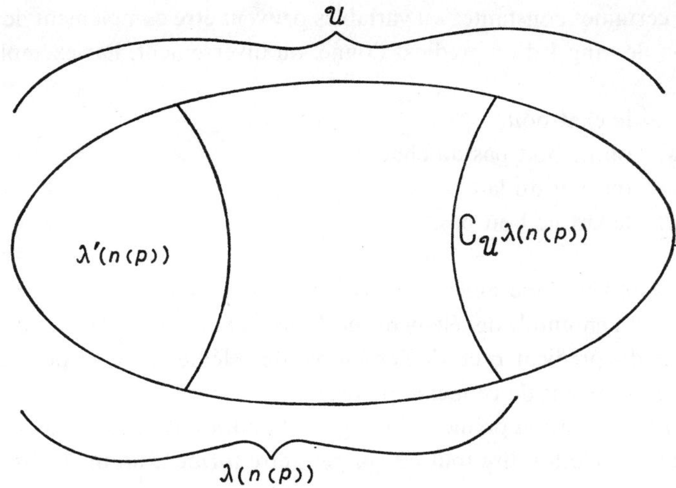

2.2. *Deuxième stade: classes résultant du choix d'une notion*

a) Le point de départ de ce deuxième stade est l'ensemble $\lambda(n(p))$ défini au 1. Cependant $\lambda(n(p))$ ne joue pas ici le rôle que jouait l'univers $\mathcal{U}$ au 1; on passe de $\lambda(n(p))$ au nouvel univers $\mathcal{L}(n(p))$, en particulier, par l'opération suivante: dans la classe de F-équivalence de la notion $n(p)$ sélectionnée au 1 on choisit un représentant. Ceci revient à dire que, ayant à notre disposition plusieurs verbes synonymes pour exprimer une idée (par exemple: être sur, se trouver sur, …) on en choisit un (par exemple: se trouver sur). C'est ce verbe qui sera conservé dans tout ce qui suit jusqu'à obtention des modalités assertives.

Cette opération de choix d'un des représentants semble pouvoir être considérée comme une opération d'extraction sur la classe de F-équivalence (cf. III).

$n(q)$ étant l'élément choisi dans la classe $\|n(p)\|_F$ on peut définir le nouvel univers par:

$$\mathcal{L}\big(n(q)\big) = \{\langle n(q), \mu_0, \mu_1 \rangle / (\mu_0 \in U) \wedge (\mu_1 \in U)\}.$$

b) Ce choix de la notion $n(q)$ impose un choix sur les arguments: étant donné un prédicat q n'importe quoi ne peut être le complément de rang 0 ou le complément de rang 1 de ce prédicat. En effet:

> la table ne mange pas
> le lapin n'écrit pas

mais: on mange du lapin

Alors que: on n'écrit pas une table.

De plus certaines constantes ou variables peuvent être complément de rang 0 mais non de rang 1 d'un prédicat donné, ou inversement. Par exemple:

$$\text{le chat boit,}$$
$$\text{mais:} \quad \text{on ne boit pas du chat,}$$
$$\text{on boit du lait}$$
$$\text{mais:} \quad \text{le lait ne boit pas.}$$

Nous sommes donc amenés à distinguer deux sous-ensembles Γ_0 et Γ_1 de U; Γ_0 est l'ensemble des éléments de U pouvant intervenir comme premier argument du prédicat q et Γ_1 l'ensemble des éléments de U pouvant être deuxième argument de ce même prédicat.

Exemple: si q est le prédicat "manger", la notion de q est "manger ou ne pas manger", c'est-à-dire tout ce qui peut être formé à partir de "manger".

$$\Gamma_0 \text{ est la classe des "mangeurs"}$$
$$\Gamma_1 \text{ est la classe des "mangeables".}$$

Remarque: les exemples précédents nous montrent que la classe Γ_0 est, en fait, déterminée par la notion "n (être p-eur)" et Γ_1 par la notion "n (être p-é)".

c) Cependant ce qui précède ne suffit pas pour assurer la cohérence sémantique d'une lexis. Si γ_0 est un élément donné de Γ_0, tout élément de Γ_1 ne peut être complément de rang 1 d'une proposition où le prédicat est q et le complément de rang 0: γ_0. (Par exemple, on peut admettre qu'un cheval ne mange pas de souris alors qu'un chat en mange.) Donc la donnée de γ_0 sélectionne un sous-ensemble de Γ_1.

En termes d'ensembles cela revient à dire que cette cohérence des deux arguments du prédicat impose de travailler non sur le produit cartésien mais sur le sous-ensemble (noté également q), de $\Gamma_0 \times \Gamma_1$, déterminé par q considéré comme une relation.

d) Les remarques précédentes nous permettent alors de décomposer l'univers $\mathscr{L}(n(q))$ d'abord en deux régions:

$$L(n(q)) = \{n(q)\} \times \Gamma_0 \times \Gamma_1$$
$$\complement_{\mathscr{L}(n(q))} L(n(q)) = \{\langle n(q), \gamma', \gamma'' \rangle / (\gamma' \in \complement_U \Gamma_0) \vee (\gamma'' \in \complement_U \Gamma_1)\}.$$

Enfin à l'intérieur de $L(n(q))$ on peut distinguer le sous-ensemble suivant:

$$L'(n(q)) = \{\langle n(q), \gamma_0, \gamma_1 \rangle / (\gamma_0 \in \Gamma_0) \wedge (\gamma_1 \in \Gamma_1) \wedge (\langle \gamma_0, \gamma_1 \rangle \in q)\}.$$

D'où le schéma:

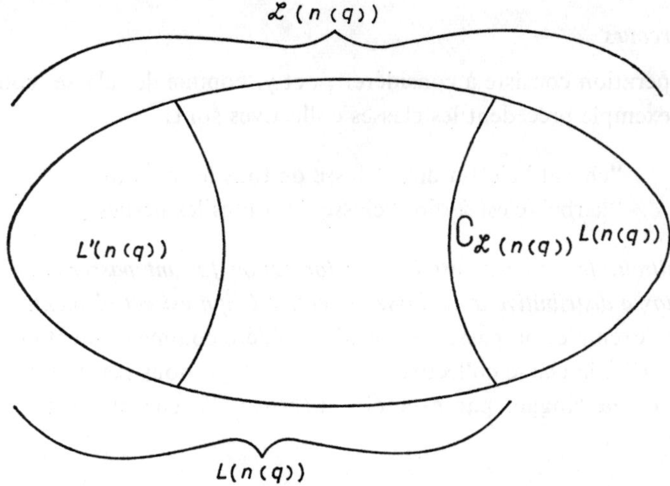

3. PARCOURS, EXTRACTION ET FLÉCHAGE

3.1. Avant de passer du schéma précédent aux modalités de type M1 (définies au IV) nous allons essayer de préciser ce que sont les opérations de parcours, d'extraction et de fléchage.

Du point de vue de la langue, ces opérations peuvent être définies comme suit:

a) Le parcours permet d'exprimer un être linguistique représentant de la classe d'équivalence de tous les êtres linguistiques possédant une même propriété (par exemple dans "*le* cheval est un animal à quatre pattes").

b) L'extraction permet de considérer un ou plusieurs êtres pris parmi les précédents (par exemple dans "*une* (ou *des*) pomme(s) se trouvent sur cette table");

c) Le fléchage permet de distinguer un ou plusieurs êtres parmi ceux du a) (par exemple dans: "*les* chevaux, que je vois, courent dans *le* pré").

Du point de vue logique, ces opérations ne sont, semble-t-il, pas très simples et ce qui suit mérite d'être précisé. Ce qui nous paraît acquis est le rôle essentiel joué ici par la notion de "classe collective" opposée à la notion de "classe distributive". En particulier, nous pouvons considérer que l'ensemble $L(n(q))$ formé de triplets du type, $\langle n(q), \gamma_0, \gamma_1 \rangle$ est tel que: γ_0 est un élément de la classe distributive Γ_0 et γ_1 est un élément de la classe distributive Γ_1.

Exemple: q est le prédicat "manger";

γ_0 l'élément "cheval" de la classe distributive "mangeur";

γ_1 l'élément "herbe" de la classe distributive "mangeable".

3.2. *Parcours*

Cette opération consiste à considérer γ_0 et γ_1 comme des classes collectives. Dans l'exemple précédent les classes collectives sont:

> "cheval" c'est-à-dire "classe de tous les chevaux"
> "herbe" c'est-à-dire "classe de toutes les herbes".

Définition: le parcours est la transformation faisant passer d'un élément d'une classe distributive à la classe collective C qui est cet élément.

Dans l'exemple: on passe de cheval considéré comme élément de la classe "mangeur" à la classe collective "cheval". Ce qui nous permettra, du point de vue de la langue, par exemple, d'écrire: "*le* cheval est un mangeur d'herbe".

3.3. *Extraction*

a) Les différents types d'extraction sont caractérisés par une condition sur le cardinal du sous-ensemble considéré: par exemple "un cheval" reviendrait, *si c'était possible*, à sélectionner un quelconque des sous-ensembles à un élément de la classe collective "cheval". De même pour "des chevaux" (cardinal >1), trois chevaux (cardinal $=3$), ...

La notion de sous-ensemble d'une classe collective n'existant pas, nous sommes amenés à *considérer la classe collective C comme une classe distributive D* (c'est-à-dire, comme un ensemble au sens ordinaire du terme). Par exemple, la classe collective "cheval" est considérée comme étant l'extension du prédicat "être cheval".

Notation: X étant un ensemble, nous noterons $\delta(\overline{\overline{X}})$ la condition imposée au cardinal de X.

b) On peut alors faire correspondre à cette classe distributive D l'ensemble $P(D)$ de ses parties, puis sélectionner dans $P(D)$ les sous-ensembles X de D qui vérifient la condition $\delta(\overline{\overline{X}})$ sur le cardinal. Dans ce dernier stade on passe donc de $P(D)$ à

$$E(C) = \{X/(X \in P(D)) \wedge \delta(\overline{\overline{X}})\}.$$

Enfin, on passe de $E(C)$ à un de ses éléments.

c) *Définition: nous appelons extraction la combinaison des opérations définies en* a) *et* b).

d) *Il ne peut y avoir extraction sans parcours préalable.*

3.4. *Fléchage*

a) *Définition:* le fléchage est une opération identique au parcours en ce sens qu'elle fait passer d'un élément X de $E(C)$ à la classe collective correspondante.

b) *Il ne peut y avoir fléchage sans extraction préalable.* (Ce qui différencie, en général, le fléchage du parcours.)

c) D'autre part, le fléchage aboutissant à une classe collective, on peut sur celle-ci faire une nouvelle extraction, etc …

Exemple: "cheval"

1) extraction: "*des* chevaux" (galopent dans le pré);
2) fléchage: "*ces* chevaux" (sont beaux);
3) extraction: "*un de ces* chevaux" (a l'œil torve);
4) fléchage: "ce dernier" …; etc …

3.5. *Schéma récapitulatif des définitions de ce paragraphe*

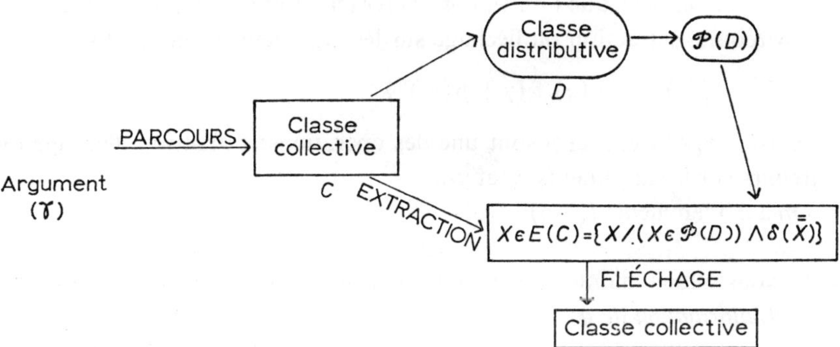

3.6. *Cas particuliers*

a) L'extraction est faite à partir d'une classe collective C obtenue par parcours et considérée comme une classe collective à un seul objet; celle-ci fournit donc une classe distributive D à un seul élément ($\bar{\bar{X}}=\bar{\bar{D}}=1$).

Exemple: La classe collective "cheval" se transforme par une extraction de ce type en "un cheval"; cette expression est prise au sens "d'un cheval quelconque". Par exemple dans "*un* cheval a quatre pattes".

b) L'extraction peut aussi être faite avec la condition $\delta(\bar{\bar{X}})\equiv(\bar{\bar{X}}=\bar{\bar{D}})$, ce qui revient à prendre, par exemple, tous les chevaux si la base de l'extraction est la classe collective "cheval". On trouve cette interprétation dans "tous les chevaux ont quatre pattes".

c) Le fléchage effectué après une extraction de l'un des deux types précédents redonne la classe collective C obtenue à l'aide du parcours précédent l'extraction. Par exemple: "le cheval est un animal à quatre pattes".

Finalement, les trois opérations de parcours, d'extraction te de fléchage semblent, dans les cas particuliers définis ci-dessus, pouvoir être employées indifféremment et il semble très difficile de différencier parcours et fléchage dans la langue.

Remarque concernant la notation: Dans ce qui suit nous noterons ε_1, ε_2, φ_1, φ_2, respectivement, les extractions et fléchages correspondant aux cas particuliers ci-dessus. ε et φ sans indice représenteront l'extraction et le fléchage dans le cas où ce dernier donne un résultat différent du parcours noté π.

4. MODALITÉS DU TYPE M1 (ASSERTION)

4.1. Le point de départ à été défini à la fin du chapitre II; il s'agit de l'ensemble:

$$L(n(q)) = \{\langle n(q), \gamma_0, \gamma_1 \rangle / (\gamma_0 \in \Gamma_0) \wedge (\gamma_1 \in \Gamma_1)\}$$
$$= \{n(q)\} \times \Gamma_0 \times \Gamma_1.$$

Le nouvel univers que l'on va considérer ici est obtenu à partir de $L(n(q))$ par parcours, extraction ou fléchage sur les arguments γ_0 et γ_1. Il s'écrit:

$$l(q) = \{\langle n(q), \alpha(\gamma_0), \beta(\gamma_1)\rangle\}$$

où $\gamma_0 \in \Gamma_0$, $\gamma_1 \in \Gamma_1$ et α et β sont une des opérations: extraction, fléchage ou parcours sur les arguments γ_0 et γ_1.

On a évidemment: $l(-q) = l(q)$.

4.2. Nous allons maintenant distinguer trois zones dans ce nouvel univers:

a) *L'affirmation de q:*

$$\text{AFF}(q) = \{\langle q, \alpha(\gamma_0), \beta(\gamma_1)\rangle\}.$$

b) *La négation de q:*

$$\text{NEG}(q) = \{\langle -q, \alpha(\gamma_0), \beta(\gamma_1)\rangle\}.$$

Dans l'affirmation et la négation γ_0 et γ_1 sont compatibles, α et β ne peuvent être que l'extraction ε ou le fléchage φ alors que dans la définition de $l(q)$ ils pouvaient également représenter le parcours et les cas particuliers d'extraction et fléchage. Ceci signifie donc que la condition $\delta(\overline{X})$ utilisée dans l'extraction ne peut être $(\overline{X} = \overline{D})$ (cf. III-6) et le résultat du fléchage est supposé être différent de celui du parcours. Remarquons également que $\text{NEG}(q) = \text{AFF}(-q)$.

c) *Le complémentaire* $\text{CONT}(q)$ *de* $\text{AFF}(q) \cup \text{NEG}(q)$ *par rapport à* $l(q)$ est formé par la réunion des quatre ensembles suivants:

C_1: ensemble de triplets $\langle q, \alpha(\gamma_0), \beta(\gamma_1)\rangle$ où γ_0 et γ_1 ne sont pas compatibles, c'est-à-dire ne peuvent pas être en même temps complément de rang 0 et complément de rang 1 du prédicat q; α et β peuvent être n'importe quelle opération d'extraction, parcours ou fléchage.

C_2: ensemble de triplets $\langle -q, \alpha(\gamma_0), \beta(\gamma_1)\rangle$ remplissant les mêmes conditions que C_1 mais partant sur la négation du prédicat.

C_3: ensemble de triplets $\langle q, \alpha(\gamma_0), \beta(\gamma_1)\rangle$.

C_4: ensemble de triplets $\langle -q, \alpha(\gamma_0), \beta(\gamma_1)\rangle$.

Pour ces deux ensembles, γ_0 et γ_1 sont compatibles par rapport au prédicat q et entre eux; une des deux opérations, α et β, au moins est une opération de parcours ou correspond à un cas particulier d'extraction ou de fléchage.

4.3. *Interprétation de* $\mathrm{AFF}(q)$ *et de* $\mathrm{NEG}(q) = \mathrm{AFF}(-q)$

Un triplet de $\mathrm{AFF}(q) \cup \mathrm{AFF}(-q)$ contient tout ce qui est nécessaire pour composer, de manière encore schématique, une phrase de la langue. Les trois composantes (prédicat et deux arguments) d'un tel triplet doivent être comprises dans un sens très général, ce que ne laissent pas voir les exemples donnés plus haut; le prédicat peut être un verbe ou tout être linguistique pouvant admettre des arguments comme "être lent" (1 seul argument); "avoir la propriété", "faire faire", etc … Les arguments seront des constantes ou des expressions plus complexes substituées à ces constantes. Ceci nous conduira à étudier les lexis de lexis, les substitutions de lexis à des arguments, etc …, c'est-à-dire l'ensemble des opérations que l'on peut faire sur les lexis.

Aux schémas de phrases ainsi définis on pourra appliquer les opérations relatives au temps, aux modalités, … Pour cela, nous définirons un nouvel univers à partir de $\mathrm{AFF}(q) \cup \mathrm{AFF}(-q)$.

4.4. *Interprétation de* $\mathrm{CONT}(q)$

a) Du point de vue linguistique $\mathrm{CONT}(q)$ contient les vérités générales (c'est-à-dire les phrases intemporelles) comme "le cheval a quatre pattes" et certains schémas de phrases qui sont du domaine de l'imaginaire dont "le cheval mange la souris" est un exemple. Nous sommes donc amenés, en utilisant les notions du chapitre III, à décomposer $\mathrm{CONT}(q)$ en deux parties:

1° – $\mathrm{CONTREEL}(q)$ contiendra les vérités générales. Ici, aucune des deux fonctions α et β ne peut représenter ε ou φ. Donc $\mathrm{CONTREEL}(q)$ est défini par la condition:

$$K'(\alpha, \beta) \equiv (\alpha, \beta \in \{\pi, \varepsilon_1, \varepsilon_2, \varphi_1, \varphi_2\}).$$

De façon précise, on a:

$$\mathrm{CONTREEL}(q) = C_2' \cup C_3'$$

$$\text{où } C_2' = \{\langle -q, \alpha(\gamma_0), \beta(\gamma_1)\rangle / (\gamma_0 \in \Gamma_0) \wedge (\gamma_1 \in \Gamma_1) \wedge$$
$$(\langle \gamma_0, \gamma_1\rangle \notin q) \wedge K'(\alpha, \beta)\}$$

$$C_2' \subset C_2$$

$$C_3' = \{\langle q, \alpha(\gamma_0), \beta(\gamma_1)\rangle/(\gamma_0 \in \Gamma_0) \wedge (\gamma_1 \in \Gamma_1) \wedge$$
$$(\langle \gamma_0, \gamma_1 \rangle \in q) \wedge K'(\alpha, \beta)\}$$
$$C_3' \subset C_3.$$

$2°$ – CONTIMA(q) appartient au domaine de l'imaginaire. Pour le définir nous posons:

$$C_3'' = \complement_{C_3} C_3' \qquad C_2'' = \complement_{C_2} C_2'.$$

Si nous introduisons la condition

$$K''(\alpha, \beta) \equiv (\alpha \in \{\varepsilon, \varphi\} \vee (\beta \in \{\varepsilon, \varphi\})$$

nous pouvons aussi définir les ensembles C_2'' et C_3'' par:

$$C_2'' = \{x/(x \in C_2) \wedge K''(\alpha, \beta)\}$$
$$C_3'' = \{x/(x \in C_3) \wedge K''(\alpha, \beta)\}$$

avec des notations évidentes.

Dans ces conditions on a:

$$\text{CONTIMA}(q) = C_1 \cup C_4 \cup C_2'' \cup C_3''$$

b) *Exemples:*

$1°$ – Soit q le prédicat "manger"; on suppose que $\langle$cheval, viande$\rangle \notin q$. Alors, on trouve dans CONT(q) les triplets:

(1) $\langle -$manger, π (cheval), π (viande)$\rangle \in C_2'$
    "le cheval ne mange pas la viande"

(2) $\langle -$manger, ε_1 (cheval), π (viande)$\rangle \in C_2'$
    "un cheval ne mange pas la viande".

$2°$ – Prenant toujours $q =$ manger, on suppose que $\langle$chat, souris$\rangle \in q$. Les triplets suivants sont également dans CONT(q):

(3) $\langle$manger, ε_1 (chat), φ_1 (souris)$\rangle \in C_3'$
    "un chat mange les souris".

(4) $\langle$manger, φ_1 (chat), φ_1 (souris)$\rangle \in C_3'$
    "les chats mangent les souris".

Remarque: dans la langue certaines formes sont ambiguës; d'autres ne sont pratiquement pas employées. On peut penser que l'opération de parcours fournira la forme la plus courante.

$3°$ – Soit q le prédicat: "avoir" (la propriété); les trois exemples suivants montrent l'emploi indifférent du parcours, de l'extraction ou du fléchage:

"un cheval a quatre pattes"

"le cheval a quatre pattes"

"(tous) les chevaux ont quatre pattes".

c) Il semble que, contrairement aux schémas de phrases de $\mathrm{AFF}(q)\cup\mathrm{AFF}(-q)$, il reste peu d'opérations à effectuer sur ceux appartenant à $\mathrm{CONTREEL}(q)$; cet ensemble nous fournira un nouvel univers indépendant de celui obtenu à partir de $\mathrm{AFF}(q)\cup\mathrm{AFF}(-q)$. Dans ce nouvel univers nous pourrons avoir des opérations de temps (pour exprimer, par exemple, les vérités générales dans le passé: au sujet des dynosaures en particulier), de modalités (fournissant: "les hommes doivent manger pour vivre"), etc …

D'autre part, comme dans le cas de $\mathrm{AFF}(q)\cup\mathrm{AFF}(-q)$, les composantes d'un triplet de $\mathrm{CONTREEL}(q)$ doivent être prises dans un sens très général.

5. *Relations entre* $\mathrm{AFF}(q)\cup\mathrm{AFF}(-q)$ *et* $\mathrm{CONT}(q)$

a) Par rapport à l'univers $l(q)$ on peut définir les ensembles:

$$\complement\,\mathrm{AFF}(q)\ \text{et}\ \complement\,\mathrm{AFF}(-q)$$

On a alors les relations:

(1) $\mathrm{CONT}(q)=\complement\,\mathrm{AFF}(q)\cap\complement\,\mathrm{AFF}(-q)$

(2) $\mathrm{AFF}(q)\subset\complement\,\mathrm{AFF}(-q)$

(3) $\mathrm{AFF}(-q)\subset\complement\,\mathrm{AFF}(q)$

b) *Exemples:* soit q le prédicat "manger"

1° – $\langle -\text{manger, le cheval, la viande}\rangle\in\complement\,\mathrm{AFF}(q)$.

Mais ce triplet ne saurait appartenir à $\mathrm{AFF}(-q)$ car, à un instant précis, il n'est pas forcément vrai que "le cheval ne mange pas la viande". Ce triplet est donc dans $\mathrm{CONT}(q)$ car

$$\complement\,\mathrm{AFF}(q)=\mathrm{CONT}(q)\cup\mathrm{AFF}(-q)$$

2° – $\langle -\text{manger, Jean, une pomme}\rangle\in\mathrm{AFF}(-q)$; en effet celà signifie non seulement "il est faux que Jean mange une pomme" – ce qui entraîne son appartenance à $\complement\,\mathrm{AFF}(q)$ –, mais aussi "il est vrai que Jean ne mange pas une pomme" à un instant donné.

3° – $\langle\text{manger, les chats, les souris}\rangle\in\mathrm{CONTREEL}(q)\subset\mathrm{CONT}(q)$.

Ce triplet n'est pas dans $\mathrm{AFF}(q)$ car il n'est pas vrai d'une manière obligatoire qu'à un instant donné, les chats mangent les souris. Mais il est faux que "les chats ne mangent pas les souris". Donc ce triplet appartient à $\complement\,\mathrm{AFF}(-q)$.

4° – $\langle\text{manger, le cheval, la viande}\rangle\in\mathrm{CONT}(q)$.

Ce triplet n'appartient pas à $\mathrm{CONTREEL}(q)$. Il appartient à $\complement\,\mathrm{AFF}(-q)$ car il signifie: il est faux que "le cheval ne mange pas la viande".

5. SCHÉMA RÉSUMANT LES RÉLATIONS ENTRE LES ENSEMBLES INTRODUITS AUX PARAGRAPHES PRÉCÉDENTS

Commentaire: On est passé du premier univers $\mathscr{U}$ au deuxième univers $\mathscr{L}(n(q))$ en transformant par extraction l'ensemble $\lambda(n(p)) = \complement_{\lambda(n(p))}\lambda'(n(p)) \cup \lambda'(n(p))$ en $\mathscr{L}(n(q))$.

On passe du deuxième univers $\mathscr{L}(n(q))$ au troisième $l(q)$ en transformant $L'(n(q)) \cup \complement_{L(n(q))}L'(n(q))$ en $l(q)$ par trois opérations liées mais différentes: le parcours, l'extraction et le fléchage. De façon précise on transforme $L'(n(q))$ en $\text{AFF}(q) \cup \text{AFF}(-q)$ par extraction et fléchage; par parcours, ou par une opération équivalente, sur au moins un argument, $L'(n(q))$ se transforme en $C_3 \cup C_4 \subset \text{CONT}(q)$. Quant à $\complement_{L(n(q))}L'(n(q))$, il devient $C_1 \cup C_2 \subset \text{CONT}(q)$ par parcours, extraction ou fléchage.

Remarque 1: le dernier univers $l(q)$ est symétrique par rapport à q et $-q$, en ce sens que $\text{AFF}(q)$ et $\text{AFF}(-q)$ ont des rôles analogues et que $\text{CONT}(q) = \text{CONT}(-q)$. Ceci n'était pas vrai dans les univers précédents.

Remarque 2: dans chaque triplet défini pour $\text{AFF}(q)$ et $\text{AFF}(-q)$, on peut considérer que la place, correspondant au deuxième argument du prédicat, peut être vide.

Cependant, il faut faire une différence entre les arguments vides γ_1 des phrases:

   la table ne mange pas (c'est-à-dire "la table n'est pas un mangeur")

et   Jean mange (ou ne mange pas à un instant donné).

La première est relative à la notion "n(être mangeur)" et correspond à une vérité générale donc intemporelle. La seconde est une phrase assertive (pouvant être temporalisée) relative à la notion "n(manger)" ou γ_1 n'est pas précisé mais existe (c'est-à-dire Jean mange ce qu'il mange).

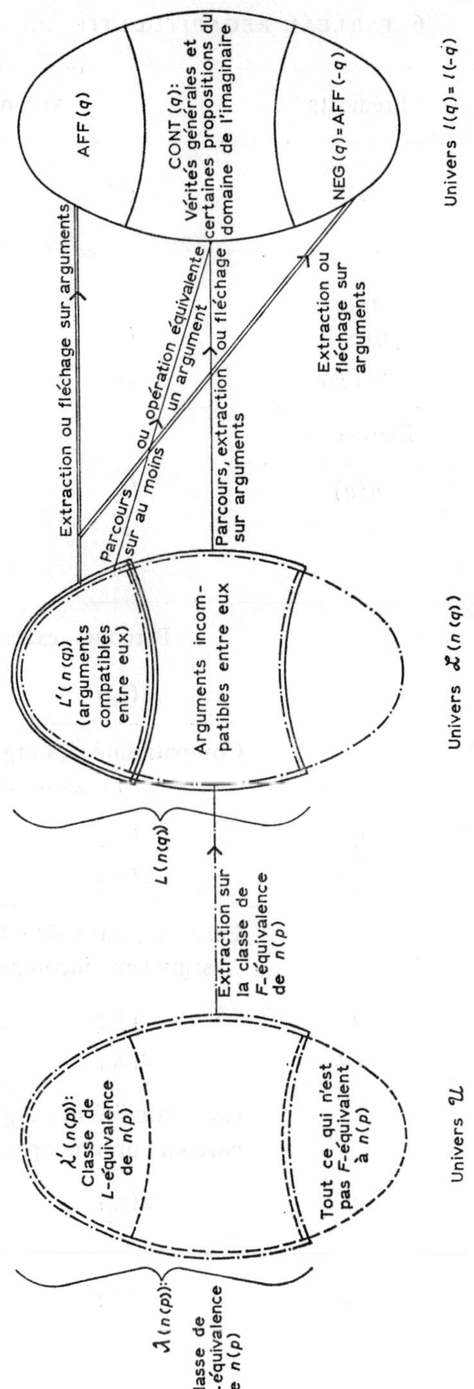

AFF (q)
CONT (q): Vérités générales et certaines propositions du domaine de l'imaginaire
NEG (q) = AFF (-q)
Univers $l(q) = l(-q)$
Extraction ou fléchage sur arguments
Parcours ou opération équivalente sur au moins un argument
Parcours, extraction ou fléchage sur arguments
Extraction ou fléchage sur arguments
$L'(n(q))$ (arguments compatibles entre eux)
Arguments incompatibles entre eux
Univers $\mathcal{L}(n(q))$
$L(n(q))$
Extraction sur la classe de F-équivalence de n(p)
$\lambda'(n(p))$: Classe de L-équivalence de n(p)
Tout ce qui n'est pas F-équivalent à n(p)
Univers $\mathcal{U}$
$\lambda(n(p))$: Classe de F-équivalence de n(p)

6 TABLEAU RÉCAPITULATIF

	Prédicats	Arguments	
Univers de départ	V	U	U
Lexis	$n(p)$ $\|n(p)\|_L$ $\|n(p)\|_F$	 U U	 U U
	Extraction		
	$n(q)$	Γ_0 $\downarrow$ γ_0	Γ_1 $\Rightarrow\quad\gamma_1$
		Parcours, extraction, fléchage	
		$\alpha(\gamma_0)$	$\beta(\gamma_1)$
		Compatibilité des arguments; ni parcours ni operation équivalente	
	q	$\alpha(\gamma_0)$	$\beta(\gamma_1)$
Modalités	$-q$	$\alpha(\gamma_0)$	$\beta(\gamma_1)$
		Parcours, extraction, fléchage; arguments incompatibles	
de type M1	q	$\alpha(\gamma_0)$	$\beta(\gamma_1)$
	$-q$	$\alpha(\gamma_0)$	$\beta(\gamma_1)$
		Compatibilité des arg.; au moins un parcours ou une operation équivalente	
	q	$\alpha(\gamma_0)$	$\beta(\gamma_1)$
	$-q$	$\alpha(\gamma_0)$	$\beta(\gamma_1)$

Ensembles

$$\mathcal{U} = \{\langle n(p), \mu_0, \mu_1 \rangle / (n(p) \in V) \wedge (\mu_0, \mu_1 \in U)\}$$

$$\lambda'(n(p)) = \{\langle n(q), \mu_0, \mu_1 \rangle / (n(q) \in \|n(p)\|_L) \wedge (\mu_0, \mu_1 \in U)\}$$
$$\lambda(n(p)) = \{\langle n(q), \mu_0, \mu_1 \rangle / (n(q) \in \|n(p)\|_F) \wedge (\mu_0, \mu_1 \in U)\}$$

$$L(n(q)) = \{\langle n(q), \gamma_0, \gamma_1 \rangle / (\gamma_0 \in \Gamma_0) \wedge (\gamma_1 \in \Gamma_1)\}$$
$$L'(n(q)) = \{\langle n(q), \gamma_0, \gamma_1 \rangle / (\gamma_0 \in \Gamma_0) \wedge (\gamma_1 \in \Gamma_1) \wedge (\langle \gamma_0, \gamma_1 \rangle \in q)\}$$

$$l(q) = \{\langle n(q), \alpha(\gamma_0), \beta(\gamma_1) \rangle / (\gamma_0 \in \Gamma_0) \wedge (\gamma_1 \in \Gamma_1) \wedge (\alpha, \beta \in \{\pi, \varepsilon, \varphi, \varepsilon_1, \varepsilon_2, \varphi_1, \varphi_2\})\}$$

$$\text{AFF}(q) - \{\langle q, \alpha(\gamma_0), \beta(\gamma_2) \rangle / (\gamma_0 \in \Gamma_0) \wedge (\gamma_1 \subset \Gamma_1) \wedge (\langle \gamma_0, \gamma_1 \rangle \in q) \wedge (\alpha, \beta \in \{\varepsilon, \varphi\})\}$$
$$\text{NEG}(q) = \{\langle -q, \alpha(\gamma_0), \beta(\gamma_1) \rangle / (\gamma_0 \in \Gamma_0) \wedge (\gamma_1 \in \Gamma_1) \wedge (\langle \gamma_0, \gamma_1 \rangle \in q) \wedge (\alpha, \beta \in \{\varepsilon, \varphi\})\}$$

$$C_1 = \{\langle q, \alpha(\gamma_0), \beta(\gamma_1) \rangle / (\gamma_0 \in \Gamma_0) \wedge (\gamma_1 \in \Gamma_1) \wedge (\langle \gamma_0, \gamma_1 \rangle \notin q) \wedge (\alpha, \beta \in \{\pi, \varepsilon, \varphi, \varepsilon_1, \varepsilon_2, \varphi_1, \varphi_2\})\}$$
$$C_2 = \{\langle -q, \alpha(\gamma_0), \beta(\gamma_1) \rangle / (\gamma_0 \in \Gamma_0) \wedge (\gamma_1 \in \Gamma_1) \wedge (\langle \gamma_0, \gamma_1 \rangle \notin q) \wedge (\alpha, \beta \in \{\pi, \varepsilon, \varphi, \varepsilon_1, \varepsilon_2, \varphi_1, \varphi_2\})\}$$

$$C_3 = \{\langle q, \alpha(\gamma_0), \beta(\gamma_1) \rangle / (\gamma_0 \in \Gamma_0) \wedge (\gamma_1 \in \Gamma_1) \wedge (\langle \gamma_0, \gamma_1 \rangle \in a) \wedge$$
$$\times [(\alpha \in \{\pi, \varepsilon_1, \varepsilon_2, \varphi_1, \varphi_2\}) \vee (\beta \in \{\pi, \varepsilon_1, \varepsilon_2, \varphi_1, \varphi_2\})]\}$$
$$C_4 = \{\langle -q, \alpha(\gamma_0), \beta(\gamma_1) \rangle / (\gamma_0 \in \Gamma_0) \wedge (\gamma_1 \in \Gamma_1) \wedge (\langle \gamma_0, \gamma_1 \rangle \in a) \wedge$$
$$\times [(\alpha \in \{\pi, \varepsilon_1, \varepsilon_2, \varphi_1, \varphi_2\}) \vee (\beta \in \{\pi, \varepsilon_1, \varepsilon_2, \varphi_1, \varphi_2\})]\}]$$
$$\text{CONT}(q) = C_1 \cup C_2 \cup C_3 \cup C_4$$

C.N.R.S.-C.E.T.A. (Grenoble)

BIBLIOGRAPHIE

Baille, A. et Rouault, J. (1966), 'Un essai de formalisation de la sémantique des langues naturelles', Document C.E.T.A. n° G-2200-A, décembre.

Clay, R. E. (1965), 'The Relation of Weakly Discrete to Set and Equinumerosity in Mereology', *N. D. J. of Formal Logic* **5**, n° 4, octobre.

Culioli, A. (1969), 'Sémantique Générale', à paraître.

Dupraz, M. et Rouault, J. (1968), 'Lexis, Affirmation, Négation: Etude fondée sur les classes', Document C.E.T.A. n° G-2400-A, juillet.

Sobocinski, B. (1949/1950), 'L'analyse de l'antinomie russellienne par Lesniewski', *Methodos*.

CHARLES J. FILLMORE

TYPES OF LEXICAL INFORMATION*

0. THE LEXICON

A lexicon viewed as part of the apparatus of a generative grammar must make accessible to its users, for each lexical item,

(i)   the nature of the deep-structure syntactic environments into which the item may be inserted;

(ii)   the properties of the item to which the rules of grammar are sensitive;

(iii)   for an item that can be used as a 'predicate', the number of 'arguments' that it conceptually requires;

(iv)   the role(s) which each argument plays in the situation which the item, as predicate, can be used to indicate;

(v)   the presuppositions or 'happiness conditions' for the use of the item, the conditions which must be satisfied in order for the item to be used 'aptly';

(vi)   the nature of the conceptual or morphological relatedness of the item to other items in the lexicon;

(vii)   its meaning; and

(viii)   the phonological or orthographic shapes which the item assumes under given grammatical conditions.

In this paper I shall survey, in a very informal manner, the various types of information that needs to be included, in one way or another, in the lexical component of an adequate grammar. I shall, however, have nothing to say about (viii) above, and nothing very reliable to say about (vii).

1. THE SPEECH ACT

I begin by assuming that the semantic description of lexical items capable of functioning as predicates can be expressed as complex statements about properties of, changes in, or relations between entities of the following two sorts: (a) the entities that can serve as arguments in the predicate-argument constructions in which the given lexical item can figure, and (b) various aspects of the speech act itself. In this section I shall deal with the concepts that appear to be necessary for identifying the role of the speech act in semantic theory.

The act of producing a linguistic utterance in a particular situation in-

F. Kiefer (ed.), Studies in Syntax and Semantics, 109–137. © D. Reidel, Dordrecht-Holland

volves a speaker, an addressee, and a message. It is an act, furthermore, which occurs within a specific time-span, and it is one in which the participants are situated in particular places. Now the time during which a speech act is produced is a span, the participants in the speech act may be moving about during this span, and even the identity of the participants may change during the speech act; but for most purposes the participant-identity and the time-space coordinates of the speech act can be thought of as fixed points. In accepting this fiction, I commit myself to regarding sentences like (1) to (3) as somewhat pathological:

(1)   I'M NOT TALKING TO YOU, I'M TALKING TO YOU.

(2)   I WANT YOU TO TURN THE CORNER … RIGHT … HERE!

(3)   THIS WON'T TAKE LONG, DID IT?

The producer of a speech act will be called the *locutionary source* (LS), the addressee will be referred to as the *locutionary target* (LT)[1]. The temporal and spatial coordinates of the speech act are the *time of the locutionary act* (TLA), the *place of the locutionary source* (PLS) and the *place of the locutionary target* (PLT).

There are certain verbs in English which refer to instances of speech acts other than the one which is being performed (e.g. SAY), and I shall refer to these as *locutionary verbs*. It is necessary to mention locutionary verbs now because we shall find that linguistic theory requires a distinction between the 'ultimate' speech act and speech acts described or referred to in a sentence. Thus in the linguistic description of some verbs reference is made to either the LS or the agent of a locutionary verb[2], and these situations must be distinguished from those in which the reference is to the LS alone.

Words in English whose semantic descriptions require reference to some aspect of the locutionary act include HERE, THIS, NOW, TODAY, COME, and KNOW. The word COME[3], for example, can refer to movement toward either the PLA or the PLT at either TLA or the time-of-focus identified in the sentence. Thus in (4)

(4)   HE SAID THAT SHE WOULD COME TO THE OFFICE THURSDAY MORNING

it is understood that the office is the location of the LS or the LT either at TLA or on the said Thursday morning. Uses of the verb KNOW allow the LT to infer the factuality of the proposition represented by a following THAT-clause. Thus, in sentence (5)

(5)   SHE KNOWS THAT HER BROTHER HAS RESIGNED

it is understood that the LS at TLA presupposes the factuality of her brother's resignation.

In the semantic description of some verbs reference is made either to the subject of the 'next locutionary verb up', or to the LS just in case the sentence contains no explicit locutionary verb. If we are to believe Ross (see note 2), the verb LURK requires of its subject that it be distinct from the subject of the first commanding locutionary verb. It may look, on just seeing sentences (6)–(7),

(6)   HE WAS LURKING OUTSIDE HER WINDOW

(7)   *I WAS LURKING OUTSIDE HER WINDOW

that what is required is simply non-identity with LS; but this is shown not to be so because of the acceptability of sentence (8)

(8)   SHE SAID I HAD BEEN LURKING OUTSIDE HER WINDOW.

From these observations it follows that sentence (9) is ambiguous on whether or not the two pronouns HE are coreferential, but sentence (10) requires the two HE's to be different.

(9)   HE SAID HE HAD BEEN LOITERING OUTSIDE HER WINDOW

(10)   HE SAID HE HAD BEEN LURKING OUTSIDE HER WINDOW.

There are apparently many speakers of English whose use of LURK fails to match the observations I have just reviewed; but for the remainder, this verb provides an example of the distinction we are after.

There is, then, a distinction in semantic descriptions of lexical items between references to properties of the higher clauses that contain them, on the one hand, and to features of or participants in the speech act itself on the other hand. The former situation falls within the area of 'deep structure constraints' (see Section 9 below), but the latter requires the availability of concepts related to the speech act.[4]

2. ELEMENTARY SEMANTIC PROPERTIES OF VERBS

I assume that what we might call the basic sense of a word is typically expressible as a set of components, and that while some of these components may be idiosyncratic to particular words, others are common to possibly quite large classes of words. The components themselves may be complex, since they may be required to characterize events or situations that are themselves complex, but the ultimate terms of a semantic description I take to be such presumably biologically given notions as identity, time, space, body, movement, territory, life, fear, etc., as well as undefined terms that directly identify aspects of or objects in the cultural and physical universe in which human beings live. In this section, we shall sample certain elementary semantic properties of verbs, in particular those relating to time, space, movement, and 'will'.

Some verbs refer to activities viewed as necessarily changing in time, others do not; this contrast is frequently referred to with the terms 'momentary' and 'continuative' respectively. SLEEP is a continuative verb, WAKE UP is a momentary verb. A continuing activity, or state, necessarily occupies a span of time, and thus it makes sense to qualify a continuative verb with a complement which identified one or both of the end-points of such a span, or a distance-measure of the span. Thus while the sentences in (11) make sense, those in (12) do not.

(11)   SHE SLEPT $\begin{Bmatrix} \text{FOR THREE DAYS} \\ \text{UNTIL FRIDAY} \end{Bmatrix}$

(12)   *SHE WOKE UP $\begin{Bmatrix} \text{FOR THREE DAYS} \\ \text{UNTIL FRIDAY} \end{Bmatrix}$.

On the other hand, the negation of a momentary verb can identify a continuing state; hence, the sentences in (13) make sense.

(13)   SHE DIDN'T WAKE UP $\begin{Bmatrix} \text{FOR THREE DAYS} \\ \text{UNTIL FRIDAY} \end{Bmatrix}$.

Momentary verbs that represent acts that are repeatable may be understood 'iteratively'. WAKE UP is not iterative, as is shown by example (12). KICK, however, can be understood iteratively, as we see in (14)

(14)   HE KICKED THE DOG UNTIL 5 O'CLOCK.

Momentary verbs that are also 'change-of-state' verbs cannot be used iteratively when a specific object is involved, as we see in example (15),

(15)   *HE BROKE THE VASE UNTIL 5 O'CLOCK

but if the same activity can be directed to an unspecified number of objects, then change-of-state verbs can be understood iteratively, too, as we see in (16)

(16)   HE BROKE VASES UNTIL 5 O'CLOCK.

It appears, in short, that a lexico-semantic theory will have to deal with those aspects of the meanings of verbs which relate to the occurrence in time of the situations which they identify.

Turning to other types of semantic properties, we note that verbs like HIT and TOUCH, though they differ in thatht e former is momentary while the latter may be either momentary or continuative, have in common the notion of surface-contact, a property they share with KNOCK, STRIKE, CONTACT,

IMPINGE, SMITE, and many others. They differ in that the impact of the described acts is apparently gentler for TOUCH than for HIT.

The verbs LEAP and JUMP agree in implying a momentary change in vertical position (one has to leave the ground in order to perform either of these actions), but they differ in that LEAP seems to imply a change in horizontal position, too. SLIDE, like LEAP, refers to position-changes along a surface, but differs from LEAP in not implying movement away from the surface. SCUTTLE, like SLIDE, suggests movement across a surface, but with the assumption that contact with the surface is interrupted and with the further sense that the motion is rapid. DART is like SCUTTLE in referring to rapid sudden motion, but fails to share with it any reference to a surface. Verbs of motion, in short, may be described by associating them with properties relating to direction, speed, gravity, surface, etc.[5]

Sometimes a verb has a built-in reference to the outcome of an activity. Conceptually it appears that the actor engages in some activity and though the activity may be directed toward some specific outcome it is the activity itself which (by chance) leads to that outcome. These have been called 'achievement verbs'. One of the tests of an achievement verb is that the modal MAY is usable in construction with such a verb only in its epistemic or predictive sense, not in its pragmatic or permission-granting sense. This is apparently because of the 'by-chance' relationship between the activity and the outcome: one doesn't grant someone permission to have good luck. Hence we find (17) and (19) understandable only in the epistemic sense of MAY, while (18) and (20) can be understood in either the epistemic or the pragmatic sense.

(17)   HE MAY ACHIEVE HIS GOAL

(18)   HE MAY TRY TO ACHIEVE HIS GOAL

(19)   HE MAY FIND THE EGGS

(20)   HE MAY LOOK FOR THE EGGS.

A final general property of verbs that we may point out in this section has to do with the intentional or non-intentional involvement of one of the participants in the events described by use of the verb. If we compare (21) and (22)

(21)   JOHN MEANS X BY Y

(22)   JOHN UNDERSTANDS X BY Y

we note that in (21), but not in (22), the association between X and Y is intentional on John's part. The word MEAN can be used in the sense which

UNDERSTAND has in (22), but in that case the sentence is differently constructed. (23) is a paraphrase of (22).

(23)   Y MEANS X TO JOHN.

3. PREDICATE STRUCTURE

I assume that most of the 'content words' in a language can be characterized
in the lexicon in terms of their use as predicates. I take this to be true of
nouns, verbs, adjectives[6], most adverbs, and also a great many conjunctions.
Thus a sentence like (24)

(24)   HARRY LIVES AT HOME BECAUSE HE LOVES HIS MOTHER

is evaluated as true or false depending not only on the joint truth-values of
the two clauses which flank BECAUSE, but on the truth or falsity of the 'causal'
connection between the two situations named by these clauses. The sentence
can be interpreted as having BECAUSE as its main predicate, a predicate which
takes two clauses as its arguments and which is used to assert a 'causal' or
'logical' connection between them.

As predicates, words can be described first of all according to the number
of 'arguments' that they take. Thus the verbs ASCEND and LIFT are both
motion verbs, they are both used to describe motion upward, but they differ
in that while ASCEND is used only of the object that moves upward, LIFT
requires conceptually two objects, one the object that is moving upward, the
other the object or being that is causing it to move upward. Another way
of stating this is: ASCEND is a one-argument predicate, LIFT is a two-argument
predicate.[7]

Many verbs are flexible in the number of arguments they take. This is true,
for example, of some motion verbs, like MOVE and ROTATE, and many change-
of-state verbs, like OPEN and BREAK. MOVE, as can be seen in sentences
(25)–(27), can occur with one, two, or three arguments.

(25)   THE ROCK MOVED

(26)   THE WIND MOVED THE ROCK

(27)   I MOVED THE ROCK (WITH A STICK).

Mention of the object which moves is required of all three uses; the two-
argument uses additionally identify either the physical force or object which
is directly responsible, or the animate being which is indirectly responsible,
for the activity of moving; and the three-argument use identified all three
of these (as in (27) with the parenthesized phrase included). The surface-
contact verbs HIT, TOUCH, STRIKE, etc., require conceptually at least two

arguments in all of their uses, namely the objects which come into contact, but they accept as a third argument the animate being that is responsible for the coming-into-contact.

The verbs ROB and STEAL conceptually require three arguments, namely those identifiable as the culprit, the loser, and the loot. The words BUY and SELL are each 4-argument predicates, the arguments representing the one who receives the goods or services, the one who provides the goods and services, the goods and services themselves, and the sum of money that changes hands.

I have referred in this section to the conceptually required number of arguments. I am distinguishing this from the number of arguments that must be explicitly identified in English sentences. The various ways in which English grammar provides for the omission or suppression of conceptually required arguments is the subject of Section 5. To say that conceptually ROB or BUY are 3- or 4-argument predicates respectively is to acknowledge that even when we say merely (28)

> (28)   SHE ROBBED THE BANK

we understand that she took something out of the bank, and when we say (29)

> (29)   SHE BOUGHT IT

truthfully, it is necessarily the case that there was somebody who sold it to her and that a sum of money was exchanged.

4. CASE STRUCTURE

In the preceding section I identified the separate arguments associated with the verb ROB by referring to their roles as 'culprit', 'loser', and 'loot'; in a similar way, I might have identified the three arguments associated with the verb CRITICIZE as 'critic', 'offender' and 'offense'. It seems to me, however, that this sort of detail is unnecessary, and that what we need are abstractions from these specific role descriptions, abstractions which will allow us to recognize that certain elementary role notions recur in many situations, and which will allow us to acknowledge that differences in detail between partly similar roles are due to differences in the meanings of the associated verbs. Thus we can identify the culprit of ROB and the critic of CRITICIZE with the more abstract role of Agent, and interpret the term Agent as referring, wherever it occurs, as the animate instigator of events referred to by the associated verb. Although there are many substantive difficulties in determining the role structure of given expressions, in general it seems to me that for the predicates provided in natural languages, the roles that their arguments play are taken from an inventory of role types fixed by grammatical theory. Since the most readily available terms for these roles are found in the literature of case theory, I have taken to referring to the roles as *case relationships*, or simple *cases*. The combination of cases that might be associated with a given predicate is the *case structure* of that predicate.

In addition to the apparently quite complex collection of complements that identify the limits and extents in space and time that are required by verbs of motion, location, duration, etc., the case notions that are most relevant to the subclassification of verb types include the following:

> Agent (A), the instigator of the event
> Counter-Agent (C), the force or resistance against which the action is carried out
> Object (O), the entity that moves or changes or whose position or existence is in consideration
> Result (R), the entity that comes into existence as a result of the action
> Instrument (I), the stimulus or immediate physical cause of an event
> Source (S), the place to which something is directed
> Experiencer (E), the entity which receives or accepts or experiences or undergoes the effect of an action (earlier called by me 'Dative').

It appears that there is sometimes a one-many relationship between an argument to a predicate and the roles that are associated with it. This can be phrased by saying either that some arguments simultaneously serve in more than one role, or that in some situations the arguments in different roles must (or may) be identical.

Thus verbs like RISE and MOVE can be used intransitively, that is with one noun phrase complement; the complement may refer just to the thing which is moving upward, or it may simultaneously refer to the being responsible for such motion. Thus in speaking simply of the upward motion of smoke we can say (30),

(30)   THE SMOKE ROSE

and in speaking of John's getting up on his own power, we can say (31)

(31)   JOHN ROSE.

The case structure of RISE, then, might be represented diagrammatically as (32). The fact that there are two case lines connecting RISE with its one argument, and that the line labeled A has its case label in parentheses, reflect the fact

(32)

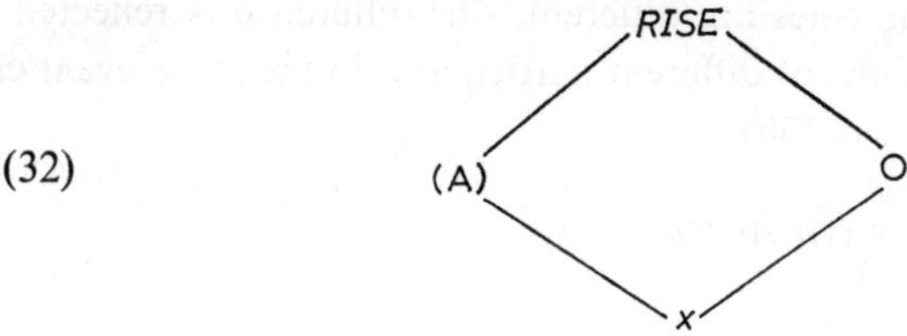

that the argument can serve in just one of these roles (O) or simultaneously in both (A and O). RISE differs from ARISE in the optionality of A; it differs from ASCEND in having an 'A' line at all, and they all differ from LIFT in that the latter requires two arguments.[8] Thus (33)–(35)

(33)

(34)

(35)

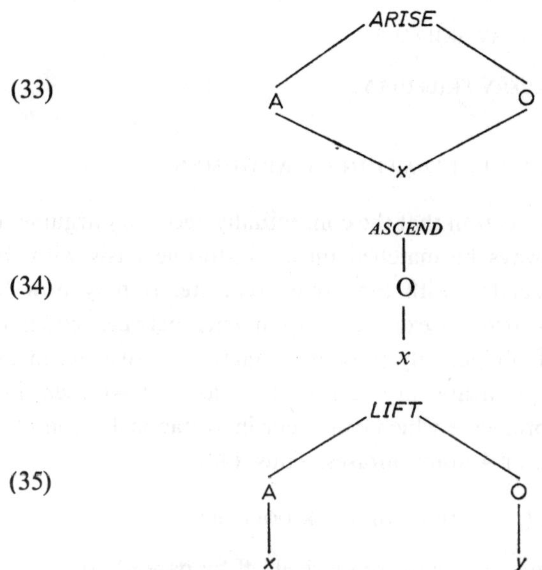

Frequently a linguistically codable event is one which in fact allows more than one individual to be actively or agentively involved. In any given linguistic expression of such an event, however, the Agent role can only be associated with one of these. In such pairs as BUY and SELL or TEACH and LEARN we have a Source (of goods or knowledge) and a Goal. When the Source is simultaneously the Agent, one uses SELL and TEACH; when the Goal is simultaneously the Agent, we use BUY and LEARN.

It is not true, in other words, that BUY and SELL, TEACH and LEARN are simply synonymous verbs that differ from each other in the order in which the arguments are mentioned.[9] There is synonymy in the basic meanings of the verbs (as descriptions of events), but a fact that might be overlooked is that each of these verbs emphasizes the contribution to the event of one of the participants. Since the roles are different, this difference is reflected in the ways in which the actions of different participants in the same event can be qualified. This we can say (36)

(36)   HE BOUGHT IT WITH SILVER MONEY

but not (37)

(37)   HE SOLD IT WITH SILVER MONEY.

Similarly, the adverbs in (38) and (39) do not further describe the activity as a whole, but only one person's end of it.

(38)   HE SELLS EGGS VERY SKILFULLY

(39)   HE BUYS EGGS VERY SKILFULLY.

5. SURFACE REALIZATION OF ARGUMENTS

I suggested in the previous section that the conceptually necessary arguments to a predicate cannot always be matched on a one-to-one basis with the 'cases' that are also associated with the same predicate. It may now be pointed out that there is also no exact correspondence between either of these and the number of obligatorily present syntactic constituents in expressions containing the predicates in question. BUY, as we have seen, is a 4-argument (but 5-case) predicate which can occur in syntactically complete sentences containing 2, 3, or 4 noun phrases. Thus, (40),

(40)   HE BOUGHT IT (FROM ME) (FOR FOUR DOLLARS)

in which optionally present segments are marked off by parentheses.

The verb BLAME has associated with it 3 roles, the accuser (Source), the defendant (Goal), and the offense (Object). Expressions with this verb can contain reference to all three, as in (41), just two, as in (42) and (43), or only one, as in (44).

(41)   THE BOYS BLAMED THE GIRLS FOR THE MESS

(42)   THE BOYS BLAMED THE GIRLS

(43)   THE GIRLS WERE BLAMED FOR THE MESS

(44)   THE GIRLS WERE BLAMED.

No sentence with BLAME, however, can mention only the accuser, only the offense, or just the accuser and the offense. See (45)–(47).

(45)   *THE BOYS BLAMED

(46)   *THE MESS WAS BLAMED

(47)   *THE BOYS BLAMED (FOR) THE MESS.

An examination of (41)–(47) reveals that the case realized here as THE GIRLS is obligatory in all expressions containing this verb, and, importantly, that there are two distinct situations in which the speaker may be silent about one of the other arguments. I take sentence (43) as a syntactically complete sentence, in the sense that it can appropriately initiate a discourse (as long as the addressee knows who the girls are and what the mess is). In this case the speaker is merely being indefinite or non-committal about the identity of the accuser. I take sentence (42), however, as one which cannot initiate a conversation and one which is usable only in a context in which the addressee is in a position to know what it is that the girls are being blamed for. Another way of saying this is that (43) is a paraphrase of (43′) and (42) is a paraphrase of (42′).

(42′)   THE BOYS BLAMED THE GIRLS FOR IT.

(43′)   THE GIRLS WERE BLAMED FOR THE MESS BY SOMEONE.

This distinction can be further illustrated with uses of HIT. In (48), a paraphrase of (48′), the speaker is merely being indefinite about the implement he used:

(48)   I HIT THE DOG

(48′)   I HIT THE DOG WITH SOMETHING.

In (49), the paraphrase of (49′), the speaker expects the identity of the 'target' (Goal) to be already known by the addressee.

(49)   THE ARROW HIT

(49′)   THE ARROW HIT IT.

The two situations correspond, in other words, to definite and indefinite pronominalization.

Sometimes an argument is obligatorily left out of the surface structure because it is subsumed as a part of the meaning of the predicate. This situation has been discussed in great detail by Jeffrey Gruber (see note 5 above) under the label 'incorporation'. An example of a verb with an 'incorporated' Object is DINE, which is conceptually the same as EAT DINNER but which does not tolerate a direct object.[10]

The verb DOFF has an incorporated Source. If I DOFF something, I remove it from my head, but there is no way of expressing the Source when this verb is used. There is no such sentence as (50)

(50)   *HE DOFFED HIS HAT FROM HIS BALDING HEAD.

There are other verbs that identify events which typically involve an entity
of a fairly specific sort, so that to fail to mention the entity is to be understood
as intending the usual situation. It is usually clear that an act of slapping is
done with open hands, an act of kicking with legs and/or feet, an act of
kissing with both lips; and the target of an act of spanking seldom needs to
be made explicit. For these verbs, however, if the usually omitted item needs
to be delimited or qualified in some way, the entity can be mentioned. Hence
we find the modified noun phrase acceptable in such sentences as (51)–(53)

(51)   SHE SLAPPED ME WITH HER LEFT HAND[11]

(52)   SHE KICKED ME WITH HER BARE FOOT

(53)   SHE KISSED ME WITH CHOCOLATE-SMEARED LIPS.

Lexical entries for predicate words, as we have seen in this section, should
represent information of the following kinds: (1) for certain predicates the
nature of one or more of the arguments is taken as part of our understanding
of the predicate word: for some of these the argument cannot be given any
linguistic expression whatever; for others the argument is linguistically
identified only if qualified or quantified in some not fully expected way; (2)
for certain predicates, silence ('zero') can replace one of the argument-expressions just in case the speaker wishes to be indefinite or non-commital
about the identity of the argument; and (3) for certain predicates, silence
can replace one of the argument-expressions just in case the LS believes that
the identity of the argument is already known by the LT.

6. MEANING VS. PRESUPPOSITION

Sentences in natural language are used for asking questions, giving commands, making assertions, expressing feelings, etc. In this section I shall deal
with a distinction between the presuppositional aspect of the semantic
structure of a predicate on the one hand and the 'meaning' proper of the
predicate on the other hand. We may identify the presuppositions of a
sentence as those conditions which must be satisfied before the sentence can
be used in any of the functions just mentioned. Thus the sentence identified
as (54)

(54)   PLEASE OPEN THE DOOR

can be used as a command only if the LT is in a position to know what door
has been mentioned and only if that door is not, at TLA, open.[12] The test
that the existence and specificity of a door and its being in a closed state

make up the *presuppositions* of (54) rather than part of its *meaning* is that under negation the sentence is used to give quite different instructions, yet the presuppositional conditions are unaffected.

(54')   PLEASE DON'T OPEN THE DOOR.

The presuppositions about the existence and specificity of the door relate to the use of the definite article and have been much discussed in the philosophical literature on referring.[13] The presupposition about the closed state of the door is a property of the verb OPEN.

Presuppositions of sentences may be associated with grammatical constructions independent of specific predicate words (such as those associated with the word *even* or with the counterfactual-conditional construction[14]), but I shall mention here only those that must be identified with the semantic structure of predicate words. If we limit our considerations to sentences which can be used for making assertions, we can separate the basic meaning of a predicate from its presuppositions, by describing the former as being relevant to determining whether as an assertion it is true or false, the latter as being relevant to determining whether the sentence is capable of being an assertion in the first place. If the presuppositional conditions are not satisfied, the sentence is simply not apt; only if these conditions are satisfied can a sentence be appropriately used for asking a question, issuing a command, making an apology, pronouncing a moral or aesthetic judgment, or, in the cases we shall consider, making an assertion.

Let us illustrate the distinction we are after with the verb PROVE in construction with two THAT-clauses. Consider sentence (55)

(55)   THAT HARRY IS STILL LIVING WITH HIS MOTHER PROVES THAT HE
         IS A BAD MARRIAGE RISK.

It is apparent that if I were to say (55) about somebody who is an orphan, nobody would say that I was speaking falsely, only that I was speaking inappropriately. If PROVE has a THAT-clause subject and a THAT-clause object, we say that the truth of the first THAT-clause is *presupposed*, and that the verb is used to assert a causal or logical connection between the two clauses and thus (when used affirmatively) to imply the truth of the second clause. That this separation is correct may be seen by replacing PROVE in (55) by DOESN'T PROVE and noting that the presuppositional aspects of (55), concerning the truth of the first THAT-clause, are unaffected by the change.

It is difficult to find pairs of words in which the presuppositional content of one is the meaning content of the other, but a fairly close approximation to this situation is found in the pair of verbs ACCUSE and CRITICIZE. The words differ from each other on other grounds, in that ACCUSE is capable of being a 'performative', while CRITICIZE is not; and CRITICIZE, unlike ACCUSE, is capable of being used in senses where no negative evaluation is intended. In sentences (56) and (57) we are using ACCUSE in a non-performative sense and we are using CRITICIZE as a 3-argument predicate in a 'negative-evaluative' sense.

(56)   HARRY ACCUSED MARY OF WRITING THE EDITORIAL

(57)   HARRY CRITICIZED MARY FOR WRITING THE EDITORIAL.

I would say that a speaker who utters (56) presupposes that Harry regarded the editorial-writing activity as 'bad' and asserts that Harry claimed that Mary was the one who did it; while a speaker who utters (57) presupposes that Harry regarded Mary as the writer of the editorial and asserts that Harry claimed the editorial-writing behavior or its result as being 'bad'. The content of the presupposition in each one of these verbs shows up in the assertive meaning of the other.

Certain apparent counter-examples to the claims I have been making about presuppositions can be interpreted as 'semi-quotations', I believe. Some utterances are to be thought of as comments on the appropriate use of words. Uses of the verb CHASE presuppose that the entity identified as the direct object is moving fast. Uses of the verb ESCAPE presuppose that the entity identified by the subject noun phrase was contained somewhere 'by force' previous to the time of focus. These presuppositions, as expected, are unaffected by sentence negation.

$$(58) \quad \text{THE DOG} \begin{Bmatrix} \text{CHASED} \\ \text{DIDN'T CHASE} \end{Bmatrix} \text{THE CAT}$$

$$(59) \quad \text{HE} \begin{Bmatrix} \text{ESCAPED} \\ \text{DIDN'T ESCAPE} \end{Bmatrix} \text{FROM THE TOWER.}$$

It seems to me that sentences like (60) and (61) are partly comments on the appropriateness of the words CHASE and ESCAPE for the situations being described. These are sentences that would most naturally be used in contexts in which the word CHASE or ESCAPE had just been uttered.

(60)   I DIDN'T 'CHASE' THE THIEF; AS IT HAPPENED, HE COULDN'T GET HIS CAR STARTED

(61)   I DIDN'T 'ESCAPE' FROM THE PRISON; THEY RELEASED ME.

It is important to realize that the difference between assertion and presupposition is a difference that is not merely to be found in the typical predicate words known as verbs and adjectives. The difference is found in predicatively used nouns as well. In the best-known meaning of BACHELOR, for example, the negation-test reveals that only the property of 'having never been married' is part of the meaning proper. Uses of this word (as predicate) *presuppose* that the entities being described are human, male and adult. We know that this is so because sentence (62)

(62)   THAT PERSON IS NOT A BACHELOR

is only used as a claim that the person is or has been married, never as a claim that the person is a female or a child. That is, it is simply not appropriate to use (62), or its non-negative counterpart, when speaking of anyone who is not a human, male adult.

7. EVALUATIVE AND ORIENTATIVE FEATURES

Jerrold J. Katz[15] and Manfred Bierwisch[16] have proposed semantic features which treat certain relations between objects and the human beings that deal with these objects. Katz has treated the semantic properties of words that relate to the ways in which objects and events are evaluated, and Bierwisch has proposed ways of associating with words information concerning the ways in which the objects they describe are related to spatial aspects of the language-user's world.

For certain nouns the evaluative information is determinable in a fairly straightforward way from their definitions. This is most clearly true in the case of agentive and instrumental nouns. Many definitions of nouns contain a component which expresses a typical function of the entity the noun can refer to. Thus the lexical entry for PILOT will contain an expression something like (63)

(63)   profession: A of [V   O   A]
            where   V is 'navigate', with the presupposition that O is an
            air vessel

and the lexical entry for KNIFE will contain such an expression as (64)

(64)   use: I of [V   O   I   A]
            where V is 'cut', with the presupposition that O is a physical
            object.

For such nouns I assume that the evaluative feature can be automatically specified from the function-identifying part of a definition. A noun which refers to a 'typical' (e.g., 'professional') Agent in an activity is evaluated according to whether the Agent conducts this activity skillfully; a noun which names a typical Instrument in an activity is evaluated according to whether the thing permits the activity to be performed easily. In these ways we can make intelligible our ability to understand expressions like A GOOD PILOT, A GOOD PIANIST, A GOOD LIAR, A GOOD KNIFE, A GOOD PENCIL, A GOOD LOCK, etc.

For nouns whose definitions do not identify them as typical Agents or Instruments, the evaluative feature apparently needs to be specified separately. Thus FOOD is probably in part defined as (65)

(65)   function: O of [V   O   A]
         where   V is 'eat'.

Food is evaluated according to properties (namely nutrition and palatability) which are not immediately derivable from the definition of FOOD, and this fact apparently needs to be stated separately for this item. To call something A GOOD PHOTOGRAPH is to evaluate it in terms of its clarity or its ability to elicit positive esthetic responses in the viewer, but neither of these notions can be directly derived from the definition of PHOTOGRAPH. Here, too, the evaluative feature needs to be stated independently of the definition of the word.

The question a lexicographer must face is whether these matters have to do with what one knows, as a speaker of a language, about the words in that language, or what one knows, as a member of a culture, about the objects, beliefs and practices of that culture. Do we know about books that they are used in our culture to reveal information or elicit certain kinds of esthetic appreciation, or do we know about *the word* BOOK that it contains evaluative features that allow us to interpret the phrase A GOOD BOOK? Do we understand the expression GOOD WATER (as water that is safe for drinking) because its semantic description has set aside that one use of water as the use in terms of which water is to be generally evaluated, or because we know that for most purposes (e.g., watering the grass, bathing) any kind of water will do, but for drinking purposes some water is acceptable and some is not? These are serious questions, but we can of course avoid facing them by making, with the typical lexicographer, the decision not to insist on a strict separation between a dictionary and an encyclopedia.[17]

The distinction between lexical information about words and non-lexical information about things must come up in dealing with Bierwischian features, too. Let us examine some of the ways in which users of English speak of the horizontal dimensions of pieces of furniture. If we consider a sofa, a table, and a chest of drawers, we note first of all that a sofa or a chest of drawers has one vertical face that can be appropriately called its *front*, but the table does not. For a non-vertically-oriented oblong object that does not have a natural front, its shorter dimension is spoken of as its WIDTH, the longer dimension as its LENGTH. For the two items that do have a front, the dimension along that front is the WIDTH (even though it may be the longer of the two dimensions), the dimension perpendicular to the front is its DEPTH.

Objects with fronts, furthermore, are typically conceived of as confronted from the outside, as is the case with the chest of drawers, or as viewed from the inside, as with the sofa. The terms LEFT and RIGHT are used according to this inner or outer orientation. Thus the left drawer of a chest of drawers is what would be to our *left* as we faced it, the left arm of a sofa is what would be to our *right* as we face it.

This information is clearly related to facts about the objects themselves and the ways in which they are treated in our culture, and cannot be something that needs to be stated as lexically specific information about the nouns that name them. It seems to me, therefore, that the truly lexical information suggested by these examples is the information that must be assigned to the words LEFT, RIGHT, WIDE, LONG and DEEP (and their derivatives), and that the facts just reviewed about the items of furniture are facts about how these objects are treated by members of our culture and are therefore proper to an encyclopedia rather than a dictionary. It is difficult to imagine a new word being invented which refers to sofas but which fails to recognize one of its facts as its 'front'; and it is likely that if a new item of furniture gets invented, the properties we have been discussing will not be arbitrarily assigned to the noun which provides the name for these objects, but rather the words WIDE, LEFT, etc., will be used in accordance with the ways in which people orient themselves to these objects when they use them. That the orientation is a property of the position- and dimension-words is further demonstrated by the fact that the uses I have suggested are not by any means obligatory. If a 3′ by 6′ table is placed in such a way that one of its 6′ sides is inaccessible, with people sitting at and using the opposite side, the table can surely be described as 6′ wide and 3′ deep. On the other hand, a sofa that is 2 miles 'wide' would probably impress us more as a physical object than as a sofa and would most likely be described as being 2 miles long.

The phenomena I have been mentioning are to be stated as part of the presuppositional components of the lexical entries for the words LEFT, WIDE, etc. Uses of the word WIDE presuppose that the object being referred to has at least one (typically) horizontal dimension; and that the dimension which this word is used to quantify or describe is either the main left-to-right extent of the object as human beings conceive their orientation to it, if that is fixed, or it is the shorter of two horizontal dimensions. The adjectives TALL and SHORT (in one sense) presuppose as HIGH and LOW do not, that the object spoken of is vertically oriented and is typically in contact with

(or is a projection out of) the ground. Similarly the noun POST, as opposed
to POLE, presupposes that the object in question is (or is at least intended
to be) vertically oriented and in contact with the ground. Many of the
features of spatial orientation treated by Bierwisch will take their place, in
other words, in the presuppositional components of the semantic descriptions of words usable as predicates.

There are, however, some spatial-orientation features that appear to enter
rather basically into the definitions of nouns. Of particular interest are nouns
that identify conceptually n-dimensional entities where these are physically
realized by m-dimensional objects, where $m > n$. Thus a LINE is conceptually
one-dimensional, and a STRIPE is conceptually two-dimensional. If a straight
mark on a piece of paper is viewed as a LINE, the dimension perpendicular
to its length is its THICKNESS, but if it is viewed as a STRIPE, the second
dimension is its WIDTH. If the stripe has a third-dimensional aspect (e.g., if
it is drawn with heavy paint), it is that which one speaks of as its THICKNESS.
These are matters that seem to be related to the 'meaning' of these nouns
rather than to presuppositions about the objects they name.

8. FUNCTIONAL SHIFT

Syntactically and semantically different uses of the same word type should
be registered in the same lexical entry whenever their differences can be seen
as reflecting a general pattern in the lexical structure of the language. I shall
call attention to certain situations in which a word that is basically a noun
can also be used verbally, and a situation in which a verb of one type is used
as a verb of another type.

I have already suggested that the 'sentential' portions of the definitions
of agent and instrument nouns serve to provide the evaluative features associated with these nouns. In many cases they also serve in identifying the
verbal use of these same nouns. If, for example, the word PILOT is defined
in part as one who flies an airplane, a dictionary entry must show some way
of relating this aspect of the meaning of the noun to the meaning of the
associated verb. Perhaps, for example, in connection with the activity characterized as (66)

(66)   V   O   A
     where V = navigate;   presupposition:
               O = air vessel

one might wish to state that the noun PILOT is the name given to one who
professionally serves the Agent role in this activity, the verb PILOT has the
meaning of the verb in this event-description. If the word is further repre-

sented as basically a Noun, a general understanding of 'metaphor' will suffice to explain why the verb PILOT can be used to refer to activities that are 'similar to', not necessarily identical with, the activity of a pilot in flying an air plane.

If the noun LOCK is defined as a device which one uses to make something unopenable, then that is related to the fact that the *verb* LOCK means to use such a device for such a purpose. If PLASTER is defined as something which one attaches to a surface for a particular range of purposes, then that fact should be shown to be related to uses of the *verb* PLASTER. I have no proposal on how this is to be done; I merely suggest that when both the verbal and the nominal use of a word refer to events of the same type, the event-description should, other things being equal, appear only once in the lexicon.

Certain fairly interesting instances of verbal polysemy seem to have developed in the following way. Where one kind of activity is a possible way of carrying out another kind of activity, the verb which identifies the former activity has superimposed onto it certain syntactic and semantic properties of the verb which identifies the second or completing activity.

Thus the verb TIE refers to particular kinds of manipulations of string-like objects, with certain results. In this basic meaning of the verb, it occurs appropriately in sentences (67) and (68)

(67)   HE TIED HIS SHOESTRINGS

(68)   HE TIED THE KNOT.

The act of tying things can lead to fastening things, and so an extension of the verb TIE to uses proper to a verb like FASTEN or SECURE has occurred. The verb can now mean to fasten something by performing tying acts, and it is this which accounts for the acceptability of TIE in (69).

(69)   HE TIED HIS SHOES.

Shoes are simply not in themselves the kinds of objects that one manipulates when tying knots.

In this second use the verb TIE continues to describe the original activity, but it has been extended to take in the result of such activity. The feature that characterizes this second use, then, will be something like (70).

(70)   extension: Result (replace FASTEN).

The verb SMEAR, to take another example, refers to the activity of applying some near-liquid substance to the surface of some physical object. The activity of smearing something onto a thing can have the result of covering that thing. The word SMEAR has, in fact, been extended to take on the syntax and semantics of COVER. Thus the 'original' and the extended uses of SMEAR are exemplified in the following sentences:

(71)   HE SMEARED MUD ON THE FENDER

(72)   HE SMEARED THE FENDER WITH MUD.

The difference by which (71) and (72) are not quite paraphrases of each other is found in the meaning of sentence (73)

(73)   HE COVERED THE FENDER WITH MUD.

By claiming that the second use of SMEAR is one in which the properties of COVER have been superimposed we have accounted for the addition to (72) of the meaning of (73), and simultaneously we have accounted for the fact that the extended use of SMEAR takes (as does COVER) the Goal rather than the Object as its direct object, setting the latter aside in a preposition-phrase with WITH.[18]

The verb LOAD, let us say, means to transfer objects onto or into a container of some sort. The activity of loading can lead to the filling of that container, and so the verb LOAD has taken on the additional syntactic and semantic functions of FILL. In this way we can account for the use of LOAD in sentences (74) and (75) and the similarities between (75) and (76)

(74)   HE LOADED BRICKS ONTO THE TRUCK

(75)   HE LOADED THE TRUCK WITH BRICKS

(76)   HE FILLED THE TRUCK WITH BRICKS.

The verbs SMEAR and LOAD have the same co-occurrences in their extended meanings as in their non-extended meanings. The verb TIE is not like that: in its FASTEN-extension it takes nouns that are not appropriate to its original sense. This means that the description of the feature indicated in the extended use will have to be interpreted (by lexico-semantic rules) in such a way that when the two verbs fail to take the same cases, those of the verb which identifies the resulting action are dominant, the characteristics of the event described by the other verb taking their place among the *presuppositions* of the verb in its extended sense. Thus it is presupposed of the FASTEN-extension of TIE that the Object is something which can be fastened by an act of tying.

If the type of extension that I have been discussing in this section can be shown to be a quite general phenomenon of lexical systems (at present it is little more than a suggestion, the 'evidence' for its correctness being rather hard to come by), then perhaps we can use this concept to eliminate certain problems connected with what Gruber has called 'incorporation'. LEAP is a verb which takes, in Gruber's system, a phrase in OVER, as seen in (77) and (78)

(77)   HE LEAPED OVER THE FENCE

(78)   HE LEAPED OVER THE LINE.

The preposition OVER can be 'incorporated' into LEAP, but only in the understanding that the associated noun is an obstacle[19]; thus, the preposition OVER may be absent from (77), but not from (78). The theoretical issue here has to do with the way in which the process of preposition-incorporation is to be sensitive to the size relationship between the entities identified by the subject and prepositional-object nounphrases. My interpretation is that there is an OVERCOME-extension to the word LEAP, and I claim that this accounts simultaneously for the 'obstacle' presupposition and for the non-occurrence of OVER in the extended-sense sentence.[20]

9. DEEP-STRUCTURE ACCEPTABILITY

Facts about lexical items that relate to the formal properties of sentences can be separated into two sets: requirements on the deep-structure and requirements on the surface structure. The former determine the acceptability of a given word in deep-structures of certain types; the latter specify those grammatical modifications of sentences whose operation is determined by lexical information. The surface conditions are provided in the grammar in the form of the rules which convert deep structures into surface structures (transformational rules), and possibly, in some cases, by the elaboration of special constraints on surface structure.

I shall take the position that content words may all be inserted as predicates, and that their realization as nouns, verbs or adjectives is a matter of the application of rules. Therefore we need not consider part-of-speech classification among the types of information relevant to the lexical insertion into deep structures. What Chomsky has referred to as 'strict subcategorization'[21] corresponds to what I have treated here in terms of the number of arguments a predicate takes and their case structure. What Chomsky has referred to as 'selection'[22] is described here with the concept presupposition and is taken as being more relevant to semantic interpretation than to lexical insertion.

The deep-structure requirements that are of chief interest for this discussion, then, are those of the type Perlmutter has been referring to as 'deep structure constraints' or 'input conditions'.[23]

Examples, due to Perlmutter, are the requirement for BUDGE that it occur in a negative sentence, as shown in grammaticality judgments on (79) and (80);

(79)   *I BUDGED

(80)   I DIDN'T BUDGE

the requirement for LURK (discussed earlier) that its Agent be non-coreferential to the Agent of the 'next higher' locutionary verb; or for TRY that its Agent be coreferential to the (eventually deleted) subject of the 'next lower' sentence, as suggested by (81) and (82)

(81)   *I TRIED [FOR YOU] TO FIND IT

(82)   I TRIED [FOR ME] TO FIND IT.

I have included deep-structure constraints in this survey of types of lexical information, but I have nothing new to say about them. I would like to suggest, however, that it may not be necessary to require the extent of detail which Perlmutter envisions or the transformational apparatus which that sometimes entails. Where Perlmutter requires that the Agent of TRY match the *Agent* of the embedded sentence, it may only be necessary to require that the coreferential nounphrase in the embedded sentence be the one which is destined to be the subject of that sentence. And where Perlmutter requires sentence (83) to be derived transformationally from the structure underlying (84),

(83)   HE TRIED TO BE MISUNDERSTOOD

(84)   HE TRIED TO GET TO BE MISUNDERSTOOD

this may not be necessary if TRY is merely described as a verb which expresses, of its Agent subject, the intension and attempt to bring about the situation identified by the embedded sentence. This may be necessary in order to account for the way in which we understand sentence (85),

(85)   HE TRIED TO SEEM CHEERFUL

a sentence which cannot be straightforwardly paraphrased in such a way as to reveal an underlying agentive notion in the embedded sentence.

10. GOVERNMENT

Once a specific predicate word is inserted into a deep structure, its presence may call for certain modifications in the rest of the sentence. The typical case of this is what is known as 'government'. For English the operation of the rules establishing 'government' associates prepositions with noun-phrases and 'complementizers' with embedded sentences and their parts.[24]

Thus – to consider only the association of prepositions with noun-phrases

– we speak of GIVING SOMETHING TO SOMEBODY, ACCUSING SOMEBODY OF SOMETHING, BLAMING SOMETHING ON SOMEBODY, INTERESTING SOMEBODY IN SOMETHING, ACQUAINTING SOMEBODY WITH SOMETHING, and so on. It is certain, of course, that many of the facts about particular choices of prepositions and complementizers are redundantly specified by other independently motivated features of predicates or are determined from the nature of the underlying case relationship, so that a minimally redundant dictionary will not need to indicate anything about the form of governed constituents directly. Until it is clear just what the needed generalizations are, however, I propose using the brute-force method and specifying the prepositions one at a time for each verb and each case relationship.

11. TRANSFORMATIONALLY INTRODUCED PREDICATORS

Certain lexical items can be used as predicates semantically, but cannot themselves occur as surface predicate words. Such words will appear in the syntactic position expected of some other constituent (usually, I think, that of the Result constituent), and there must therefore be lexically associated with them some predicator word, a word that is capable of bearing the tense and aspect properties that can only be attached to verb-like elements. The constructions I have in mind are those of the type HAVE FAITH IN, GIVE CREDENCE TO, BE LOYAL TO, etc., and the predicator words I have in mind include BE, DO, GIVE, HAVE, MAKE, TAKE and a few others.

12. SUBJECT AND OBJECT

One of the subtlest but at the same time most apparent aspects of the syntax of the predicate is the set of ways in which the subject/verb and verb/object constructions can be set up. These constructions have as their purpose – generally, but not always – a focusing on one terminal of a multi-argument expression, a focusing on one particular role in the situation under discussion.

I have suggested elsewhere[25] that the normal choice of subject is determined by a hierarchy of case types, and only those predicates which require something 'unexpected' as their subjects need to have such information registered in their lexical entry. I believe that, at least in the vast majority of cases, those noun-phrases capable of becoming direct objects of a given verb are at the same time the ones which can appear as the subjects of passive constructions made with the same verb. Thus such information at least does not need to be stated twice, and at best may not need to be stated at all for most verbs, since it is most likely subject to rather general statements about combinations of cases.[26]

There is an extremely interesting set of subject- and object-selection facts that seem to operate in connection with expressions of 'quantity' and 'contents'. The verb SLEEP refers to an 'activity' of an animate being in a particular place, where the one who sleeps is typically mentioned as the subject; but when the focus is on the place and at issue is the *number* of different beings that can sleep in that place, the verb permits the Place nounphrase to appear as subject. We see this in sentence (86)

(86)   THIS HOUSEBOAT SLEEPS EIGHT ADULTS OR SIXTEEN CHILDREN.

The verb FEED has its use as a 'causative' of EAT, but it can be used to express other kinds of relations with eating, too. To indicate the typical relation between the Agent and a description of the 'contents' of his eating activity, we use sentences like (87)

(87)   THE CHILD FEEDS ON RAISINS.

There is a relation between a recipe (which identifies, among other things, quantities of food) and the number of people who can (with satisfaction) eat the food one prepares by following the recipe, and this is the relation we see expressed in a sentence like (88)

(88)   THIS RECIPE FEEDS EIGHT ADULTS OR FOUR CHILDREN.

In the case of FEED, the connection between the Place and a quantity of 'eaters' requires the latter quantity to be a 'rate'. Thus we get sentences like (89)

(89)   THIS RESTAURANT FEEDS FOUR HUNDRED PEOPLE A DAY.

It is not clear to me how one can capture facts of the sort I have just suggested in any way short of providing (in effect) separate lexical descriptions for each of these uses. It is clear, anyway, that examples (86)–(89) cannot be understood as merely exemplifying 'causative' extensions of these verbs.

13. SAMPLE LEXICAL ENTRIES

In this last section I exhibit extremely tentative suggestions for the lexical entries for BLAME (in two senses[27]), ACCUSE, and CRITICIZE (in one sense). The feature-pair ± Locutionary indicates whether the verb does or does not refer to a linguistic act; the feature + Performative marks verbs which can be used in first-person simple-present utterances in the performance of an explicitly marked illocutionary act[28]; the feature-pair ± Momentary indicates whether or not the verb can be used, in the affirmative, to refer to an event that takes place at a specific point in time. The variables x, y, and z are argument variables whose case-role and preposition-selection properties are indicated by first, second or third position in the next two items. All are normal transitive verbs, and the normal subject-selection for active sentences is in each case the noun-phrase that fills the Source role. For BLAME the direct object is either the Goal or the Object, since we have both 'BLAME Y FOR Z' and 'BLAME Z ON Y'; for ACCUSE the direct object is necessarily the Goal noun-phrase; for CRITICIZE it is the Goal noun-phrase if that is explicit in the sentence, otherwise the Object noun-phrase. The verbs ACCUSE and CRITICIZE require the Goal noun-phrases to identify human beings; BLAME does not, since one can blame an event on, e.g., an inanimate force. The items identified as 'zero for indefinite' and 'zero for definite' indicate the conditions under which the explicit mention of an argument may be omitted, in the sense mentioned in Section 5.

There are many types of lexical information not found in these sample entries, for example those mentioned in sections 7 and 8 above. There are many facts about these particular verbs that are ignored in these descriptions provided here, for example the information that the situation named by the Object noun-phrase for BLAME and CRITICIZE is necessarily understood as something for which factuality is claimed (notice (90) and (91)); that the linguistic event capable of constituting a criticism is necessarily more complicated that the linguistic or gestural event capable of constituting an accusation; and that the presupposed seriousness of the offense for an act of criticism is not as great as that appropriate for acts of accusation (compare (92) and (93)). It is hoped, nevertheless, that from these examples some suggestions can be gleaned for the design of canonical representations in a lexicon.

(90)   I ACCUSED JOHN, WHO HAS NEVER LEFT OHIO, OF TAKING PART IN THE BERKELEY RIOTS.

(91)   *I CRITICIZED JOHN, WHO HAS NEVER LEFT OHIO, FOR TAKING PART IN THE BERKELEY RIOTS.

(92)   I ACCUSED JOHN OF MURDERING HIS MOTHER-IN-LAW.

(93)   I CRITICIZED JOHN FOR MURDERING HIS MOTHER-IN-LAW.

BLAME (i): −Locutionary, −Momentary

arguments:	x, y, z
cases:	Source & Experiencer, Goal, Object
prepositions:	by, on, for

normal subject:	x
direct object:	y or z
presuppositions:	x is human
	z is an activity z' or the result of z'
	x judges [z' is 'bad']
meaning:	x judges [y caused z']
zero for indefinite:	x
zero for definite:	z

BLAME (ii): $-$Locutionary, $-$Momentary

arguments:	x, y, z
cases:	Source & Experiencer, Goal, Object
prepositions:	by, on, for
normal subject:	x
direct object:	y
presuppositions:	x is human
	z is an activity z' or the result of z'
	x judges [y caused z']
meaning:	x judges [z' is 'bad']
zero for indefinite:	x
zero for definite:	z

ACCUSE: $+$Performative, $+$Locutionary, $+$Momentary

arguments:	x, y, z
cases:	Source & Agent, Goal, Object
prepositions:	by, $\emptyset$, of
normal subject:	x
direct object:	y
presuppositions:	x and y are human
	z is an activity
	x judges [z is 'bad']
meaning:	x indicates [y caused z]
zero for indefinite:	x
zero for definite:	z

CRITICIZE: $+$Locutionary, $+$Momentary

arguments:	x, y, z
cases:	Source & Agent, Goal, Object
prepositions:	by, $\emptyset$, for
normal subject:	x
direct object:	z if $y=\emptyset$, otherwise y

presuppositions: x and y are human

z is an activity z' or the result of z'

x judges [y caused z']

meaning: x indicates [z' is bad]

zero for indefinite: x and z; and y if z is a 'result' and $z \neq \emptyset$

zero for definite: none

The Ohio State University, Columbus

REFERENCES

* Sponsored in part by the National Science Foundation through Grant GN-534.1 from the Office of Science Information Service to the Computer and Information Science Research Center, The Ohio State University. This article is also going to appear in: *Semantics: An Interdisciplinary Reader in Philosophy, Linguistics, Anthropology and Psychology* (ed. by D. D. Steinberg and L. A. Jakobovits), University of Illinois Press Urbana (Ill.), 1969.

[1] I have borrowed these terms from philosopher Richard Garner, to whom I am also indebted for a number of suggestions on the content and phrasing of several sections of this paper.

[2] The disjunction in this statement may be unnecessary if we accept John R. Ross's arguments that declarative sentences have phonetically unrealized embedding sentences representable as something like I DECLARE TO YOU THAT.... On Ross's view every sentence contains at least one locutionary verb, so that the difference we are after is a difference between references to the 'next higher' locutionary verb and reference to the 'highest' locutionary verbs. See John R. Ross, 'On Declarative Sentences', to appear in *Readings in English Transformational Grammar*, Ginn and Blaisdell, 1969.

[3] See Charles J. Fillmore, 'Deictic Categories in the Semantics of "COME"', *Foundations of Language* **2** (1966) 219–27.

[4] There is an additional use of deictic words, and that is this: in a third person narrative, one can express one's 'identification' with one of the characters in the narrative by letting that character be the focus of words that are primarily appropriate to *hic-nunc-ego*. Thus we may find in an exclusively third-person narrative a passage like (i)

(i)   here was where Francis had always hoped to be, and today was to mark for him the beginning of a new life

in which the words HERE and TODAY refer to the place and time focused on in the narrative, not to the place and time associated with the author's act of communication. In what might be referred to as the 'displaced ego' use of deictic words, the author has shown us that he has for the moment assumed Francis's point of view.

I propose that a rather subtle test of psycho-sexual identity can be devised which makes use of a story in which two characters, one male and one female, do a lot of cross-visiting, but in their other activities do nothing that makes one of them clearly more lovable than the other. The subject's task is to listen to the story and then retell it in his own words. The writer of the original story must not use the words COME and GO; but if the subject, in retelling the story, states, say, that BILL CAME TO MARY'S HOUSE (using CAME rather than WENT), this fact will reveal that he is experiencing the story from Mary's point of view.

[5] Possibly the richest source of insights into verbs of motion is the recent output of Jeffrey S. Gruber. See his dissertation, *Studies in Lexical Relations*, M.I.T., 1965 (unpublished); 'Look and See', *Language* **43**, 4 (1967) 937–47; and *Functions of the Lexicon in Formal Descriptive Grammars*, Technical Memorandum TM-3770/000/00, System Development Corporation, Santa Monica, California, 1967.

[6] In other words, I accept the part-of-speech identities argued by George Lakoff in Appendix A of *On the Nature of Syntactic Irregularity*, Report No. NSF-16, Computation Laboratory of Harvard University, 1965; as well as the extension of such identities to 'nouns' proposed by Emmon Bach in 'Nouns and Noun Phrases', in *Universals in Linguistic Theory* (ed. by E. Bach and R. Harms), Holt, Rinehart and Winston, 1968.

[7] Of course, as motion verbs each of them may take time and space complements as well, as is seen in THE BALLOONS ASCENDED TO THE RAFTERS JUST AFTER THE SPEECH ENDED. Since in general the nature of the time and space complements is predictable from properties of the type discussed in Section 2, we may permit ourselves to ignore such matters while discussing the typing of predicates on the basis of the number of arguments they accept.

[8] In truth, however, LIFT also requires conceptually the notion of Instrument. That is, lifting requires the use of something (perhaps the Agent's hand) to make something go up. It is conceivable that the basic case structures of ARISE and LIFT are identical, with grammatical requirements on identity and deletion accounting for their differences. Thus the two are shown in (i) and (ii).

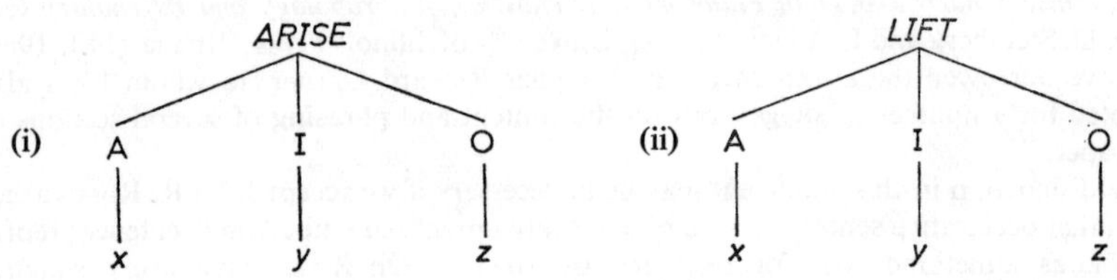

For ARISE, however, it is required that $z = y = z$, and hence only one noun will show up. The meaning expressed by JOHN AROSE is that John willed his getting up, that he used his own body (i.e., its muscles) in getting up, and that it was his body that rose. For LIFT, however, there may be identities between x and z, resulting in a sentence like JOHN LIFTED HIMSELF, or there may be identities between y and z, resulting in a sentence like JOHN LIFTED HIS FINGER. RISE, then, must be described as (iii)

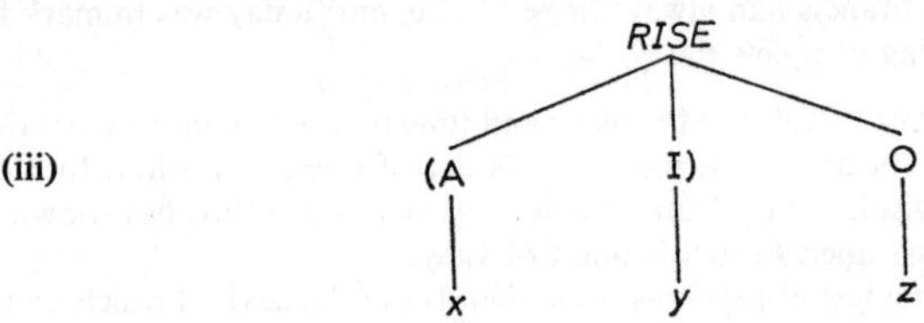

where the identity requirements of ARISE obtain just in case x and y are present.

[9] This has, of course, been suggested in a great many writings on semantic theory; most recently, perhaps, in the exchanges between J. F. Staal and Yehoshua Bar-Hillel in *Foundations of Language*, 1967 and 1968.

[10] One can, however, indicate the content of the meal in question, as in an expression like HE DINED ON RAISINS.

[11] At least in the case of SLAP, the action can be carried out with objects other than the usual one. Thus it is perfectly acceptable to say SHE SLAPPED ME WITH A FISH.

12 I am only dealing here with those presuppositions which are relatable to the *content* of the utterance. It is also true, of course, that (54) can be used appropriately as a command only if the LT understands English, is believed by the LS to be awake, is not totally paralyzed, etc. These matters have more to do with questions of 'good faith' in speech communication than with information that is to be understood as knowledge about individual lexical items.

13 On referring see "On referring", by P. F. Strawson, *Mind* **50** (1950) 320–344.

14 For some examples see my mistitled paper, 'Entailment Rules in a Semantic Theory', *Project on Linguistic Analysis* Report No. 10, 1965.

15 Jerrold J. Katz, 'Semantic Theory and the Meaning of "Good"', *Journal of Philosophy* **61** (1964).

16 Manfred Bierwisch, 'Some Semantic Universals of German Adjectivals', *Foundations of Language* **3** (1967) 1–36.

17 As evidence for the linguistic validity of 'evaluative features' I would accept a pair of words which differ *only* in the evaluative features associated with them. If, for example, English FOOD and FEED could always refer to the same objects but served in the expressions GOOD FOOD and GOOD FEED to refer to food that was *palatable* and *nutritious* respectively, such a pair would provide a good argument for the existence of evaluative features as an aspect of linguistic competence.

18 I believe that (72) can be read as a paraphrase of (71). If this is so, a correct description of the situation must be that in its original meanings, SMEAR permits the direct-objects choices seen in either (71) or (72), but in its extended meaning it permits only that exemplified by (72).

19 Gruber (1965), p. 24. The condition for incorporation of OVER into LEAP, in Gruber's words, is this: "The object of the preposition must be of significant height with respect to the subject".

20 This argument is certainly not directed against Gruber's incorporation process as such, only against the proposed need to state separately its applicability to words like LEAP, JUMP, HOP, etc. The quite literal 'incorporation' of OVER in OVERCOME has not escaped my notice.

21 Noam Chomsky, *Aspects of the Theory of Syntax*, M.I.T. Press, 1965, esp. pp. 95–100.

22 *Ibid*, pp. 148ff.

23 My knowledge of Perlmutter's work on deep-structure and surface-structure constraints comes from Perlmutter's presentations at the January, 1968, San Diego Syntax Conference and from references in papers and presentations by J. R. Ross.

24 The term 'complementizer' is taken from Peter Rosenbaum, *The Grammar of English Predicate Complement Constructions*, M.I.T. Press, 1968, and refers to the provision of THAT, -ING, etc., in clauses embedded to predicates.

25 'The Case for Case', in *Universals in Linguistic Theory* (1968) (see note 6).

26 Incidentally, verbs which are obligatorily passive are verbs with one associated noun-phrase designated as 'direct object' but none as 'normal subject'. An automatic consequence of this situation is that the expression will be cast in the passive form.

27 There is a third use of BLAME in which it refers to a linguistic or otherwise symbolic act. Thus, if John wrote an offensive letter himself and did something which gave others to believe that I has done it, I could report that John blamed the letter on me.

28 In the sense of John L. Austin, as presented in his posthumous work *How to do Things with Words*, Oxford University Press, 1965.

S.-Y. KURODA

REMARKS ON SELECTIONAL RESTRICTIONS AND PRESUPPOSITIONS*

1. INTRODUCTION

McCawley disputes the syntactic treatment of selectional restrictions Chomsky expounded in *Aspects of the Theory of Syntax* (cf. McCawley (1968a) and (1968b)). He instead claims that phenomena of selectional restrictions are nothing but aspects of more general semantic phenomena of presupposition, the idea previously introduced by Fillmore. In particular, it is claimed that inherent and selectional features that are introduced in the base component in the Chomskian scheme do not exist as syntactic features.

The problem of selectional restriction is unquestionably a moot point in the semantico-syntactic theory, and a sweeping solution to the problem should not naturally be expected to obtain easily. The primary concern of this paper is rather restricted. I shall take up the particular method of refutation of Chomskian selectional features by McCawley and try to show that his argument is not quite acceptable. In his argumentation against Chomsky's selectional features McCawley ingeniously has recourse to the fact that some nouns, e.g. *neighbor*, are neutral with respect to gender. However, the full implication of this fact is not sufficiently appreciated within a language like English, where grammatical gender plays only a marginal role. I shall try to show below that in languages like French, where natural and grammatical genders interact in an intricate way, this problem of 'neutral' nouns remains syntactic. In the course of the discussion I shall reinterpret and reformalize some transformations partially as wellformedness conditions rather than solely as structure-changing operations. I would claim that the Chomskian type of selectional features, and consequently inherent features, too, cannot entirely be abolished from syntax, although I would give a somewhat different interpretation to features that appear formally similar to Chomskian selectional features. This amounts, as will be claimed, to formalizing some aspects of semantic presupposition within syntax and reinterpreting Chomskian selectional features as a special type of such rules of presupposition.

As the reader will notice the framework proposed here is closely related to the one proposed by Weinreich. For convenience of presentation I shall postpone commenting on his work until the final concluding section.

F. Kiefer (ed.), Studies in Syntax and Semantics, 138–167. © *D. Reidel, Dordrecht-Holland*

2. CHOMSKIAN FRAMEWORK AND MCCAWLEY'S CRITICISM

First I shall summarize to the extent necessary for our present purposes Chomsky's framework of selectional restriction and McCawley's criticism of it.

McCawley points out quite rightly that in the Chomskian framework the feature *Male* would have to be introduced in the base component as one of the inherent features of a noun, since choice of pronouns *him* and *her* must depend on this feature. For example, the sentence

(1)   A waitress hurt herself.

would be derived, irrelevant details omitted, from the base form:

(2)   A waitress hurt a waitress.

The pronoun *herself* in (1) inherits, so to speak, the feature specification − *Male* of the noun *waitress* in (2) through a pronominalization process. In the Chomskian framework an inherent feature such as *Male* that participates in operations of the syntactic component must be introduced in the pre-terminal string underlying the base form (2) by means of a rewriting rule, say, of the form:

(3) $[+ Human] \rightarrow [\pm Male]$.

The lexical entry *waitress* is also assigned the specification − *Male*; the lexical insertion rule, operating under the nondistinctness convention, inserts the lexical entry *waitress* in a slot where the specification − *Male* has been provided by rule (3).

Once introduced as a syntactic inherent feature, the feature *Male* would not be restricted to serving in gender agreement between anaphoric pronouns and their antecedents, but also to characterizing selectional restrictions; selectional features referring to the feature *Male* would serve to distinguish the well-formedness of, for example,

(4)   The waitress is buxom.

and the anomaly of, say,

(5)   The bachelor is buxom.

More specifically, *buxom* would be assigned the feature specification $+[- Male \rule{1.5em}{0.4pt}]$, and in the Chomskian framework it may only be inserted in the environment − *Male*..._____, which is satisfied in (4), but not in (5).

But this machinery with inherent features and selectional features referring to them leads one to peculiar situations, as McCawley rightly observes. Consider the sentence

(6)   The neighbor is tall.

The slot that is filled by the noun *neighbor* must be specified either as $+Male$ or $-Male$ by the rewriting rule (3). The lexical entry *neighbor*, on the other hand, would be unspecified with respect to feature *Male*. The nondistinctness convention allows *neighbor* to be inserted in a slot of a preterminal string that is specified either $+Male$ or $-Male$. Thus, the slot underlying *neighbor* in the speech form (6) may be either $+Male$ or $-Male$, which implies that the speech form (6) is ambiguous in the sense of the syntactic theory.

This conclusion is obviously bizarre; the theory conflicts with the intuition it is supposed to formalize. It is true that when the speech form is applied to an actual situation the real referent of the word *neighbor* in the world must be either male or female; but it is perfectly possible for us to hear about a speaker's *neighbor* without knowing his or her sex, or even for a speaker to talk about his neighbor without knowing the neighbor's sex.

But this theory has also apparent advantages. For when one hurts oneself, one is compelled to reveal one's sex, so that either one has to say

(7)   The neighbor hurt himself.

or

(8)   The neighbor hurt herself.

The base form of these speech forms may appear to be identical:

(9)   The neighbor hurt the neighbor.

but the Chomskian theory would be able to differentiate two different base forms underlying (7) and (8), respectively, by assuming that in one both occurrences of *neighbor* are $+Male$ while in the other they are $-Male$.

Furthermore, the Chomskian framework of selectional restriction would predict the natural reading of sentences like:

(10)   The neighbor is buxom.

Upon hearing this sentence the hearer would naturally assume that the person referred to by the word *neighbor* is female. In fact, only *neighbor* with the specification − *Male* may occupy the subject position of (10) since *buxom* would be assumed to have the specification + [− *Male* _____]. Any criticism against the bizarre ambiguity of (6) implied by the Chomskian framework must give some solutions to these two points where the Chomskian framework works well.

McCawley's criticism against Chomsky in the matter of selectional restriction does not, of course, end with the difficulty connected with sentences like (6). McCawley points out that a selectional restriction imposed by a verb or adjective is a restriction on the entire noun phrase as its subject, object, etc., rather than on just the head of that noun phrase. For example, he says, the sentence

(11)   My buxom neighbor is the father of two.

violates the same selectional restriction as does

(12)   My sister is the father of two.

Thus, in general, what brings about violation of a selectional restriction is entire syntactic constituents rather than some distinguished lexical items contained in them. Furthermore, as McCawley claims, any piece of semantic information that may figure in semantic representation, and only such information, may figure in selectional restrictions. Finally McCawley concludes that 'the matter of selectional restrictions should be totally separate from the base component and that the base component thus be a device which generates a class of deep structures without regard to whether the items in them violate any selectional restrictions (McCawley 1968b, p. 135).

3. MCCAWLEY'S TREATMENT OF SELECTIONAL RESTRICTIONS AND PRESUPPOSITION

I shall return later to comment on McCawley's general claim just cited. My immediate concern in this section is to review McCawley's treatment of sentences like those discussed in the preceding section in the Chomskian framework.

McCawley does not introduce rules like (3) in the base component, or for that matter any inherent features like *Male*; neither maleness nor femaleness is introduced in the preterminal string that underlies (6). Nor is the lexical item *neighbor* specified + *Male* or − *Male* in the lexicon. (6) is structurally unambiguous and does not carry any information on the sex of the person referred to by *neighbor*, a natural conclusion.

Then how would one account for the fact that in the natural reading of (10) *neighbor* is understood to be famale? McCawley says that the meaning of *buxom* 'presupposes' femaleness of its subject; this is a semantic phenomenon. The selectional restriction illustrated by the pair consisting of the normal and the anomalous form (4) and (5) is also explained as a matter of presupposition. Both forms are syntactically well-formed in the McCawleian framework, i.e. well-formed outputs of the base component. In (4) the semantic presupposition of the meaning of *buxom* is satisfied by the meaning of *waitress*, resulting in a normal sentence. On the other hand, in (5) the same semantic presupposition of the meaning of *buxom* is contradicted by the meaning of *bachelor*, resulting in a semantically anomalous form.

McCawley's argument for accounting for selectional restrictions as exemplified by (4) and (5) in terms of presupposition is reinforced by the claim that the notion of presupposition is needed anyway in the general framework of semantics. For one thing, McCawley points out, the Chomskian framework of selectional features can cover in any case only a fraction of the phenomena of selectional restrictions. To quote his favorite example, there isn't any syntactic or semantic feature to characterize matrixhood of lexical items so that they may be the object of the verb *diagonalize*; rather, the verb *diagonalize* presupposes that the intended referent of the object be a matrix. A selectional violation would arise if the assertions and presuppositions made by various parts of a sentence contradict each other. For another thing, presupposition may also account for selectional restrictions of a lexical item 'on itself', quoting McCawley's phrasing, i.e. 'presupposition' on the referent of a lexical item by its meaning itself. Thus, for example, as McCawley rightly comments following Fillmore, the meaning of *bachelor* is 'unmarried' or 'not having a wife' and humanness, maleness, etc. are presupposed by this meaning. (For details of justification of this claim the reader is referred to McCawley (1968a).) Thus it would appear, and in fact I would agree, with certain qualifications which will be made clearer later, that the idea of presupposition is the correct generalization of the notion of selectional restriction and the latter is now to be subsumed under the former in the theory of grammar.

According to McCawley, maleness and femaleness to be assumed in *neighbor* in (7) and (8), respectively, are also semantic phenomena of presupposition, they are presupposed, presumably, by the meanings of *himself* and *herself*. An anomalous form like

(13)   A waitress hurt himself.

is now considered, according to McCawley, to be syntactically well-formed but only semantically anomalous just as (5); the assertion of femaleness of the lexical item *waitress* contradicts the presupposition by the word *himself* that its antecedent is male. In fact, McCawley says, as generally is the case with semantic anomaly, either of these two contradictory elements may be taken to be metaphorical, indicating either effeminacy of a waiter or masculinity of a waitress.

4. CRITICISM AGAINST MCCAWLEY'S CLAIM, 1; GENDER AGREEMENT IN THE GENERAL CASE OF PRONOMINALIZATION

So far McCawley's contention appears convincing, and in fact I do not deny that it contains interesting insights, particularly in bringing together the phenomena of selectional restriction and presupposition. Nonetheless, his argumentation does not seem to be perfect and, in particular, I do not believe that he has established a proof that inherent features, selectional features, or things like that are totally abolished from syntax. Some subtleties remain in the relationship of selectional restrictions with the syntactic mechanism of language.

To begin with, McCawley's contention that gender agreement of a pronoun with its antecedent is a matter of semantic presupposition is not as clear and plausible as it may appear at first glance with such examples as (13). First of all, one encounters some difficulty when one tries to go beyond an informal understanding of the claim to see what such a contention may mean in more exact formal terms. This is because McCawley neither proposes any formal mechanism for presupposition, nor does he specify, in the papers under discussion, the formal mechanism of pronominalization he would adopt; more specifically, it is not clear whether his claim on the semantic nature of gender agreement of a pronoun is meant to be crucially dependent on one or the other formulation of pronominalization prevalent at present, in particular, on the one he proposed in another paper of his, McCawley (1969) (cf. also 1968b). The claim may bring different implications to the relationship between syntax and semantics, depending on the particular formulation of pronominalization.

This point is not my main concern at present, however. The reason I am going to dwell on it for a while is mainly to make the second point – to which I shall come shortly – clearer. It suffices for us, then, to assume for the time being the mechanism of pronominalization proposed in McCawley's papers cited above. According to this proposal, here drastically simplified only to serve our present purpose, nouns as lexical items are not inserted into slots under node N in the preterminal string in the sense that such slots are generally understood; rather, such slots are filled only by variables with referential indices like x_1, x_{27}, etc. To the sentence are attached as many extra occurrences of node N as there are different referential index variables in it where each variable is 'defined' in terms of a noun. Thus sentences (1) and

(14)   A waitress hurt a bachelor.

would have base forms like

(15)   (x_1 hurt x_1), $x_1 = $ a waitress.

(16)   (x_1 hurt x_2), $x_1 = $ a waitress, $x_2 = $ a bachelor.

respectively. It is assumed that there is an operation that inserts the defining noun phrase into the corresponding variable, or if there are many occurrences of the variable, one of its occurrences; the rest of the same variable are filled in by pronouns. To return to examples (15) and (16), the first occurrence of x_1 in (15) is filled by *a waitress*, the second occurrence by *herself*, to yield sentence (1); in (16) x_1 and x_2 are filled by *a waitress* and *a bachelor*, respectively, to yield sentence (14).

Then, presumably, the presupposition relation among the elements of a sentence is established after this operation of replacement of variables by words which, in a sense, exerts the effect of both the lexical insertion rule and the pronominalization rule at the same time. And, presumably, choice of *himself* or *herself*, which is to fill the second slot of x_1 in (15) is made independently of any inherent features that the lexical item *waitress* may have; only the semantic presupposition of one or the other of these pronouns may contradict some assertions that the lexical item may make, yielding 'semantically' anomalous forms like (13).

Thus, the claim to the effect that forms like (13) are semantically anomalous, which seems quite compatible with intuitive judgment on such forms, appears to fit well in the mechanism of pronominalization proposed by McCawley himself. This I do not dispute. But now to the second point. This is essentially nothing to do with what particular formalization of pronominalization one would adopt, but rather with intuitive judgment on some anomalous forms. To repeat partially, I could accept the judgment that forms like (13) are semantically anomalous with, characteristically, two possible metaphorical readings. On this is based the claim that gender agreement of pronouns is in nature identical to semantical presupposition related to selectional restrictions. However, my point is that forms like (1) and (13) are too special for a general conclusion to be drawn on the semantic implication of pronominalization in general. Take, thus, sentences like

(17)   A waitress hurt herself when someone hit her and she dropped
          glasses.

The base form, according to McCawley, would be something like

(18)   (x_1 hurt x_1 when x_2 hit x_1 and x_1 dropped x_3), $x_1 = $ a waitress, $x_2 = $ someone, $x_3 = $ glasses.

Now if one fills the second occurrence of x_1 and those after that by pronouns independently with respect to gender, i.e. without making gender agreement, one might get forms like

(19)   A waitress hurt himself when someone hit her and he dropped glasses.

(20)   A waitress hurt herself when someone hit him and she dropped glasses.

But in such cases, I would dare assume, though I am not a native speaker of English, that the forms thus obtained are mere word strings under the condition that referential identity is presupposed by the base form (18); (19) or (20) may not cause a metaphorical or humorous reading, indicating that the waitress changes successfully her (or his?) femininity or masculinity so frequently.

To avoid generating forms like (19) and (20) syntactically, one would have to have recourse to the feature of gender by some means, whatever formulation pronominalization might be assumed to take. Of course, one could still claim that forms like (19) and (20) are *by mere definition* syntactically well-formed and only semantically anomalous or semantically filtered out. But then the attempt at justifying *intuitively* the claim for semantic anomaly for (13), pointing to two possible resolutions in anomalous readings of the contradiction of meaning, becomes irrelevant. Besides, to call forms semantically anomalous to which presumably no semantically anomalous reading may even be assigned is hardly acceptable.

To summarize, Chomsky would, as McCawley points out, need the feature *Male* as an inherent syntactic feature and would introduce it by a rule like (3), because it is required in the formulation of gender agreement of a pronoun[1]; on the contrary, McCawley would claim that such a feature as a syntactic feature is not required in the formulation of gender agreement of a pronoun, since gender agreement and violation of it are to be accounted for semantically in terms of presupposition. But I believe his argument based on forms like (13) is insufficient to establish this general claim; the fact remains that a feature like *Male* must be referred to in the operation of pronominalization. It is another question how pronominalization is to be formalized, how features like *Male* are to be introduced in the syntactic component, or whether or not such features play any role in selectional restrictions within or outside the syntactic component.

5. CRITICISM AGAINST MCCAWLEY'S CLAIM, 2; GENDER AGREEMENT IN FRENCH

Would the above observation on pronominalization imply that human nouns must be specified as to their gender so that their gender may be referred to by pronominalization, and hence would it lead us to go back to the Chomskian framework in which (6) emerges as an ambiguous form? I shall hold on this question for the time being. In this section I shall discuss another example in which the gender feature is called for by a syntactic process. In fact, I shall take this to be more crucial than the above observation on pronominalization in connection with the problem of whether or not inherent features such as *Male* may be considered to be asyntactic in the general theory of grammar in the sense that they are not involved in the working of the syntactic component. It is also more crucial in determining how selectional restrictions are related to the syntactic mechanism of language.

After all, English is not a very good testing ground for possible involvement of the gender feature in the syntactic mechanism of language since gender plays rather a marginal role in grammar. A language such as French would testify to a more intricate involvement of gender in syntax. In French some nouns are grammatically masculine but semantically neutralized as to their referentialibility to a male or female person. One may say

(21)   Un professeur sera surpris.

without excluding the possibility that the referent of the subject will be female. The sentence

(22)   Le professeur a épousé Pierre.

is not semantically anomalous, *le professeur* in the natural reading of the sentence being taken to refer to a female professor. If a sentence like (22) is embedded by relativization into a matrix sentence as a modifier of *le professeur*, some, if not all, speakers of French make gender agreement of a particle, if necessary, according to the natural, rather than grammatical, gender of *le professeur*.[2] Thus we have

(23)   Le professeur qui a épousé Pierre sera surprise.

or

(24)   C'est le professeur qui a épousé Pierre que Charles a surprise.

It would be quite all right to say that femaleness of *le professeur* in (23) and (24) is presupposed by the meaning of the modifying clause *qui a épousé Pierre*; to this extent the femaleness of *le professeur* could be just a matter of semantic interpretation, just as the femaleness of *neighbor* would be presupposed by the meaning of *buxom* in the sentence

(25)   The buxom neighbor was surprised.

In this English case with *neighbor* the story ends here; in the French case with *le professeur* it doesn't. Apparently the femaleness presupposed by the modifying clause is responsible for the feminine ending of the participle *surprise* in (23) and (24). Gender agreement transformation would be quite naturally understood if it can refer to the feature *Female* of *le professeur* in (23) and (24); but this would mean that the femaleness of *le professeur* in these sentences is not simply a matter of semantic presupposition.

Although it may seem hardly necessary, let me elaborate this point a little further. Let us compare the case of English pronominalization exemplified by (1), (7), (8), etc. with the case of French gender agreement exemplified by (23) and (24). Let us for the time being disregard the criticism directed towards the 'semantical' treatment of pronominalization in Section 4. Thus, in examples like (1), (7), or (8), where only one anaphoric pronoun is concerned, or more specifically, where only an occurrence of a reflexive pronoun is concerned, the account of gender agreement (or disagreement) in terms of presupposition appears to have some reasonable basis. Let us accept for the time being the reasonableness, to this extent, of presuppositional treatment of gender agreement in English pronominalization and compare it with possible presuppositional treatment of gender agreement in French participles. (In fact, later I shall accept a somewhat modified version of a 'presuppositional' account of gender agreement of English pronouns in the general case.) Let us then go back to McCawley's framework and consider the McCawleian base form

(26) $(x_1 \text{ hurt } x_1)$, $x_1 = \text{neighbor}$.

which would supposedly underlie both (7) and (8); the first x_1 is replaced by *neighbor*; (7) and (8) are obtained if the second x_1 is replaced by *himself* and *herself*, respectively. After this replacement maleness and femaleness are presupposed in *neighbor* by *himself* and *herself*. Variables like x_1 are, so to speak, vessels, and insertion of lexical items like *neighbor* or pronouns like *himself* fills those vessels with semantic information. Even before such bestowment of semantic information, those vessels are related semantically to each other to some extent in the schemata like

(27) $x_1 \text{ hurt } x_1$, or, $x_1 \text{ hurt } x_2$.

These schemata themselves represent already primitive forms of units of meaning. Lexical insertion and pronoun insertion represent further refinement of such primitive forms of meaning. In the structure of English it happens that the third person singular pronoun must carry a piece of information, i.e. gender, that may not be carried by a human noun like *neighbor*, and in cases like (26), even though the two vessels represented by the two occurrences of x_1 are supposed to be coreferential, they may be filled with different pieces of information. Then pieces of information that are lacking in one of the two vessels are presupposed in it by the information filled into the other.

But in a case like gender agreement in French, particles with such a 'natural' interpretation for presupposition may not be available. Informally speaking, it would be quite obvious that to assume that the position filled by the feminine ending of *surprise* in (23) and (24) represents some kind of 'slot for meaning' is unnatural. Formally such an assumption would result in two kinds of redundancy. First of all, the information that *le professeur* is feminine is given in the relative clause; there is no need to reserve room after a participle to store that information. Secondly, the French past participle agrees in gender with the *deep* object only in case some transformation happens to bring the object before the participle; the 'nonclefted' sentence corresponding to (24) is

(28)   Charles a surpris le professeur qui a épousé Pierre.

Accordingly, if one assumes that there is a slot for a meaning after *surpris* in the base structure to indicate the gender of its direct object, it must be later deleted from structures like (28) where the direct object does not precede the participle in the surface structure; thus this semantically redundant assumption does not buy anything on the formal side, either.

The gender agreement of French participles is to be recognized to be a syntactic process that belongs to a layer much closer to the surface structure and a kind of process the standard transformational technique is supposed to be particularly fitting to describe.

It appears clear, then, that feature specifications $\pm$ *Male* must be referred to in a syntactic process of gender agreement of French participles and not simply semantic in the sense that their role is restricted in semantic interpretation and presupposition. Would this observation lead us to the original Chomskian framework?

6. AN ALTERNATIVE PROPOSAL INDICATED

I have claimed that both the Chomskian and the McCawleian framework are not appropriate to deal with the phenomenon of gender agreement in general, or more specifically, with the particular gender agreement found in French between a participle and its deep object. Some alternative proposal is now in order. In the following I shall submit a solution that would be a plausible one developed from the original Chomskian framework. However, as it will be pointed out later, the insight of Fillmore and McCawley that relates the notion of selectional restriction with the idea of presupposition is also in a sense incorporated in the framework to be proposed now.

The informal guideline underlying the formal framework to be proposed is to formalize the intuitively, I believe, plausible assumption that the gender of the participle *surprise* in (23) and (24) is determined by the natural gender of *le professeur*, which in turn is determined by the natural gender of the subject of the embedded sentence, which, finally, is determined, semantically speaking, by the meaning of the phrase *a épousé Pierre* and, syntactically speaking, by the context _____ *a épousé Pierre*.

Let us then start from the beginning. How would the statement 'the context _____ *a épousé Pierre* determines the natural gender of the subject' be reflected in the formal machinery of the Chomskian framework? It would be reflected in a statement like 'the verb *épouser* is assigned, among others, a specification of a selectional feature $+ [- Male]$ _____ $[+ Male]$.

For completeness' sake, let me here recall how selectional features like this are to be interpreted in the Chomskian framework. Chomsky proposed two alternative interpretations of the use of such features. Let me explain them, for the sake of simplicity, with examples from English. Presumably the adjective *buxom* is assigned the selectional feature specification 'take a female subject', or formally $+ [- Male]$ _____ or something like it. Now, according to one alternative, selectional features like this are introduced by rewriting rules in the base component of a form something like

$$(29) \qquad Adj \rightarrow + [- Male] \underline{\qquad} \quad \text{in env.} \quad [- Male] \dots \underline{\qquad}$$

Adjectives are subcategorized by this rule into those that take female subjects and the others. Each adjective in the lexicon is assigned a specification with respect to this selectional feature, $[- Male]$ _____ after all redundancy rules and conventions are applied to it inside the lexicon. Thus, *buxom*, for example, is assigned the specification $+ [- Male]$ _____. Now an adjective with this specification may be inserted into a slot in the preterminal string where the same feature specification has been introduced by rule (29). Since rule (29) is context sensitive, referring to the inherent feature $- Male$ of the subject slot, which is assumed to have been introduced by a rule like (3), the mechanism sketched above insures getting (4) to the exclusion of (5).

According to the other alternative, rewriting rules like (29) are not introduced in the base component; in a preterminal string an adjective slot is not

assigned any specification with respect to the selectional feature $[-Male]$
_____. Only in the lexicon is the specification of the feature assigned to
adjectives. Then, each lexical entry is assumed to represent a *transformation*
that replaces a dummy symbol *Delta* by itself and the selectional feature
specifications assigned to it are assumed to describe structural indices of this
particular transformation. For example, the adjective *buxom* is assigned the
specification $+[-Male]$ _____ in the lexicon. This specification means that
the lexical entry *buxom* may replace a *Delta* that is found in a string that
has a proper analysis $[-Male], ..., [+Adj]$ or something like it.

Note that in either of the alternatives it is assumed that slots for nouns
are assumed to have been assigned inherent feature specifications like $\pm Male$
in the base component by the time rewriting rules like (29) or transformations
that insert lexical entries are applied.

It is argued in McCawley (1968a) that there is little empirical evidence to
support the first alternative over the second; then, the first alternative is
simply overloaded with extra machinery. I do not substantiate this point
and refer the reader to McCawley (1968a). I simply state here that my
proposal, to be submitted now, may be considered an improvement over
the second alternative, not the first.

Thus, each lexical entry is assumed to represent a transformation which
inserts 'itself' into a preterminal string. But I shall provide a selectional
feature specification like $+[-Male]$ _____ with a different interpretation
so that we may get rid of spurious specifications of inherent features like
$\pm Male$ in preterminal strings. Let us continue to observe *buxom waitress*,
neighbor, and *bachelor*. As McCawley rightly observes, the meaning of *buxom*
presupposes femaleness of its subject. He does not provide us with any
formulation of such a 'rule of presupposition' in a formalized semantic
theory, to which, according to McCawley, it belongs. But once one starts
speculating on a possible formalism of such a presupposition rule one would
come to reinterpret a selectional feature specification like $[-Male]$ _____
as a presupposition rule saying, to put it informally, that femaleness is presupposed in the subject of *buxom*. Such a selectional feature specification
might now be considered to be a kind of semantic redundancy rule to predict
femaleness of the subject noun from the meaning of the adjective *buxom*.
Note that, according to this reinterpretation of selectional feature specifications, which is intended to give a formal basis, at least partially, to Mc-
Cawley's presupposition theory, selectional features are not syntactic features.
Take sentence (10). The syntactic component would generate it without any
specification as to male/female distinction of *neighbor*; the semantic component operating on this syntactically well-formed string would assign a
semantic feature specification $-Male$ to *neighbor* which is predicted by a

presupposition rule, or a kind of semantic redundancy rule, that is assigned to the lexical entry *buxom*. No particular syntactic process would be involved that assigns the specification − *Male* to *the waitress*, or the slot it fills, in sentence (4), either; but in this case the lexical entry *waitress* would be assigned a semantic feature specification − *Male* in the lexicon unlike *neighbor*, which is neutral, and accordingly the semantic redundancy rule represented by the selectional feature specification + [− *Male*] _____ would apply to (4) only vacuously. Sentence (5) would also be generated by the syntactic component as a syntactically well-formed sentence. The semantic redundancy rule would contradict the semantic inherent feature specification of the lexical entry *bachelor* and marks the sentence semantically anomalous.

This would be one plausible way in which one might formalize (a portion of) McCawley's presupposition theory. Note that as a kind of redundancy rule a presupposition rule is not allowed to 'rewrite' a specification already given. In fact, it is a perfectly reasonable assumption that 'inherent' feature specifications may never be rewritten; they may only be supplied or predicted by their contexts.

Essentially the only thing I need now to go from the McCawleian framework to the one I am proposing, though its implication for the general theory is all crucial, is simply to add that presuppositional redundancy rules such as discussed above may not entirely be enclosed in the semantic component. This would be a direct consequence from our observation on gender agreement of French participles made earlier. In the next section I shall recapitulate this conclusion and discuss some other consequences of our observation.

7. SELECTIONAL FEATURE AS STRUCTURAL CHANGE
OF A TRANSFORMATION

It was claimed that the feature specification − *Male* of *le professeur* in (23) and (24) must be available when gender agreement transformation operates on the participle *surpris*. It follows that prediction of femaleness of the subject of the phrase *a épousé Pierre* may not be realized strictly within the semantic component totally independently of the transformational component of French grammar. It must be assumed that the redundancy rule that is assumed to be represented, some way or other, by a selectional feature specification like + [− *Male*] _____ [+ *Male*] is a syntactic rule. The Chomskian framework may now be modified to accommodate this requirement simply by dropping rewriting rules like (3) that introduce inherent features into preterminal strings and interpreting a selectional feature specification like + [− *Male*] _____ [+ *Male*], not as a structural index of the transformation represented by a lexical entry that is so specified, but rather as a structural change of the transformation, with slight modification in understanding this term, as will be proposed shortly.

Let me go back, for simplicity's sake, to the English examples, to explain the point. Consider how forms like (4), (5), and (10) would be generated or blocked. The preterminal string underlying these forms would have the form

(30)   N is Adj

where the slot N is not specified as to its male/female distinction. The transformations, presumably unordered, that correspond to the lexical entries *waitress*, *bachelor*, or *neighbor*, on the one hand, and *buxom*, on the other, replace N and *Adj*, or more exactly, the occurrences of *Delta* dominated by them, by the lexical entry *waitress*, *bachelor*, or *neighbor*, on the one hand, and *buxom*, on the other, respectively. The selectional feature specification $+[-Male]$ _____ assigned to the lexical entry *buxom* is now assumed partially to read 'specify the subject as $-Male$', or in other words, the lexical entry might be interpreted to represent a transformation something like

$$(31)\qquad N, ..., [Delta]_{Adj} \quad \begin{bmatrix} 1 \\ -Male \end{bmatrix}, 2, buxom$$
$$1 \quad 2 \quad 3 \;\rightarrow$$

I said 'partially' because it appears that, strictly speaking, the specification of $+[-Male]$ _____ is assumed to represent at the same time the structural condition of the transformation, $N, ..., Adj$, N being predictable from $-Male$, and a part of its structural change. I shall propose shortly to interpret the specification $+[-Male]$ _____ to stand solely for the structural change of the transformation, with appropriate modification of its meaning to be specified later, so that a pleasing uniformity may be regained. But for the time being let us return to the formulation given in (31) and finish rough examination as to how forms like (4), (5), and (10) would be generated or blocked.

Assume that replacement of N by *waitress*, *bachelor* or *neighbor* takes place before replacement of *Adj* by *buxom*. Then, when rule (31) is applied in the process of derivation of (4), (5), and (10), the slot N in (30) is specified as $-Male$, $+Male$ and unspecified with respect to *Male*, respectively. In the first case, rule (31) applies vacuously, and (4) obtains. In the second case, the inherent feature specification $+Male$ assigned to *bachelor* in the lexicon contradicts the specification $-Male$ prescribed in the structural change of rule (31); by *convention* an inherent feature specification may not be changed; hence the blocking of the derivation of (5). In the third case rule (31) applies nonvacuously and specifies *neighbor* as $-Male$ and generates (10) as a syntactically well-formed form *with the specification* that *neighbor* is female.

Assume, next, that replacement of *N* takes place after replacement of *Adj*. Then when the nouns *waitress, bachelor,* and *neighbor* are to be inserted into the slot *N*, this slot has been assigned the feature specification $-Male$; this specification is vacuously supplied to *waitress*, contradicts the specification $+Male$ of *bachelor*, and is nonvacuously supplied to *neighbor* to generate, to block, and to generate (4), (5), and (10), respectively.

Thus, the modification proposed above to interpret lexical entries as transformations would yield the desired result concerning forms like (4), (5), and (10) under the same assumption that such transformations are mutually unordered as in the Chomskian framework. The above exposition still leaves some lack of clarity as to which feature specifications of a lexical entry are to be interpreted as representing structural change and which others as structural index of the transformation the lexical entry represents. As mentioned above, such distinction of the role of the feature specifications in a lexical entry will be removed later.

Note that in the proposed framework sentences like (6) do not emerge from the syntactic component as structurally ambiguous sentences, unlike in the original Chomskian framework. The lexical entry *neighbor* is not specified at the feature *Male* in the lexicon, no 'selectional feature' is assigned to *tall* that would introduce a gender specification in its subject, nor is any specification of the inherent feature *Male* introduced by a rewriting rule like (3).

8. RELATIVIZATION AND PRONOMINALIZATION AS FEATURE AGREEMENT TRANSFORMATION

Leaving for later consideration the problem of how feature specifications in a lexical entry should be interpreted exactly, let us now proceed to see how French examples like (23) and (24) would be generated, since this is more crucial to the main theme of the paper. The way a sentence like

(32)   Le professeur a épousé Pierre.

is generated parallels the way (10) is generated and needs no more clarification; presumably, the verb *épouser* is assigned specifications $+[\omega Male]$ ______$[-\omega Male]$, and in the derivation of (32) the first of these supplies the specification $-Male$ and $+Male$ to *le professeur* and *Pierre* nonvacuously and vacuously, respectively. *Le professeur* in (32) is syntactically specified as $-Male$. On the other hand, in the base form of the matrix sentence of (23) and (24):

(33)   Le professeur sera surpris.

or more exactly

(34)   Delta surprendra le professeur.

le professeur is unspecified at feature *Male* because *surprendre* does not demand selectional restriction on its subject or object based on male/female distinction.

The mechanism we still need to complete the derivation of sentences (23) and (24) is to 'shift' the specification — *Male* that has been assigned to *le professeur* in the constituent sentence by a 'selectional restriction' to *le professeur* in the matrix sentence which no 'selectional restriction' assigns such specification.

This problem is dependent on how the entire process of relativization is to be formalized. For our present purposes, however, it suffices to recognize that some sort of cross-reference of identity is involved in relativization as well as in pronominalization. Consider the base form that underlies sentence (23):

(35)   Le professeur # le professeur a épousé Pierre # sera surpris.

Here, as indicated above, the second *le professeur* gets specified as — *Male* while the first is unspecified at feature *Male*. In order to 'shift' the specification — *Male* from the constituent to the matrix sentence, one might formulate (a portion) of the relativization transformation as follows:

$$(36) \quad \begin{array}{ccccccccc} N & \# & X & N & Y & \# & & & \\ & & & \alpha Male & & & & & \\ 1 & & 2 & 3 & 4 & & \rightarrow & 1 & 2 \quad \emptyset \quad 4 \\ & & & & & & & & \alpha Male \end{array}$$

where $1 = 3$ except for some feature specifications including $\pm Male$.

This would suffice to derive (23) from (35) with additional application of a gender agreement rule that would refer to the specification — *Male* introduced into the matrix occurrence of *le professeur* in (35) by (36). The rule is a kind of regressive agreement rule.

I shall return shortly to formalization of the mechanism of regressive agreement connected with relativization. At this point let us return to the problem of gender agreement of pronouns in English. How would forms like (1), (7), (8), or (13) be generated or blocked? Let us base our examination of the problem on the 'classical' formulation of pronominalization, according to which pronominalization would be formulated as follows:

(37)   N X N
         1 2 3 → 1 2 $\begin{bmatrix} 3 \\ +\text{Pro} \end{bmatrix}$

where 1 = 3 (identity appropriately understood).

In the Chomskian framework the gender specifications of the pronoun and its antecedent are given in the base component; in the base form (2) of (1) both occurrences of *waitress* are assigned − *Male*, and this specification is inherited by *herself* in (1) through pronominalization. 'Identity appropriately understood' in the formulation of pronominalization in (37) is understood to include identity of gender. Two different base forms are responsible for derivation of (7) and (8), one with the specification + *Male*, the other with − *Male*, assigned to *neighbor*. In our framework, as in the McCawleian, *neighbor* is not assigned gender specification which may be inherited by a pronoun. Pronominalization itself must introduce gender specification of the anaphora of *neighbor*, which means a rule like

(38)   N X N
         1 2 3 → 1   2   3
                     αMale   αMale
                              + Pro

where 1 = 3 (identity appropriately understood)

is necessary. The common base form of (7) and (8) has not yet polarized its meaning into its two possible realizations, (7) and (8). Rule (38) has this effect of polarization, and one could say it is a rule of 'simultaneous' or 'nondirected' assimilation or agreement.

Note that this formulation is compatible with the derivation of (1); with alpha taken to be minus, rule (38) only vacuously supplies the specification − *Male* to the two occurrences of *waitress* in the base form (2) of (1). On the other hand, form (13) may be generated only at the expense of violation of the structural change specified by (38).

9. TRANSFORMATIONS AS PARTIAL WELL-FORMEDNESS CONDITIONS

We have now all the machinery needed to generate desired gender specifications in the grammatical examples discussed above, and also to block derivation of the ungrammatical ones. Some simplification of the formalism involved in the proposed framework is now in order. Let me note the following two points on the shape of rules (36) and (38). First of all, information is somewhat redundantly given in rule (38); the information contained in the structural index of the rule is repeated in the structural change, since feature

Male is lexically determined by the category noun. Thus, we might just as well state only the structural change of the rule in the form

$$(39) \qquad \alpha\text{Male} \quad X \quad + \text{Pro}$$
$$\alpha\text{Male}$$
$$1 \qquad 2 \qquad 3$$

where $1 = 3$ (identity appropriately understood).

This rule may be regarded as partially a blank-filling rule and partially a wellformedness condition.[3] This is made possible on the assumption that inherent features may not change their specifications. Secondly, one may note essentially the same kind of redundancy in the formulation of (36) as in that of (38). It may not be immediately seen from the way relativization is formulated in (36), but this is due to the fact that the formulation is insufficient; the third term may not be deleted entirely but certain features of it must be inherited by a relative pronoun. In fact, in French gender must also be kept in a relative pronoun in such cases as

$$(40) \qquad \text{La femme avec laquelle Pierre s'est marié a été surprise.}$$

Instead of (36) one may have a rule

$$(41) \qquad N \quad \# \quad X \quad N \quad Y \quad \#$$
$$\alpha\text{Male}$$
$$1 \qquad 2 \quad 3 \quad 4 \qquad \rightarrow \qquad 1 \qquad 2 \quad 3 \qquad 4$$
$$\alpha\text{Male} \quad \text{Pro}$$

This rule must be supplemented by the rules that propose the relativized term and form an appropriate relative pronoun from it. But note now that it does not matter whether the specification α *Male* of the third term appears in the structural index or the structural change of the transformation, again on the assumption that inherent features may not be respecified. And if this specification is shifted from the structural index part to the structural change part of the rule, the same kind of redundancy becomes apparent as with rule (38). Thus one might as well reformulate it as

$$(42) \qquad N \quad \# \quad X \quad N \quad Y \quad \#$$
$$\alpha\text{Male} \qquad \alpha\text{Male}$$
$$+ \text{Pro}$$
$$1 \qquad 2 \quad 3 \quad 4$$

where $1 = 3$ (identity appropriately understood).

This may again be considered to be partially a blank-filling rule and partially a well-formedness condition.

To return to example (23), the blank at feature *Male* in *le professeur* in the matrix is filled by rule (42); on the other hand, the specification $-Male$ which is inherent in the lexical entry *femme* is 'tested' by rule (42) in derivation of (40).

We are now in a position to return to the meaning of lexical entries as transformations. Some nonuniformity was noticed concerning interpretation of feature specifications given in lexical entries; some seem to have been interpreted as describing structural indices and some others structural changes of lexical transformations that insert 'themselves'. But now these transformations are also regarded as 'uni-sided'; i.e. they are transformations describable only by their structural change and they act partially as blank-filling rules and partially as well-formedness conditions like transformations (39) and (42).

Let us recall how sentence (23) would be derived in the framework proposed above. The rewriting rules of the base component would generate, irrelevant details omitted, the preterminal string of the form

$$(43) \qquad \# \ \ N_1 \ \ V_1 \ \ N_2 \ \ \# \ \ N_3 \ \ V_2 \ \ N_4 \ \ \# \qquad \text{where } N_2 = N_3.$$

The lexicon contains the following entries:

(44)   *surprendre,...*

(45)   *épouser,* $+[\omega\text{Male}]$ _____ $[-\omega\text{Male}],...$

(46)   *Pierre,* $+$ Male,...

(47)   *professeur,*   blankMale,....

Application of transformations (46) and (47) to (43), and some other irrelevant adjustment, would yield

$$(48) \qquad N \ \ V_1 \quad \underset{\text{blankMale}}{\text{le professeur}} \quad \# \quad \underset{\text{blankMale}}{\text{le professeur}} \quad V_2 \quad \underset{+\,\text{Male}}{\text{Pierre}}$$

Application of transformation (45) would assign $-Male$ to *le professeur* in the constituent and 'test' the specification $+Male$ of *Pierre*:

$$(49) \qquad N \ \ V_1 \quad \underset{\text{blankMale}}{\text{le professeur}} \quad \# \quad \underset{-\,\text{Male}}{\text{le professeur}} \quad \text{a épousé} \ \underset{+\,\text{Male}}{\text{Pierre}} \quad \#$$

Transformation (44) simply inserts itself into V_1; passive transformation will then yield

$$(50) \qquad \underset{\text{blankMale}}{\text{Le professeur}} \quad \# \quad \underset{-\,\text{Male}}{\text{le professeur}} \quad \text{a épousé} \ \underset{+\,\text{Male}}{\text{Pierre}} \ \# \ \text{sera surpris.}$$

Transformation (42) would assign − *Male* to *le professeur* in the matrix and
'test' − *Male* in *le professeur* in the constituent:

(51)   Le professeur # le professeur   a épousé Pierre # sera surpris.
          − Male   − Male   + Male
                               + Pro

Then, finally, gender agreement transformation, the nature of which is to be
examined below, changes *surpris* into *surprise*, making reference to specification − *Male* of *le professeur* in the matrix.[4]

I have finished presenting the framework of the base component of a
transformational grammar which is claimed to overcome shortcomings of
both the Chomskian and the McCawleian frameworks. It may be regarded
as a sublation of these two earlier proposals. Like the Chomskian and unlike
the McCawleian framework, some selectional features are introduced in the
lexicon, though they are given a somewhat different interpretation than in
the Chomskian framework. Like the McCawleian and unlike the Chomskian
framework, inherent features like *Male* are not introduced into preterminal
strings by rewriting rules; they are introduced into base forms by lexical
insertion transformations, some originating from inherent specifications of
lexical entries and some others from 'prediction' or 'presupposition' of 'selectional restrictions'.[5]

10. GENDER AGREEMENT; GRAMMATICAL AND NATURAL GENDER

The reader will have noticed that gender agreement in French of participles
or, more generally, participles and adjectives needs more careful treatment
than the foregoing discussion may directly show. Let us consider sentences
like

(52)   La théorie que le professeur a proposée a été mise en doute par
          Pierre.

The participle *mise* agrees in gender with *la théorie*. Nothing particularly
remarkable is involved here except that *la théorie* is feminine only in the
grammatical sense. The specification − *Male* that appears, for example, in
selectional restrictions of *épouser* is not supposed to refer to this feminine
feature of *la théorie*, so that one may not get

(53)   *La théorie a épousé Pierre.

Naturally, then, the inherent feature of 'natural' gender that we have been
discussing must be distinguished from another syntactic feature of grammatical gender. Let us continue to denote the natural gender feature by *Male*

and denote the grammatical gender by *Masculine*. The lexical entry *professeur* is specified as + *Masculine* and unspecified at feature *Male*. The lexical entry *théorie* is specified as − *Masculine*, but is it also unspecified at *Male*? If it is unspecified at *Male*, how would it be possible that (53) is blocked? Perhaps a plausible answer to these questions is to introduce the convention that whenever the specification + *Male* or − *Male* is referred to the specification + *Human* (and + Animate, too) is also implicitly understood. Selectional feature specification + [− *Male*] _____ [+ *Male*] implies automatically another specification + [+ *Human*] _____ [+ *Human*]. This convention blocks (53) in an obvious way.

Now there must be two gender agreement rules, one referring to grammatical gender and the other to natural gender. How are these two related to each other? From the examples treated so far it might appear that gender agreement of the participles follows natural gender if natural and grammatical genders conflict. But the whole story is not that simple. In our previous example, (23), a masculine noun phrase has acquired a feminine meaning. Take now the case of the conflict in the opposite direction: a feminine noun which acquires a masculine meaning, as in

(54)   La victime qui a épousé Marie.

How does the participle *surpris* agree with this noun phrase if it becomes the subject of the verb phrase

(55)   a été surpris.

If gender agreement follows the natural gender one would get

(56)   La victime qui a épousé Marie a été surpris.

However, it is reported that (56) sounds much worse than, say, (23). The form

(57)   La victime qui a épousé Marie a été surprise.

seems to be preferable to (56), although it is reported to be not quite pleasing, either. Thus, the gender agreement rule would be at best stated informally somewhat as follows:

(58)   If the head noun is feminine the participle agrees with the grammatical gender, although the resulting form acquires a somewhat lesser degree of grammaticalness if the natural gender of the noun conflicts with its grammatical gender. If the head noun is masculine the participle agrees with its natural gender.[6]

The fact that the gender agreement rule is more complicated than it may first appear, however, only shows, if anything, that the way inherent features are involved in the syntactic working of the French language is more subtle and complicated. A detailed and more exhaustive account of gender agreement in French is not essentially relevant to our main concern in this paper and naturally is beyond the scope of this paper.[7]

Important to note in the scope of our present study is the essentially syntactic character of gender agreement of French participles. Comparison of this gender agreement with gender agreement in pronominalization will be instructive. In the case of pronominalization one might say, and in fact rightly, that the process of pronominalization to be formulated as in (39) is a *semantic* process in a certain sense; it is supposed to introduce semantic information during the process of generation of a sentence. In sentences like

(59)   A neighbor hurt himself.

(60)   A neighbor hurt herself,

pronominalization, possibly even inadvertently, serves to give information on the sex of the referent of the noun *neighbor*. Even in sentences like (1), where it might appear that the meaning of the noun *waitress* is solely responsible for the information that the subject of the verb *hurt* is female and the process of pronominalization is simply syntactic, semantic implication of the process of pronominalization may be pointed out. This is because if the right process of pronominalization is violated and forms like (13) are generated we get, as McCawley rightly observes, semantic anomaly rather than purely syntactic anomaly. In other words, (13) is anomalous in much the same way as (5) is, both resulting in conflict of semantic 'presupposition'. But this is not the case with French gender agreement of participles. It might be possible that the form

(61)   Le professeur qui a épousé Pierre sera surpris.

is taken to be semantically anomalous, but this is not the only way (61) would be given an interpretation. It might as well be taken to be a form intended to be semantically natural but syntactically anomalous, violating the syntactic rule of gender agreement. The essentially syntactic character of gender agreement of French participles is more clearly revealed by the fact that neither (56) nor (57) is felt, as is reported to me, to be quite the right form. If gender agreement of French participles is essentially of the same semantic nature that the process of pronominalization is, then anomaly must be explained in terms of conflict of semantic presuppositions. Note that semantically anomalous forms can be uttered with good intentions of producing some particular semantic effects. But when forms like (56) and (57) are said to be somewhat anomalous it is not meant that they may be uttered successfully with good intentions of producing some particular semantic effects, but rather that the particular intended meaning fails to materialize in forms such as (56) and (57). They are purely syntactically anomalous in this sense and so are, or rather so can also be, forms like (61). This is the reason why one can say that gender agreement of French participles reveals in a more decisive way than the process of pronominalisation the fact that the inherent feature *Male* can be involved in the syntactic process of language.

11. CONCLUDING REMARKS

Chomsky called a feature "syntactic" if it is mentioned in some syntactic rule. According to Chomsky, the inherent feature *Male* would be a syntactic feature in this sense. According to McCawley, inherent features are semantic and, furthermore, he claims that selectional restrictions, which are dealt with by means of selectional features in the Chomskian framework, are not to be treated in syntax.

I claimed that McCawley's argument that inherent features are not syntactic in the sense that they are not involved in the syntactic working of language cannot be accepted in general; feature *Male* is claimed to be syntactic; furthermore, some features that are formally similar to Chomsky's selectional features are also recognized to be syntactic in the same sense.

This may give an impression that the system of grammar described in the preceding lines is very close to Chomsky's original. But the general implication of the kind of grammatical phenomenon we have been concerned with may not be fully revealed in a direct way if our observation is limited to the type of example discussed so far. We have seen that in example (23) the noun *le professeur* obtains feature specification $-Male$ through 'selectional' feature specification $+[\omega Male \underline{\hspace{1cm}} -\omega Male]$ assigned to the verb of the embedded sentence, *épouser*. Formally speaking, the meaning of the embedded sentence "presupposes", according to Fillmore-McCawley terminology, the femaleness of the subject of the matrix sentence. However, as Fillmore and McCawley rightly point out, selectional features of the kind that the Chomskian framework would allow represent only special instances of "presupposition". In the case of *épouser* the meaning of the verb and the natural gender of its object determine the natural gender of the subject of the verb. But consider a verb phrase like *wear a skirt*. Presumably (except in Scotland) this verb phrase presupposes that its subject is female. But it is not a feature independently inherent in the verb *wear* or in the noun *skirt* that is responsible for this presupposition; a male professor may well wear a shirt or buy a skirt. Perhaps, then, one would have to introduce a feature something like *To-be-worn-by-female* and assume that *skirt* is assigned feature specification $+[$*To-be-worn-by-female*$]$ and *wear* the selectional feature specification $+[-[$*Male*$]$ _____ $+[$*To-be-worn-by-female*$]]$. But this would still not be sufficient. Any specification, say, P, which gives a description of *skirt* would give rise to the presupposition that the subject of the phrase *wear clothes of the type P* (or *which are P*) is female; one would have to devise machinery to "calculate" the feature specification $+[$*To-be-worn-by-female*$]$ from the structure of expression P.

It is an issue that must be settled by careful observation whether any semantic process, however complicated, that operates on a constituent sentence and assigns a specification of gender feature to a noun in the matrix sentence contributes to a syntactic process like gender agreement or there is any syntactic limit, so to speak, that blocks too complicated semantic intervention into syntax. I would think it would be best to leave the problem open for investigation by native linguists of a language where the issue discussed in this paper exists. The purpose of the present study is to show that at least the type of presupposition that would formally correspond to Chomskian selectional features may be involved in the syntactic working of grammar.

Thus, I would agree with McCawley when he says that selectional restrictions are actually semantic if by this is simply meant that a variety of operations that would be involved in semantic presupposition are automatically involved in description of selectional restrictions; but I disagree with him when he adds to the above phrase "rather than syntactic" and by doing so means that the syntactic component is independent of matters related to selectional restrictions.

The reader will have noticed that Weinreich's notion of transfer feature is closely related to our topic. On the informal level much of what was presented in Sections 6 and 7 of this paper would be restatement of the idea underlying Weinreich's theory. I have so far bypassed Weinreich's transfer feature, since, for one thing, I am primarily concerned with reinterpretation of the particular formalism of Chomskian selectional features and, for another, mechanism of 'semantic process' itself is not my present concern. My concern is rather syntactic; I want to establish necessity of the direction suggested in Weinreich's work strictly in the syntactic framework.

In Weinreich's theory 'semantic process' and the transformational component are not assumed to be independent as the semantic and the syntactic component are assumed to be in the standard theory of transformational grammar; Weinreich's semantic calculator, a part of his 'semantic process', is assumed to precede 'transformations and morphophonemics' (cf. Weinreich (1966), diagram (76), p. 445). He gives argument for placing semantic calculator before 'morphophonemics', but he does not seem to give any reason why it is also placed before 'transformations'. Perhaps he tacitly assumes that 'transformations' and 'morphophonemics' constitute syntax and must be in the same 'box', as his diagram would indicate, where 'transformations' and 'morphophonemics' are separated only by a dotted line and surrounded by a solid line. In the framework proposed above the process that would correspond Weinreich's transfer rule must precede the transformational component.

As a conclusion of his exploration Weinreich argues for the deep interpenetration of syntax and semantics. In his paper he deals also with some problems that are not directly related to the issue discussed here and this is not the place to examine to what extent this claim as a whole is valid. So far as the aspect related to his transfer feature is concerned, the discussion in this paper would seem to confirm his conclusion, perhaps more convincingly. Syntactic processing of the matrix sentence may depend on the effect of semantic presuppositions on its constituent sentences; semantic presuppositions may be represented, in the simplest case, by means of formalism much like that of selectional features, but to single out only such a kind of presupposition would perhaps be quite arbitrary. We have no reasonable basis to assume that presuppositions in general cases may also be accountable by means of transformation-like formalism.

After this much is said, however, I must add that the implication of a comment like the above would not be taken too loosely. In fact, the effect of presupposition rules would be to provide and/or test elements of the base form with some semantically significant feature specifications that are predictable from their environments. But operations with such effect must be distinguished from what should properly be called semantic interpretation rules. Semantic interpretation rules are operations that map configurations on the syntactic deep level onto semantic representations, which, whatever they may be, have presumably different types of configurations, if anything, and obey different types of laws of organization and interrelation from those which belong to the level of syntactic deep structure.[8] The configurations that arise form the deep structure after only semantic presupposition rules have been applied may well be considered still to belong to the syntactic deep structure rather than to the level of semantic representation. What has been discussed above reveals interpenetration of semantics into syntax only to the extent that the syntactic component may depend on certain types of semantic presuppositions, and as yet not to the extent that it depends directly and essentially on semantic interpretations. Those semantic presuppositions which may affect syntactic processes like gender agreement may far exceed the complexity transformational techniques can describe. But this

     S.-Y. KURODA

possibility itself does not automatically imply that semantic interpretations are involved in syntax. So far as presupposition rules can be conceived as operations on syntactic deep representations whether they belong to syntax or semantics would not be much more than a terminological question.

In some sense I have restored Chomsky's selectional features which Mc-Cawley discarded. One might object to their rehabilitation because, after all, they can represent only a fraction of the entire phenomenon of selectional restriction or semantic presupposition. But it seems to me to be a mistake to ridicule Chomskian selectional features simply because one can easily enumerate anomalous examples that cannot be excluded by them, such as those given by McCawley: *John diagonalized that differentiable manifold, I ate three phonemes for breakfast*. Although analogy is not always a very commendable technique in rhetoric or in historical linguistics and may lead to unexpected confusion, it may be permissible to conclude this paper submitted to a seminar on mathematical linguistics by saying, or recalling, that the problem of selectional restrictions is of topological nature rather than algebraic. The essential interest in the study of selectional restriction should lie not in locating *exactly* every single element in the structure of grammaticalness but rather in investigating the structure of approximation of grammaticalness and deviancy. It seems very doubtful that the problem, for example, of determining *exactly* what items may or may not make a normal or anomalous sentence from the frame *I ate _____* is by itself of any real linguistic interest. A complete solution, if possible, of such a problem would only amount to enumerating all eatable things, or if one likes to talk formally, to recognition of a feature something like $[+ Human - eat \_\_\_\_\_]$ and to assigning plus or minus specifications for this feature to each single noun. It would be more significant to investigate the mutual relationship of redundancy among features like this one. Thus, one could introduce a rule to the effect that abstract nouns are negatively specified at $[+ Human - eat \_\_\_\_\_]$. This rule would predict, so one would say, the anomaly of *I ate three phonemes*. But however many redundancy rules of this sort one may establish, it would be easy to ridicule the system of rules by presenting deviant forms that defy the refinement attained by introduction of those rules if one's interest remained in just determining whether or not every single form is normal or anomalous. This sort of interest in the problem of selectional restriction may be compared with that of a person who is interested in knowing the *exact* decimal expansion of π. The mathematician could give him as many consecutive digits of the decimal expansion of π as the person is ready to be satisfied by. Likewise, the linguist may possibly enumerate as many normal and/or anomalous forms with the frame *I ate _____* as he wishes. But these would not be mathematically or linguistically interesting problems; only the structure of approximation that is concealed under such problems is worthy of mathematical or linguistic interest. Any criticism against the Chomskian notion of selectional restriction would have to be directed along the line that would show that it is useless, misleading, or mistaken for the purpose of taking a step towards a significant theory of the structure of grammatical approximation.

University of California, San Diego

BIBLIOGRAPHY

Bach, Emmon (1968), 'Nouns and Noun Phrases', in Bach and Harms (1968, pp. 91–122).
Bach, Emmon and Harms, Robert, (Eds.), (1968), *Universals in Linguistic Theory*, Holt, Rinehart and Winston, Inc., New York.
Chomsky, Noam (1965), *Aspects of the Theory of Syntax*, The M.I.T. Press, Cambridge (Mass.).
Kuroda, S.-Y. (1969): 'Remarks on English Manner Adverbials', in *Papers in General and Oriental Linguistics. A volume dedicated to Dr. Shiro Hattori* (ed. by R. Jakobson and S. Kawamoto).
McCawley, James D. (1968a), 'Concerning the Base Component of a Transformational Grammar', *Foundations of Language* **4**, 243–69.
– (1968b), 'The Role of Semantics in a Grammar', in Bach and Harms (1968, pp. 124–69).
– (1969), 'Where Do Noun Phrases Come from?', in *Readings in English Transformational Grammar* (ed. by R. Jacobs and P. S. Rosenbaum), forthcoming.
Weinreich, Uriel (1966), 'Explorations in Semantic Theory', in *Current Trends in Linguistics*, Vol. III. (ed. by Th. A. Sebeok), Mouton and Co., The Hague.

REFERENCES

* An earlier version of this work was presented at the Symposium on Mathematical Linguistics, Balatonszabadi (Hungary), September, 1968. I am indebted to Nicolas Ruwet for reading an earlier draft of this paper, giving valuable comments, and drawing my attention to more complicated aspects of French gender agreement which are not all taken up in this paper.

[1] Chomsky proposed two different formalisms for the base component as will be recalled briefly in Section 6. In the second of his proposals in which the lexical rule is assumed to be a substitution transformation one may also assume that inherent features like *Male* is introduced into the base form from the lexicon by this substitution, thus obliterating context-free selectional rules like (3). But, then, there must be two lexical items *neighbor*, one marked $+ Male$ and the other $- Male$. At any rate the essential point is that in Chomskian frameworks in derivation of a base form inherent features must be available in the string under production when lexical items are to be inserted in the string.

[2] Apparently the description given here and below contradicts the rules of some other speakers of French who prefer putting the participle *surpris* in (23) in the masculine form. Yet the issue discussed in this paper is not totally irrelevant for the language of such speakers; see Section 10. On the other hand the issue simply disappears with the speakers of another variant of French in which the form *la professeur* is permitted. Dialectological and/or sociolinguistic status of these variants of French is not our concern in the present paper.

[3] More exactly pronominalization would have to be formulated as a kind of rule schema that may be applicable to cases where more than two coreferential occurrences of a noun are involved and simultaneously pronominalize all of them other than the antecedent. But how such a rule schema is to be formulated is out of the scope of the present paper. The reader may also note that introduction of a rule like (39) violates, when applied to the underlying form of a sentence like (7), the currently prevalent principle of meaning invariance under a grammatical transformation unless pronouns are assumed to be generated in the base and (39) is taken to be completely a well-formedness condition. But here I shall not pursue this issue further.

[4] Here I must insert a remark on formulation of (45). Up to now (45) is implicitly assumed to follow the usual convention about alpha-rules, according to which it is a conventional abbreviation of two disjunctive rules where ω takes the values plus and minus, respectively. But consider sentences like *Un professeur a épousé un docteur*. Interpreted as an alpha-rule (45) would generate two different base forms that underlie this speech form, one with + *Male* and − *Male* assigned to *professeur* and *docteur*, respectively, and the other with the inverse assignment; then the sentence would have to be assumed formally ambiguous. This is precisely the kind of consequence we wanted to avoid concerning sentences like (6). Presumably, the sentence above, in the normal reading, only implies that the sex of *un professeur* is opposite to that of *un docteur*. But the desired result cannot be obtained within the current framework of alpha-convention, in which alphas may only appear in rules and not in generated representations. This framework suffices for accounting for assimilation and dissimilation in phonology; there two segments to be assimilated or dissimilated must be materialized in one or the other of the two possible ways of assimilation or dissimilation. Here we are faced with a new situation and a new convention is called for. Thus, it will be assumed that omega-symbols may appear in generated strings and rule (45) consists of three subrules:

$$[\omega\text{Male}] \underline{\hspace{2em}} [-\omega\text{Male}]$$
$$[+\text{Male}] \underline{\hspace{2em}} [-\text{Male}]$$
$$[-\text{Male}] \underline{\hspace{2em}} [+\text{Male}];$$

the first subrule applies obligatorily, if possible, and then the last two following the convention on application of alpha-rules. (Hence the second rule is optional and the third is obligatory if the second has not been applied.)

Rules (39) and (42) must be understood according to the usual alpha-convention.

I am indebted to Osamu Fujimura for pointing out to me the inadequacy contained in an earlier draft of the paper concerning the problem discussed here.

[5] Selectional restriction features conceived as well-formedness conditions applied cyclically may also serve to 'test' well-formedness of sentences in which selectional restriction apparently operates on a deeply embedded constituent, e.g.

> Bill cannot believe what John forced Tom to tell.

but

> *Bill cannot believe what John forced Tom to buy.

(Cf. Bach (1968) and Kuroda (1969).)

[6] Even those who prefer the masculine form *surpris* to the feminine *surprise* in sentences like (23), at least some of them, would seem to agree that forms like (56) are much worse than those like (23), which amounts to indicating that they also possess some kind of rule somehow resembles (58), if not on the level of full grammaticalness.

[7] There would be no need to recall that the masculine form sometimes serves as the unmarked member in the dimension of natural gender. For our present purposes our simplied treatment, in this respect, of natural gender suffices. Only would I remark informally that the asymmetry exhibited in rule (58) would perhaps be related to this unmarkedness characteristic of the masculine gender.

[8] To make the point clearer it might be instructive to consider a hypothetical, and obviously unrealistic, situation in which syntax depends essentially on semantic interpretation rules. Thus, just for the sake of exposition let us assume that some familiar logistic system of predicate calculus provides semantic representations of sentences. Consider a language in which the position of the main verb of a sentence, say, vis-à-vis that of the subject, depends on the number, say, modulo three, of factors in the disjunctive normal form of the semantic representation of the sentence. In such a language the transformational component must await disconfiguration of the base form by semantic interpretation rules.

I am not saying that the semantic interpretation can possibly intervene in syntax only in an odd fashion like this, nor do I mean to imply with this example that to consider possibility of involvement of semantic interpretation in syntax is an enterprise to be ridiculed. We know too little about semantic representations and semantic interpretation rules and not much even about semantic presuppositions.

DAVID M. PERLMUTTER

EVIDENCE FOR DEEP STRUCTURE CONSTRAINTS
IN SYNTAX*

0. THE PROBLEM

In *Aspects of the Theory of Syntax*, Chomsky proposed the introduction of contextual (strict subcategorizational and selectional) features into linguistic theory to specify the types of deep structures into which particular lexical items could be inserted. He also introduced into theory generalized phrase markers generated by recursive phrase structure rules of the base component capable of reintroducing the symbol S in deep structures any number of times. Each S would then be expanded further by the rewrite rules of the base. Lexical items would then be inserted into the generalized phrase markers produced in this way.

This theoretical framework gives rise to the question of whether the insertion of lexical items into generalized phrase markers will result in ill-formed deep structures, and what grammatical devices are necessary to prevent this. It was to state constraints on the distribution of a lexical item within a given simplex S that Chomsky proposed contextual features associated with the lexical item. No specific provisions were made in *Aspects* for constraints on lexical items extending across S boundaries within generalized phrase markers. Chomsky pointed out, however, that un-constrained[1] insertion of lexical items into generalized phrase markers would produce deep structures which underlie no well-formed sentences. Considering relative clauses, he pointed out that a relative clause must contain a noun phrase identical to the antecedent, and that unconstrained[1] insertion of lexical items into deep structures would give rise to deep structures in which this condition was not satisfied. Some device was needed to characterize such deep structures as ill-formed. Rather than introduce some kind of constraint on deep structures themselves, Chomsky proposed the device of transformational blocking of derivations. In the case of relative clauses which contain no noun phrase identical to the antecedent, the obligatory relativization transformation would 'block' because the condition requiring two identical noun phrases would not be satisfied. The 'blocking' of the derivation caused by the inability of this obligatory transformation to apply would characterize the sentence as ungrammatical. The notion 'well-formed deep structure' thus was not defined solely in terms of constraints on deep structures themselves, but was a derivative notion, defined

F. Kiefer (ed.), Studies in Syntax and Semantics, 168–186. © *D. Reidel, Dordrecht - Holland*

transformationally. Only those generalized phrase markers which passed through the transformational component with no transformations causing the derivation to 'block' would qualify as deep structures. To quote Chomsky:

Not all generalized Phrase-markers generated by the base will underlie actual sentences and thus qualify as deep structures. What, then, is the test that determines whether a generalized Phrase-marker is the deep structure of some sentence? The answer is very simple. The transformational rules provide exactly such a test, and there is, in general, no simpler test. A generalized Phrase-marker M_D is the deep structure underlying the sentence S, with the surface structure M_S, just in case the transformational rules generate M_S from M_D. The surface structure M_S of S is well formed just in case S contains no symbols indicating the blocking of obligatory transformations. A deep structure is a generalized Phrase-marker underlying some well-formed surface structure. Thus the basic notion defined by a transformational grammar is: *deep structure M_D underlies well-formed surface structure M_S*. The notion "deep structure" itself is derivative from this. The transformational rules act as a "filter" that permits only certain generalized Phrase-markers to qualify as deep structures.[2]

Given the framework of *Aspects*, Chomsky's proposal to characterize ill-formed deep structures with relative clauses as ungrammatical by means of transformational blocking of the derivation is well-suited to the particular constraint under consideration. What is required is that some noun phrase in the relative clause be identical to the antecedent. The constraint, then, is not a property of any particular lexical items, and could not be handled by means of contextual features associated with lexical items. Second, the constraint is one that requires identity between two noun phrases. The contextual features introduced in *Aspects* referred to strict subcategor-izational and selectional features of noun phrases, but not to identity between two noun phrases. This was, however, a condition found re-peatedly in the statement of transformations. Since the relativization transformation had to require identity between the relativized noun phrase and the antecedent in any case, it seemed natural to make use of this re-quirement as a means of characterizing as ill-formed any deep structure in which this requirement was not met.

It is the purpose of this paper to show that there exist in natural languages ill-formed generalized phrase markers generated by the base component which cannot be characterized as such by means of the blocking of trans-formations. The data on which this conclusion is based comes from sen-tences which manifest identity or non-identity constraints between the subjects of certain verbs and the subjects of their complements.[3] Two types of arguments are given to show that these constraints cannot be stated transformationally. One type of argument is based on the fact that if identity or non-identity constraints on noun phrases are to be stated transfor-mationally, the constraints must require that the relevant noun phrases be identical or non-identical at the stage in derivations at which the relevant transformation applies. It is shown here that there are subject-subject constraints which cannot be stated in this way, for they are constraints on underlying rather than derived subjects. A second type of argument is based on cases where the subject of a verb and the subject of its complement must be identical, but there is no obligatory transformation which applies to such structures. In one such case the relevant transformation is optional, while in another there is no transformation in the language which states an identity condition between the two noun phrases which must be identical. There is therefore no transformation available which can be said to cause the derivation to 'block'. It is concluded that for both types of cases it is necessary to impose a constraint requiring identity (or non-identity, as the case may be) of the subjects of certain verbs and the subjects of their complements prior to the application of transformations. We refer to these constraints as *deep structure constraints*.

The deep structure constraints proposed here go beyond the contextual features of *Aspects* in two respects. First, their domain extends beyond the boundaries of the simplex S in generalized phrase markers. Second, they refer crucially to identity and non-identity of noun phrases. One could regard them as an extension of the device of contextual features introduced in *Aspects*. In this view, they would specify conditions on the insertion of particular verbs into deep structures. Within the framework of recent work in generative semantics, the constraints proposed here could likewise be viewed as conditions on lexical insertion. Alternatively, within either the *Aspects* theory or that of generative semantics one could view them as filters imposed on trees which already contain lexical items. In this view, their role would be that of discarding or filtering out ill-formed underlying structures. It is not clear at present whether there are any empirical differences among these differing views of the deep structure contraints proposed here, or whether they are merely notational variants. At any rate, we are not concerned here with differentiating among them. It is our purpose here only to show that the ill-formed structures in question can not be characterized as such by means of transformations.

1. THE UNLIKE-SUBJECT CONSTRAINT IN ENGLISH

In his study of complementation in English, Rosenbaum (1967) pointed out that in certain complement constructions the subject of the embedded sentence must be non-identical to the subject of the matrix sentence.

(1)   I screamed for Clyde to commit himself.

(2)   a. *I screamed for me to commit myself.

            b. *I screamed to commit myself.

The question which concerns us here is one which lay beyond the scope of Rosenbaum's study – that of how such restrictions are to be stated in grammars.

The first attempt to state this restriction precisely was made by Lakoff (1965). Since the ill-formedness of *(2) is due not to any ill-formedness of either simplex S by itself, but rather to the fact that a sentence with *I* as subject is embedded beneath the sentence *I screamed* with infinitival complementizer, Lakoff sought to account for the deviance of *(2) by extending Chomsky's proposal that it is the blocking of an obligatory transformation that 'filters out' ill-formed generalized phrase markers as ungrammatical. In order to do this Lakoff proposed the notion of 'absolute exceptions' to transformational rules, marking the verb *scream* as an 'absolute exception' to the rule of Equi-NP Deletion. This meant that *scream* had to be marked in the lexicon as requiring:

(a) that the structural description of Equi-NP Deletion *not* be met, and

(b) that Equi-NP Deletion *not* apply.

A verb marked only for (b) would be a 'simple exception', in Lakoff's terminology. If *scream* were only a simple exception, however, *(2b) would be characterized as ungrammatical but *(2a) would not. The fact that *(2a) is ungrammatical as well led Lakoff to add requirement (a), making *scream* an 'absolute exception' to the rule of Equi-NP Deletion. A violation would be registered in sentences with *scream*, marking the sentence as ungrammatical, in the event that the structural description of Equi-NP Deletion were met or in the event that the rule applied.

If one assumes that violations of grammaticality due to embedding of independently well-formed simplex S's in generalized phrase markers must be accounted for transformationally, one would be driven to some such notion as absolute exceptions. Since the constraint that accounts for the difference between (1) and *(2) requires non-identity between the subject of a sentence and the subject of a sentence embedded beneath it, the only transformation we could possibly make use of to characterize the relevant sentences as ungrammatical would be a transformation that looks at the two subjects. The only transformation that does this is Equi-NP Deletion. The notion of absolute exceptions to Equi-NP Deletion, then, is a logical result of the attempt to account for the data transformationally.

There is a very simple way to test the correctness of this solution. If it is correct and the unlike-subject constraint is transformational in nature, then the grammaticality of the resulting sentence will depend on whether or not the subject of the embedded sentence and the matrix subject are non-identical *at the stage of derivations at which the Equi-NP Deletion transformation applies.* If, on the other hand, we are dealing with a deep structure constraint, then it is the identity or non-identity of the two subjects before the application of any transformations that is relevant to the grammaticality or ungrammaticality of the resulting sentence. To decide between the two hypotheses, then, we must pick an example in which the embedded sentence no longer has the same subject when Equi-NP Deletion applies that it had in deep structure. One such example is:

(3)   I screamed to be allowed to shave myself.

The deep structure of (3) is something like [4]

(4)

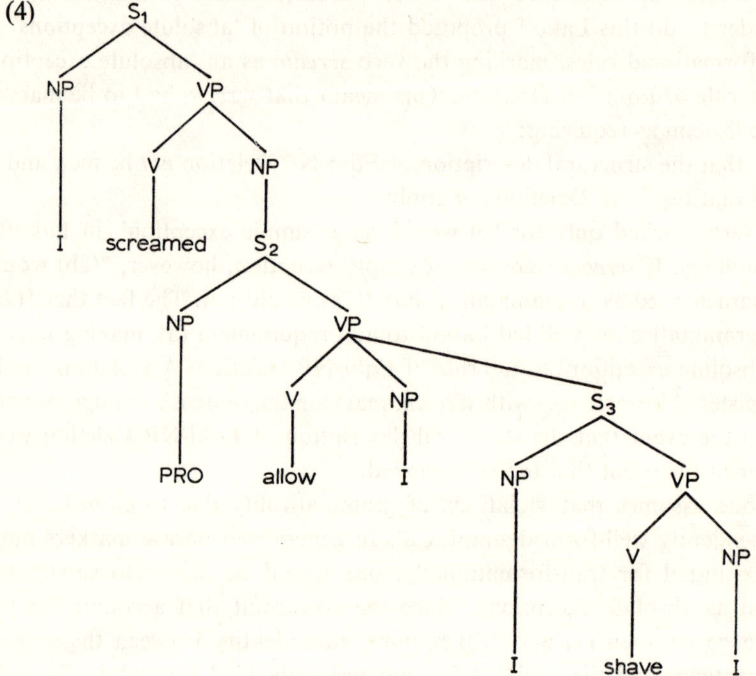

Reflexivization applies in S_3 on the first cycle, and on the second (S_2) cycle the subject of S_3 is deleted by Equi-NP Deletion and the passive transformation applies in S_2, so that *I* becomes the derived subject of S_2. After the second cycle, then, we have a derived structure like (5).

On the third (S_1) cycle, the (derived) subject of the sentence embedded beneath *scream* is in fact identical to the subject of *scream*. The structural description of Equi-NP Deletion is therefore met, and Equi-NP Deletion in fact applies. According to Lakoff's formalism, either of these two occurrences in the course of the derivation of a sentence with *scream* should cause the resulting sentence to be ungrammatical. But (3) is perfectly grammatical. We must conclude that this formalism is incorrect.

(5)

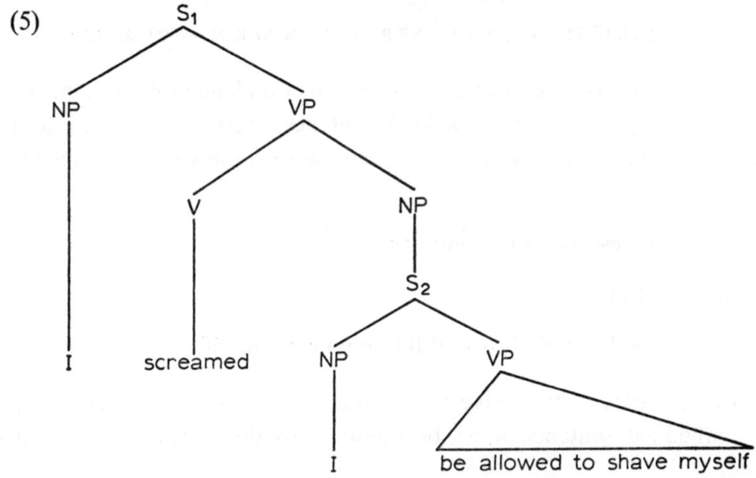

If, on the other hand, the unlike-subject constraint is a deep structure constraint, as proposed here, it does not matter whether or not the structural description of Equi-NP Deletion is met or the rule applies, as long as the subject of a sentence embedded beneath *scream* is not identical to the subject of *scream* in deep structure.[5] This condition is satisfied in (4), the structure underlying (3). The grammaticality of (3) is therefore evidence that the unlike-subject constraint is a deep structure constraint.[6]

It might be thought that a deep structure constraint like the unlike-subject constraint in English is essentially a 'null transformation' which would require that the subject of a sentence embedded beneath verbs like *scream* be non-identical to the subject of *scream*. But this constraint differs from a transformation not only in that it effects no change in phrase markers, but, more important, in that its 'structural description' must be met if a grammatical sentence is to result. For this reason, the unlike-subject constraint is not like an obligatory transformation, which applies *if* its structural description is met, but it is rather a well-formedness condition on the input to the transformational component. To call it a 'null transformation' is therefore to use the term 'transformation' in an entirely new way. Furthermore, if well-formedness conditions on trees like the unlike-subject constraint were transformations, they could be ordered with respect to other transformations. This would be an exceedingly powerful device, since such filters could be applied at any stage of derivations. However, it seems that we can constrain this filtering device and claim that they are to be applied only to phrase markers which constitute the *input* to the transformational component.[7] For this reason we call the device that is needed to state the unlike-subject constraint in English a deep structure constraint.

2. THE LIKE-SUBJECT CONSTRAINT IN SERBO-CROATIAN

Rosenbaum (1967) pointed out that in certain complement constructions in English the subject of the embedded sentence must be identical to the subject of the matrix sentence. This is the case with the verb *condescend*, so that

(6)   I condescended to commit myself.

is grammatical, but

(7)   *I condescended (for) Bill to commit himself.

is not. In examples of transitive verb phrase complementation, the subject of the embedded sentence must be identical to the object of the matrix sentence.

(8)   I forced Fred to commit himself.
(9)   *I forced Fred (for) Roxanne to commit herself.

Lakoff (1965), extending Chomsky's suggestion that ill-formed generalized phrase markers be characterized as such by the blocking of an obligatory transformation, proposed that the verbs *condescend* and *force* be marked in the lexicon as 'absolute exceptions' to the rule of Equi-NP Deletion, requiring that the structural description of Equi-NP Deletion be met and that the transformation actually apply. In this section we shall see that there are identity constraints of exactly the same kind in Serbo-Croatian. In Serbo-Croatian, however, the rule of Equi-NP Deletion is optional in the case of subject-subject identity, while in the case of object-subject identity Equi-NP Deletion does not apply at all.[8] There is therefore no obligatory transformation whose failure to apply (and to have its structural description met) we can use to characterize as ungrammatical those sentences in which the identity constraint is not met. We shall see that to characterize such sentences of Serbo-Croatian as ungrammatical it is necessary to introduce deep structure constraints into linguistic theory.

In Serbo-Croatian an embedded sentence may be introduced by the complementizer *da* in sentences like

(10)   a. Želim da idem.
            'I want that I go: I want to go.'
         b. Želim da ideš.
            'I want that you go: I want you to go.'
         c. Želim da Rastko ide.
            'I want that Rastko go: I want Rastko to go.'

There is also an infinitival complementizer. Serbo-Croatian does not have an 'accusative plus infinitive' construction, and the distribution of the infinitival complementizer is much more restricted than that of the *da* complementizer. Whereas *da* occurs in full paradigms like (10), we may use the infinitival complementizer only in the realization of the deep structure underlying (10a). Its use in sentences like (10b) and (10c) results in ungrammaticality:

(11)   a. Želim ići.
          'I want to go.'
      b. *Želim te ići.
          'I want you to go.'
      c. *Želim Rastka ići.
          'I want Rastko to go.'

In a paradigm in which the verb *željeti* 'want' has a second person singular subject we find:

(12)   a. *Želiš me ići.
          'You want me to go.'
      b. Želiš ići.
          'You want to go.'
      c. *Želiš Rastka ići.
          'You want Rastko to go.'

The appearance of the infinitival complementizer, then, is predictable: it can occur only in sentences in which the subject of the embedded sentence is identical to the subject of the matrix sentence. The subject of the embedded sentence must have been deleted in order for the infinitival complementizer to appear, for the embedded subject never shows up together with the infinitival complementizer.

We can capture these generalizations by positing an optional rule of Equi-NP Deletion in Serbo-Croatian which deletes the subject of an embedded sentence if it is identical to the subject of the matrix sentence. In just those cases in which the subject of the embedded sentence has been deleted by Equi-NP Deletion will the embedded sentence be reduced to an infinitive. It is in this way that the infinitival complementizer will be introduced. In this I am following Kiparsky and Kiparsky (1969), who have proposed a similar analysis for English.[9]

This analysis squares with the facts of verb agreement in Serbo-Croatian. In sentences with the *da* complementizer the embedded verb is inflected to agree with its subject. (10a) derives from a structure like[10]

(13)

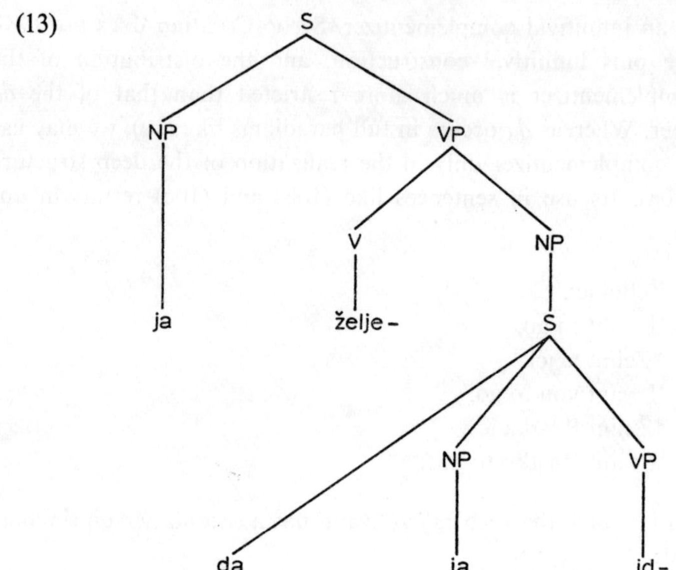

želje- and *id-* will now be inflected to agree with their subjects – *ja* in both cases. This will yield

(14)   Ja želim da ja idem.
        'I want that I go.'

Similarly, at this stage of derivations (10b) and (10c) are

(15)   a. Ja želim da ti ideš.
           'I want that you go.'
        b. Ja želim da Rastko ide.
           'I want that Rastko go.'

The embedded subjects *ja, ti,* and *Rastko* trigger verb agreement, so that the embedded verbs *idem, ideš,* and *ide* agree with their subjects *ja, ti,* and *Rastko* respectively. These inflected verb forms therefore testify to the presence of *ja, ti,* and *Rastko* in their respective sentences. At a later stage in derivations, all non-emphatic subject pronouns in Serbo-Croatian are deleted. At this point, (14), (15a), and (15b) are converted into (10a), (10b), and (10c) respectively. Now, we have postulated that in sentences with the *da* complementizer in surface structure Equi-NP Deletion has not taken place. The fact that in (10a) the embedded verb *idem* is inflected to agree with its subject *ja* supports this, since *ja* had to be present in order to trigger verb agreement. We hypothesized that the embedded infinitive results when the subject of the embedded sentence has been deleted by Equi-NP Deletion.

In these cases the embedded verb is the infinitive *ići*, which is invariant in form. The lack of agreement on the infinitive squares with our hypothesis, which entails that since the subject of the embedded sentence has been deleted by Equi-NP Deletion, there is no subject for it to agree with. The fact that the embedded verb agrees with its subject in embeddings with the *da* complementizer but not in embeddings with the infinitival complementizer thus squares with our hypothesis, according to which the embedded subject has been deleted in the latter case but not in the former.

Some additional support for this analysis comes from the so-called 'impersonal construction' *(bezlična konstrukcija)* of Serbo-Croatian. I will not justify the analysis of the impersonal construction here, but the essential point is that sentences in the impersonal construction have a [+Pro, +Human] subject in deep structure which I will refer to simply as 'Pro'; by this is meant not any pronoun, but rather the same entity that appears in surface structure as *on* in French and as *man* in German. In Serbo-Croatian, the underlying Pro subject is deleted in the course of the derivation, and the morpheme *se* is inserted into structures from which this underlying subject has been deleted.[11] This 'impersonal *se*' acts as a clitic pronoun in surface structure. As a result, a deep structure like

(16)

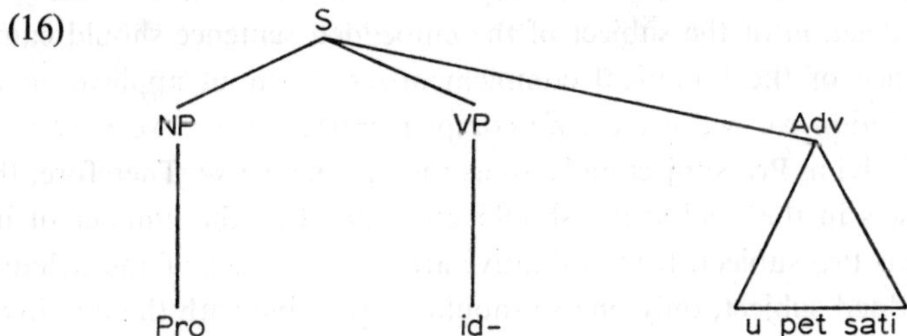

ends up as the sentence

(17)   Ide se u pet sati.
         go *se* at five o'clock
         'Pro is going at five o'clock; on va à cinq heures.'

If this sentence is embedded beneath a sentence in which *ja* ('I') is the subject of *želje-* ('want'), we get the sentence

(18)   Želim da se ide u pet sati.
         'I want that Pro go at five o'clock; je veux qu'on aille à cinq heures.'

The essential point is that sentences with the [+Pro, +Human] subject end up with the morpheme *se* in surface structure.

Now, the underlying Pro subject of the impersonal construction, like any
other subject noun phrase, is subject to the application of Equi-NP Deletion
if it is identical to the subject of the matrix sentence. Hence, if we have a
deep structure like

(19)

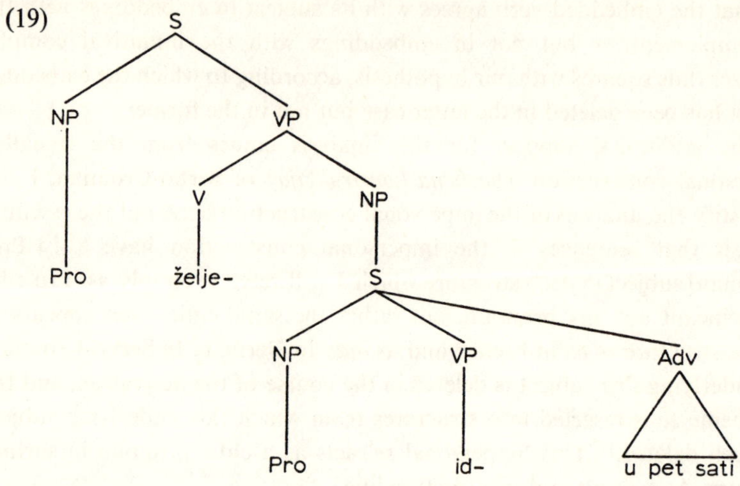

Equi-NP Deletion should be able to apply optionally. If our hypothesis is
correct, the deletion of the subject of the embedded sentence should cause
the appearance of the infinitival complementizer. Without application of
Equi-NP Deletion we will get the *da* complementizer. Now, we have seen
that the underlying Pro subject ends up as the morpheme *se*. Therefore, the
number of *se*'s in the final string should correspond to the number of instances of this Pro subject. If the infinitive arises as a result of the deletion
of the embedded subject, only one *se* should be possible with the infinitival
complementizer. This is indeed the case.

(20)   Želi se ići.
          'Pro wants to go; on veut aller.'
(21)   *Želi se ići se.

If the embedded subject has not been deleted, we should have two instances
of the Pro subject, hence two instances of *se* in the surface structure. This
too is the case.

(22)   Želi se da se ide.
          'Pro wants to go; on veut aller.'

(20) and (22) are synonymous, as are (10a) and (11a). The fact that we get
two *se*'s with the *da* complementizer but only one with the infinitival complementizer supports our hypothesis that the infinitive arises as a result of
the removal of the subject of the embedded sentence.

Having established that the infinitival complementizer results from the deletion of the subject of the embedded sentence, we are now in a position to consider the evidence that certain verbs in Serbo-Croatian manifest a *deep structure constraint* to the effect that the subject of a sentence embedded beneath them must be identical to their own subject. We will see that Lakoff's notion of 'absolute exception' to the rule of Equi-NP Deletion, requiring both that the structural description of Equi-NP Deletion be met and that the rule actually apply, cannot adequately account for the facts in Serbo-Croatian.

The verb *namjeravati* 'intend' exhibits the properties in question. We find sentences like

(23)   Namjeravam da idem.
          'I intend that I go; I intend to go.'

with the *da* complementizer and inflection of the verb *idem* to agree with its first person singular underlying subject *ja*. In addition there are grammatical sentences with the infinitival complementizer like

(24)   Namjeravam ići.
          'I intend to go.'

in which Equi-NP Deletion has deleted the subject of the embedded sentence, resulting in an infinitive. (23) and (24) are analogous to (10a) and (11a). What makes *namjeravati* different from *željeti* is the fact that whereas (10b) and (10c) with *željeti* are grammatical, the corresponding sentences with *namjeravati* are not.

(25)   a. *Namjeravam da ideš.
             'I intend that you go.'
          b. *Namjeravam da Rastko ide.
             'I intend that Rastko go.'

Sentences with *namjeravati* are grammatical just in case the subject of the embedded sentence is identical to the subject of *namjeravati*. The paradigm with a second person singular subject is therefore:

(26)   a. *Namjeravaš da idem.
             'You intend that I go.'
          b. Namjeravaš da ideš.
             'You intend to go.'
          c. *Namjeravaš da Rastko ide.
             'You intend that Rastko go.'

It is clear that the formalism of 'absolute exceptions to Equi-NP Deletion' cannot account for these facts. To use this formalism we would have to require that the structural description of Equi-NP Deletion be met and that the rule actually apply. But in (23) and (26b) Equi-NP Deletion has not applied. If it had, an infinitive would have resulted. The constraint on the subject embedded beneath verbs like *namjeravati*, then, is not statable as a constraint on the Equi-NP Deletion transformation.

It is now reasonable to ask whether it might be possible to devise some other way of stating this constraint as a transformational constraint. Two ways of doing this suggest themselves, and we shall examine them in turn.

The first way that comes to mind of stating the like-subject constraint in Serbo-Croatian by means of transformations would be to require that the structural description of the Equi-NP Deletion transformation be met, even though the rule need not actually apply. To do this would require a change in the theory of grammar, but it would be able to account for the facts of (23), (25), and (26). While this seems a highly dubious maneuver, rather than discuss its undesirability I will simply point out that there are other facts in Serbo-Croatian which it cannot handle. The Equi-NP Deletion transformation in Serbo-Croatian must be constrained so that the subject of the embedded sentence will be deleted only if it is identical to the *subject* of the higher sentence; it is never deleted upon identity to the *object* of the higher sentence.[12] As a result, Equi-NP Deletion does not apply with verbs like *prisiliti* 'force' and other verbs which occur in the type of structure that Rosenbaum calls "transitive verb phrase complementation". But the verbs which occur in these structures require that the subject of the embedded sentence be identical to the *object* of the matrix sentence. With a first person singular object in the matrix sentence, then, we find

(27)   a. Prisilio me je da idem.
         'He forced me that I go; he forced me to go.'
    b. *Prisilio me je da ideš.
         'He forced me that you go.'
    c. *Prisilio me je da ide.
         'He forced me that he go.'

while with a second person singular object in the matrix sentence we find

(28)   a. *Prisilio te je da idem.
         'He forced you that I go.'
    b. Prisilio te je da ideš.
         'He forced you that you go; he forced you to go.'
    c. *Prisilio te je da ide.
         'He forced you that he go.'

In each case the subject of the embedded sentence must be identical to the *object* of the matrix sentence. But there is no possibility of stating this constraint by requiring that the structural description of Equi-NP Deletion be met, for the structural description must specifically be constrained so as to exclude its application to these structures in order to avoid converting the structures underlying (27a) and (28b) into the ungrammatical

(29)   *Prisilio me je ići.
         'He forced me to go.'

and

(30)   *Prisilio te je ići.
         'He forced you to go.'

respectively. Hence it simply will not do to require that the structural description of Equi-NP Deletion be met.

A second possibility might be to look for some other transformation in terms of which to state the like-subject constraint as a transformational constraint. Such an attempt would be misguided, however, because in the case of verbs like *namjeravati* ('intend') the constraint holds between the subjects of two (vertically) adjacent sentences and Equi-NP Deletion is the only transformation that states an identity constraint between these two noun phrases. In the case of verbs like *prisiliti* ('force'), moreover, the constraint holds of a pair of noun phrases which is not looked at by any transformation in the grammar.

For these reasons, we cannot use the transformations of Serbo-Croatian to reject as ungrammatical any sentence in which the subject of a sentence embedded beneath *namjeravati* is not identical to the subject of *namjeravati*, or a sentence in which the subject of a sentence embedded beneath *prisiliti* is not identical to the object of *prisiliti*. We need *deep structure constraints* to do this. As was pointed out in connection with the unlike-subject constraint in English, these constraints differ from transformations not only in that they effect no change in phrase markers, but also in that their 'structural description' must be met if a grammatical sentence is to result. They are therefore different from obligatory transformations, which apply *if* their structural description is met. Furthermore, if they were transformations they could be ordered with respect to other transformations. This would give us an exceedingly powerful device. It seems that we can constrain these filtering devices and claim that they apply only to the input to the transformational component.

Brandeis University,
Dept. of English

BIBLIOGRAPHY

Chomsky, N. (1965), *Aspects of the Theory of Syntax*, The M.I.T. Press, Cambridge, Mass.
Kiparsky, P. and Kiparsky, C. (1969), 'Fact', in *Progress in Linguistics* (ed. by M. Bierwisch and K. Heidolph), Mouton and Co., The Hague.
Lakoff, G. (1965), *On the Nature of Syntactic Irregularity* (Report No. NSF-16, The Computation Laboratory of Harvard University).
Lees, R. and Klima, E. (1963), 'Rules for English Pronominalization', *Language* **39**, 17–28.
Perlmutter, D. (1970), *Deep and Surface Structure Constraints in Syntax*, Holt, Rinehart and Winston, Inc., New York.
Rosenbaum, P. (1967), *The Grammar of English Predicate Complement Constructions*, The M.I.T. Press, Cambridge, Mass.

REFERENCES

* This paper is a portion of Chapter I of my book *Deep and Surface Structure Constraints in Syntax* (Holt, Rinehart and Winston, Inc., New York, 1970). It was originally part of my doctoral dissertation (M.I.T., 1968). This work was supported in part by a graduate fellowship in linguistics from the American Council of Learned Societies and in part by the National Science Foundation through grant No. GS-2005 to Brandeis University. I am most deeply indebted to Paul Postal, who first suggested the idea of deep structure constraints, and to Wayles Browne, who first pointed out to me the difficulty of handling the facts of Serbo-Croatian by means of 'absolute exceptions,' and who has been more than helpful in the obtaining and interpretation of Serbo-Croatian data. I am also indebted to Noam Chomsky, Morris Halle, George Lakoff, and John Ross for many helpful comments and criticisms. Ljubivoje Aćimović, Velimir Kuftinec, and Rastko Maglić kindly consented to serve as informants for Serbo-Croatian. Responsibility for errors, of course, is mine alone.

[1] Unconstrained except for the constraints stated by means of contextual features.

[2] Chomsky (1965), 138–9.

[3] We will also consider cases where the object of certain verbs must be identical to the subject of the complement sentence. In the discussion which follows we refer to subject-subject constraints, but always with the understanding that object-subject constraints are included.

[4] All tree diagrams given here are highly oversimplified, ignoring any aspects of the tree which are not directly relevant to the points under discussion. For this reason such things as verb tense, auxiliary verbs, and complementizers are systematically ignored. The general framework is that of Chomsky (1965) and Rosenbaum (1967), but some changes have been made in the deep structures posited in those works. In particular, I am following Kiparsky and Kiparsky (1969) in omitting the *it* of noun phrase complements posited by Rosenbaum where they are not relevant to the points under discussion. Rosenbaum's 'pronoun replacement transformation' is sometimes referred to here as 'It-Replacement' and sometimes by the Kiparskys' term of 'Raising'. No justification is offered here either for the basic framework or for the modifications made in it, since nothing that is crucial to the argument developed here seems to hinge on these points.

[5] Another way to test this hypothesis would be to consider a deep structure like (i).
  Here the subject of the sentence embedded beneath *scream* is identical to the subject of *scream* in deep structure. If the unlike-subject constraint is indeed a deep structure constraint, then this sentence should be ungrammatical no matter what happens in the course of its derivation. Using the notion of 'absolute exception' to Equi-NP Deletion, on the other hand, the resulting sentence should be grammatical if the structural description of Equi-NP Deletion is not met and the rule does not apply. We can satisfy these two conditions in the following way. After Reflexivization has applied on the first (S_3) cycle and

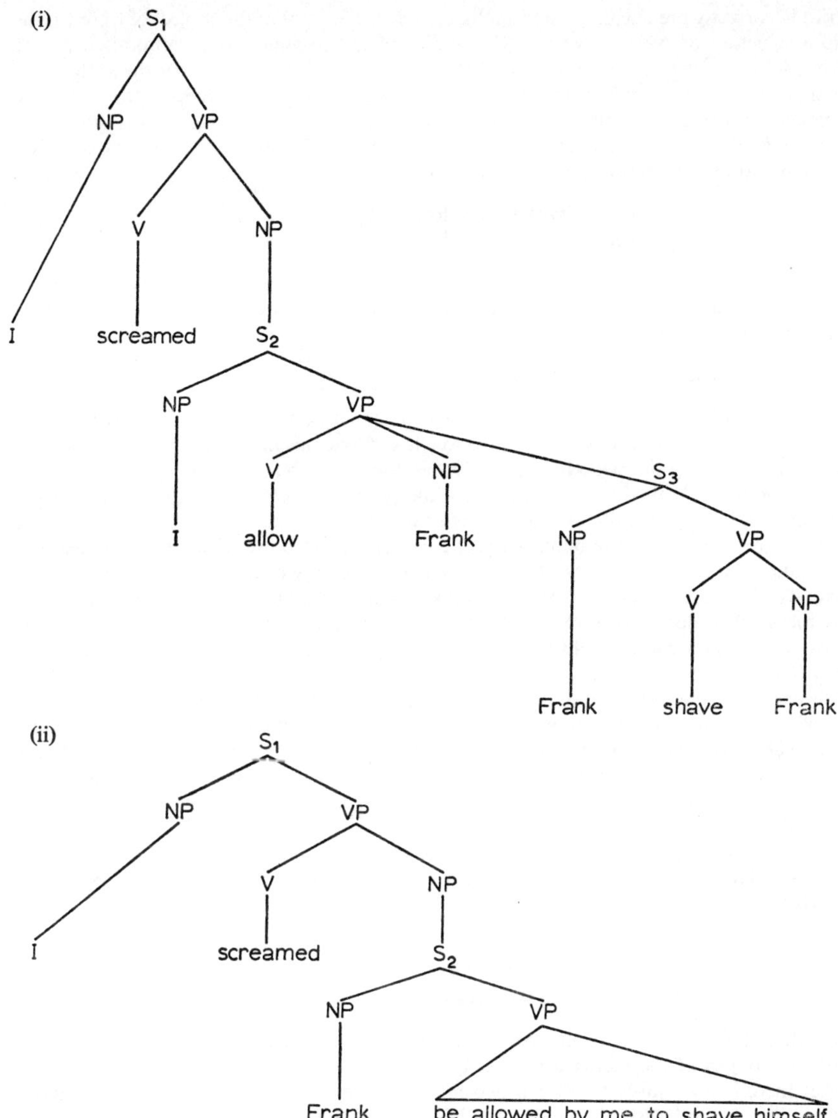

Equi-NP Deletion has deleted the subject *Frank* of S₃ on the second (S₂) cycle, let the passive transformation apply in S₂. This will yield a derived structure like (ii).

Now the (derived) subject of the sentence embedded beneath *scream* is non-identical to the subject of *scream*, so that on the third (S₁) cycle, the structural description of Equi-NP Deletion is not met and the rule can not and does not apply. According to Lakoff's formalism, the resulting sentence should be grammatical. But it is not:

(iii)   a. *I screamed for Frank to be allowed by me to shave himself.
           b. *I screamed for Frank to be allowed to shave himself by me.

If the unlike-subject constraint is a deep structure constraint, the ungrammaticality of

*(iii) is correctly predicted, since the subject of S_2 is identical to the subject of S_1 in (i), the deep structure of *(iii). However, the validity of this argument is compromised by the fact (pointed out to me by John Ross) that regardless of whether or not the verb in the matrix sentence is an unlike-subject verb, in sentences in which the subject of the embedded sentence is identical to the subject of the matrix sentence, the passive transformation cannot apply in the embedded sentence without producing an ungrammatical sentence. If we substitute *expect* for *scream* in (i) and *(iii), then, the result is equally ungrammatical.

(iv)   a. *I expected Frank to be allowed by me to shave himself.
            b. *I expected Frank to be allowed to shave himself by me.

[6] Note in passing that there are perfectly grammatical sentences with the verb *scream* in which the subject of the embedded sentence *is* identical to the subject of *scream* in deep structure. For example:

(v)   I screamed that I would go.

The unlike-subject constraint is operative in sentences like (1) and *(2), but not in (v). We are therefore faced with the question of how to characterize this difference. At first glance the difference between the two kinds of sentences appears to be due to the fact that (1) and *(2) have the infinitival complementizer, while (v) has the *that* complementizer. If this is the correct characterization of the difference between (1) and *(2), on the one hand, and (v), on the other, then the unlike-subject constraint must be restricted to sentences with the infinitival complementizer. If complementizers are present in deep structure, then this fact would not run counter to any claim that the unlike-subject constraint must be stated at the level of deep structure. A promising line of investigation for anyone desirous of disputing such a claim would be to show that sentences in which a complement is embedded beneath *scream* with the infinitival complementizer are themselves derived from 'deeper' underlying structures. This would open up the possibility that the unlike-subject constraint is in fact a constraint on the transformation which introduces the infinitival complementizer in a subset of *scream* sentences with complements. We will not follow up this line of investigation here. It suffices here to have pointed out that the unlike-subject constraint does not apply to every sentence with a verb having the phonological shape *scream*.

[7] For justification and discussion of surface structure constraints, another class of such filtering devices, applied to the *output* of the transformational component, see Perlmutter (1970).

[8] Some speakers accept sentences like

(vi)   Pomagao sam mu graditi kuću.
            'I helped him build the house.'

in which the subject of the embedded sentence has been deleted upon identity with the (dative) object of the matrix sentence. For this reason it is an oversimplification to say that there is no Equi-NP Deletion dependent on identity to the matrix object in Serbo-Croatian. Nonetheless, this statement is true of most cases of transitive verb phrase complementation in Serbo-Croatian, as it is of the cases to be examined here.

[9] The situation is somewhat more complicated in English, since in English there is also a rule of Raising or It-Replacement which takes an NP out of the embedded sentence and moves it up into the higher sentence. This rule converts structures like (vii), to structures like (viii), yielding sentences like

(ix)   I believe Frank to be a crackpot.

That the NP *Frank* is indeed moved up into the higher sentence can be seen from such examples as

(x)   I believe myself to be a crackpot.

(vii)

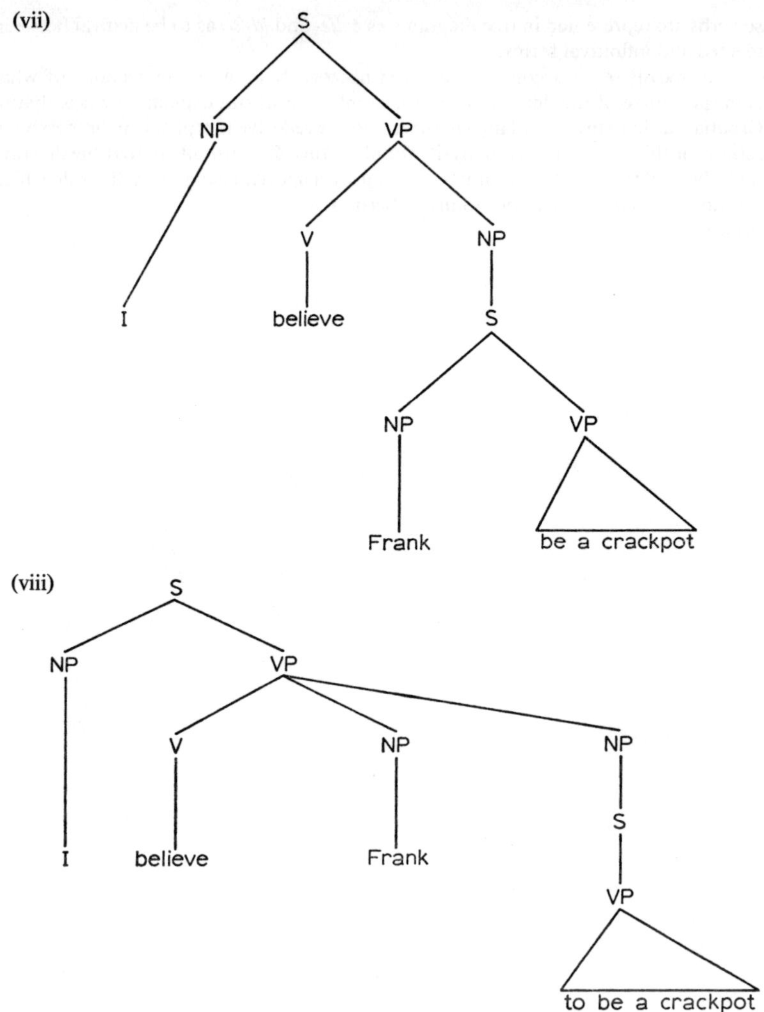

(viii)

where the reflexive pronoun *myself* could not have arisen if the subject *I* of the embedded sentence had not been moved up into the higher sentence, since, as Lees and Klima (1963) have shown, Reflexivization in English must be limited to a single simplex sentence in order to prevent such ungrammatical sentences as

(xi)   *I believe Bill to have insulted myself.

Now, the appearance of the infinitive in sentences like (ix) and (x) does not run counter to the Kiparskys' proposal, since the correct generalization is that the infinitive appears whenever the subject NP has been removed from the embedded sentence during the course of a derivation, regardless of whether the subject NP has been removed by a deletion rule, such as Equi-NP Deletion, or by some such rule as Raising. Nevertheless, there are occurrences of the infinitival complementizer in English which cannot be accounted for in this way. One such case is discussed in Perlmutter (1970).

[10] These verbs are represented in tree diagrams as *želje-* and *id-* so as to be neutral between their inflected and infinitival forms.

[11] This is not meant to be a complete or even necessarily an accurate account of what happens in the course of the derivation. For example, it does not explain why it is that in Serbo-Croatian, as in many other languages, we find the reflexive morpheme in 'impersonal' constructions of this sort. A better analysis would do this. It is also likely that the deletion of the underlying Pro subject is accomplished not by a special rule, but by the rule which deletes all non-emphatic subject pronouns in Serbo-Croatian.

[12] See note 8.

JÁNOS S. PETŐFI

ON THE STRUCTURAL ANALYSIS AND TYPOLOGY OF POETIC IMAGES

0. INTRODUCTION

The polyphonic character and unique semantic load of verbal works of art is of diverse origin. It stems

in part from the free (or specifically restricted) use of the verbal code,

in part from the superposition of the grammatical (syntactic, semantic) and sound-textural (euphonetic, rhythmic) structure components,

and finally from the text-structure interwoven by various repetitive returns.

As already suggested elsewhere[1] I feel that there are three particularly important phenomena if we consider the results of the past decades from the point of view of developing a method suitable for analyzing the text structure of verbal works of art. These are: the attempts to discover the structure layers of verbal works of art, the birth of the generative linguistic theory and the research into repetitive returns extended to more and more levels and layers of text structure.

A model capable of analyzing and describing text structure and able to unite all the aspects of the analysis of verbal works of art could only be created by utilizing and further developing the results of these fields of research.

This study aims at showing how the analysis of poetic images in such a model is an organic part of the complete text analysis that is closely related to all the other aspects and not an analysis of a single particular aspect. In my opinion this method of analysis is capable of answering all the linguistic questions that arise in connection with poetic images.

My study deals with the following themes:

1. Problems of poetic images in general.
2. The definition and analysis of poetic image, the typology of images.
3. The analysis of single images.
    3.1. The construction of the inherent structure of lexical units. (The semantic characterization of words that belong to the perception fields.)
    3.2. The syntactic-semantic characterization of the individual images. (The characterization of synaesthetical images.)
4. The analysis of the "image-field" of a work of art.

F. Kiefer (ed.), Studies in Syntax and Semantics, 187–230. © *D. Reidel, Dordrecht - Holland*

1. ON THE PROBLEMS OF POETIC IMAGES IN GENERAL

"There are countless studies on the images, symbols, synaesthesies of various authors, literary genres and epochs, but the theory, the definition and classification of imagery is still wanting. When I say 'wanting', I mean that there are at least fifty of it." – writes P. Guiraud in 1954.[2]

I do not intend to give even a sketchy survey of the special literature on imagery. All I would like to do is to quote one or two more significant books and discussions of the last decade in order to outline the present problems concerning poetic images.

1.1.   The monograph of Chr. Brooke-Rose[3] published in 1958 deals with the study of metaphors and divides the possible methods of doing this into two groups: i) analysis by a *philosophical approach* and ii) analysis by a *linguistic approach*.

The analysis of metaphors by *species-genus* (Aristotle), by the *animate-inanimate* confrontation (the successors of Aristotle, for example, Quintilian and Donatus), by the *domain of thought* (Cicero, some Rennaissance rhetoricians and H. Parkhurst, Ch. Bally, H. Wells and I. A. Richards of the 20th century for example) and finally by the *dominant trait* (the German school of today) belong in Brooke-Rose's opinion to the analysis by a *philosophical* approach.

The authoress herself deals with the field of *linguistic* approach and analyzes the role of verbal elements belonging to different grammatical categories in the formation of metaphors. (In it she refers among many others to such pioneers as G. Stern, H. Konrad, D. Davie etc.)

1.2.   In 1959 there was a discussion on the problems of images in the columns of *Voprosi Literaturi*.[4] Summing up the discussion V. Vinogradov classed the participants into three groups.

In Vinogradov's opinion those who regard the *image as the basic form of artistic language* belong to the first group. He draws the conclusion that the attitude of these researchers is primarily epistemological and psychological.

The second group defended the *'primacy' of the word* both in connection with the questions of image-like quality of a work of art and in the general field of problems itself that includes the problems related to the form – and thus to the important aspect of the content – of the work in question. Vinogradov criticizes this point of view by pointing out that the word is but one of the building stones of a work and it is related to the other elements of the composition. Its content structure is widened and increased by that additional artistic and expressive *plus* in meaning that emerges within the structure of the work. The task of the science dealing with the language of literature is exactly the discovery and explanation of these new strata of meaning. Without taking into consideration the complete structure of a verbal work of art, several of the types of literary images are neither definable nor understandable.

The third group admits the importance of research into the *image-system of verbal works* but holds the opinion that the methods of linguistics are inadequate to approach the problem as this is one of the problems of the analysis of creative processes. In Vinogradov's opinion there is some truth in this though the whole of it has many linguistic aspects that need further research.

Concerning the whole of the discussion he draws the conclusion that the participants paid little or no attention to such basic problems as the structural variations and various types of literary images or the functions of similar images in different genres. According to the general opinion stylistics is not yet in the position to solve the basic problems of the language of literature.

1.3.   Stephen Ullmann, in a study[5] published in 1961, differentiates the "image" as a "figure of speech" and the "image" as a "mental representation". He deals exclusively with the former and analyzes the problems of typology in the first place.

The "figures of speech" are classed into two large groups depending whether they come into being through similarity or contiguity. The metaphor and the simile are classed into the first metonimy and all the others are classed into the second group.

In Ullmann's opinion the distinction between simile and metaphor as explicit and implicit images is of fundamental importance.

He also differentiates between single and complex images. The single images may be described in purely grammatical terms. The situation is more complicated if two images arise simultaneously and develop in parallel or joined to each other. The development itself may be static or dynamic. It is static if the development of its various aspects stays within the framework of the single image, and dynamic if it takes place in a "chain-reaction" of the single images in the same theme.

When classifying on the basis of structure Ullmann employs I. A. Richard's categories (*tenor*: what we talk about, *vehicle*: what we say and to what the tenor is compared to, *ground*: the common characteristics of both).

Accordingly he maintains that the images may be classified on the basis of the tenor, of the vehicle or of the ground. In his opinion the case when a sphere of experience is expressed consistently and systematically by the terms of another sphere within a single work of art deserves special attention.

Finally, taking into consideration the role that an image may play the author deduces the following functions: symbolization, motivation, implicit evaluation, expression of philosophical ideas and personal aspirations, the possibility to express certain experiences, etc.

1.4. The discussion that took place in Bochum not long ago on the semantic analysis of images was interesting as well as instructive. The text of the discussion was published in the first issue of *Poetica* 1968.[6]

Professor Harald Weinrich, a member of the team who compiled the theses to start the discussion with, says in his thesis and replies to questions addressed to him:

It is not enough to consider the metaphor simply as a stylisticum or a figure of rhetorics. The metaphor is a semantic phenomenon. Its definition may only be given in the framework of a co-textual semantics.

Every word of the text needs a certain context, the actual context, however, may differ from it. The metaphor may be defined as a text element that appears in a counter-determining context (in a context into which the given text element does not fit).

Regarding the linguistic character of the metaphor in Weinrich's opinion the fact that the constituent elements belong to the same or different paradigms, is of decisive significance. (This problem was already presented in one of his studies published earlier.[7]) He drew the conclusion that in the formation of metaphors it is not the so-called 'tertium comparationis' but the "genus proximum" (der Oberbegriff) dominating the constituent elements of the metaphor, that is decisive. The metaphors, whose elements are near to each other in meaning, in other words, the ones that belong to the same "genus proximum", are the most effective. The synaesthesies whose elements have as their common "genus proximum" the "field of perception" serve as a good example.

The author emphasizes the significance of "co-textual semantics" "on the basis of the present state of research", to quote his words. He thinks that the traditional word 'semantics' could be widened in three directions: towards the text, towards the elements that possess meanings capable of forming words (monemes) and towards a so-called "word field" semantics.

We must select as our starting point the fact that the elements of a text mutually determine each other. In Weinrich's opinion the statement that syntax governs semantics, could be said universally valid. (If we compare the metaphor to non-metaphoric speech, the comparison could never take place "with an isolated normal word".) The counter-determining contexts of the individual elements could never be isolated sharply enough from the wider contexts that contain them. Accordingly, in a given case even a whole poem may be regarded as a single metaphor.

In connection with the "image-field" that is analogous with the "word field" the author remarks that this notion may only be used if we employ it for individual works of art and not for the entire language.

From these studies and discussions the outlines of three fundamental problems emerge: the definition of images, the methods of analysis and the problem of typology.

2. THE DEFINITION AND ANALYSIS OF IMAGES. THE TYPOLOGY OF IMAGES

Taking into consideration the conclusion of the above outlined studies and discussion about the definition of poetic image and the problems of their analysis and classification the following can be said.

2.1. *The Definition of 'Image'*

The meaning of the words 'image', 'figure of speech', 'trope', 'metaphor' (or rather the circle of notions expressed by these words) is not clearly defined, as appears also from the above studies. To avoid terminological misunderstandings let us introduce the notion of 'gramatically generated image' (GGI).

Figurative speech may manifest itself in various ways. In one of its forms of appearance it possesses grammatic characteristics, in others it does not. The introduced notion of image refers to the former. This is the type that may be approached by linguistic analysis.

I shall use the 'image' (=GGI) designation with the following meaning, according to a generalization of the definition of metaphor by Weinrich: I call an 'image' any part of a text made up of at least two syntactically related but semantically incompatible elements. In this definition both the expression 'syntactically related' and the expression 'semantically incompatible' need further explanation.

An analysis of 'syntactic relatedness' may be needed in three layers of the text.

The first of these is the layer of words. The rules of syntactic structure for derived and compound words must be contained in the so-called micro-syntax.

The next layer is the layer of text units or communication units as I call them. (The communication unit is about the same size as a sentence. I feel it necessary to introduce this term in part to make myself independent of the individual text segmentation given by various authors, and in part to ensure the superposition of the structures of various structure components –

grammatical, sound-textural.) To discover the syntactic structure of communication units – in my opinion – a generative transformational grammar is the most suitable as its semantic components may be constructed to allow the interpretation of the images as well.

To find the textual relationships of units larger than communication units a special compositional syntax must be elaborated. In this layer the structures of so-called "paragraphs" may be described purely in terms of grammar. To recognize the relationships among units greater than paragraphs the knowledge of the various fields of words, a thesaurus constructed to serve text analysis, is needed. The methods of analysis of these layers are still undeveloped.

There are two things needed to recognize "semantic incompatibility": an intensional semantic characterization of words (morphemes) that contains the characteristics necessary to discover the image-like quality that could be found by linguistic analysis, and a system of rules suitable to test the compatibility or incompatibility of the semantic characteristics (or set of characteristics).

However, both the correct syntactic conjunction and the semantic compatibility may only be meaningful when applied to a given model. The construction of such a model, on the other hand, may only be possible on the basis of the correct interpretation of the verbal code. I agree with J. Kristeva that the poetic language is *the* infinite verbal code and every "language" – the common language of every age, too – is a subset of this infinite code.[8] This subset, however, contains elements that are quite diverse in character. It is not possible to construct such a model that generates *all* the grammatically correct sentences of the common language *and nothing else* but those. Therefore for each model a list of the auxiliary or prohibited constructions and semantic interpretations must be given. Only the model and this list together may give the complete system of reference. (It is another question whether the found incompatibilities as the means of poetic expression, may be interpreted, and if so, how it could be done. I shall only concern myself with the methods of recognition.)

2.2. *The Analysis of Images*

When analyzing a verbal work of art in my opinion first of all a work-centered analysis is needed and progress should be made from this starting point towards the more general structures.

The work-centered analysis developed by me makes no distinction between the analysis of images and that of non-imagelike structure units.[9] The principal parts of the analysis of the grammatical component are the following:

segmentation (the identification of the communication units), the analysis of the communication units (finding and attaching the appropriate deep structures to the communication units, their semantic interpretation, syntactic and semantic characterization),

the recognition of the composition units that belong to different layers, their analysis and characterization.

The result of the first stage of the linguistic analyzing process is a characterization of the structure units of different complexity together with that of the images of different complexity that may be discovered in this phase. In part we obtain a description of the single images in themselves, in part the recognition of how the single images become constituent elements of the hierarchical structures of the work of art in each layer and level.

The second stage is the examination of the repetitive returns within the grammatical component. This analyzing process discovers the linguistic relationships between the images of the text structure and between the images and the non image-like units of the text structure within the linear patterning of the work.

This mesh of interrelations is further refined by projecting the sound-textural structure obtained in a similar manner over the grammatical structure. Thus we can establish what new relationships are produced by the sound-textural structure between those structure units that are not related on the basis of grammatical patterning, how the existing grammatical relationships are strengthened or weakened.

The examination of the grammatical and sound-textural component gives us the complete work-centered analysis of the particular structuring of the structure units, the analysis of its special unity of "content and form".

The text structure thus described is interpreted, later evaluated from the point of view of the secondary (poetical, esthetical, ideological) structures, as well as from that of the more general synchronous and diachronous structures (the life-work of the author, the contemporary works and history of the national and world literature) that include the work. The images characterized in the work-centered analysis thus obtain their additional characterization.

2.3. *The Typology of Images*

As a result of the analysis we may attach paradigmatic and syntagmatic characteristics to the images that form the basis of the formation of a non-predetermined typology.

Here I would especially like to emphasize the lack of predetermination. In the characterization of verbal works of art something similar must take place to the intensional characterization of phonemes in phonology.

The extensional form of typology (the classification of elements into certain categories of a given system of categories) can no longer be used with results either in the theory of images or in that of genres. There are very few elements that represent a pure type. The elements that are identical from the point of view of certain characteristics prove to be different regarding others. Therefore such characteristics must be found that possess those internal structures which make the sorting of the set under analysis (either works or set of images) possible according to any group of points of view determined at will.

According to the work-centered text analysis the characteristics of images are classed into the following classes:

general characteristics (resulting from the structure of the system of language):

SYNTACTIC CHARACTERISTICS:

those of complexity of structure elements that make up the image, and

the characteristics of the relationships that exist between the elements, i.e. the character of the "deep structure" of the part of the text that expresses the image;

SEMANTIC CHARACTERISTICS:

the semantic markers of the elements that make up the image,

the characteristics of the incompatibility of the elements, i.e. the semantic interpretation of that part of the text that expresses the image;

individual characteristics (resulting from the structure of the given work of art):

SYNTACTIC CHARACTERISTICS:

the text structure characteristics of the part of the text that expresses the image, i.e. the character of the "surface structure" of the image,

the character of the formal relationships between the image and the other image-like and non-image-like structure units (concerning both the deep and the surface structure);

SEMANTIC CHARACTERISTICS:

the function of the image in the hierarchical structure of the work,

the character of the semantic relationships between the image and the other image-like and non-image-like structure units of the work and determined by the grammatical component,

the character of the semantic relationships between the image and the other image-like and non-image-like structure units of the work and determined by the sound-textural component.

In addition to these characteristics other characteristics will be determined by further analysis. Let us call these additional characteristics.

Additional characteristics:

these are partly general, partly individual ones that have resulted from analyses conducted from the point of view of the secondary and the more comprehensive structures.

The number of the classes of these characteristics is finite, the number of the elements of each class may be extended freely, in other words this extension does not bring about changes in the system of characterization.

Such a set of features meets the requirements of typology mentioned above.

The clarification of theoretical problems here, as in any other field, is only one half of the solution of the problem. Having taken these *necessary* steps, to create the *sufficient* conditions of the solution an appropriate model must be built.

However, in the case of such an inconsistent system as a natural language this is far from easy. As in my experiments generally here I only wish to investigate but a single aspect of the basic problem (the analysis of works of art) more thoroughly. I hope that this experiment will also contribute to a satisfactory solution of the problem.

3. THE ANALYSIS OF SINGLE IMAGES

In an earlier study I dealt with the problems of the syntactic-semantic interpretation of verbal works of art in general. Consistently with my reasoning there and in this paper so far, in the course of the analysis I will make no distinction between the analysis of images and non-image-like structure units (the image-like quality will only become obvious during the analysis itself). It is only this method of analysis that makes the characterization of images, as organic parts of verbal works of art, possible; in other words their characterization should be such that it allows a comparison with non-image-like structure units according to any point of view at any time. Therefore, all that I have said about the syntactic analysis there, is also valid for images.

In the following – while further developing the analysis of the problems already raised in my above cited study – I will examine the problems of characterizing single images as far as synaesthetic images are concerned.

When analyzing single images the first task is the recognition of those general characteristics that arise from the system of the language. To be able to do this, first of all the elaboration of the system of semantic characteristics is needed.

3.1. *On the Construction of the Inherent Structure of Lexical Units*

Nowadays we hear more and more about the lexical component of generative grammar.

Here I do not wish to deal with the problem of the construction of the complete inherent structure of the lexical units. I would like to point out, however, some aspects of a relatively closed set of words, that must be taken into consideration when semantically characterizing words that belong to this set, if we want to find the incompatibilities formed by them.

The chosen set is the set of words that belong to various perception fields. In my opinion the fact, that all types of perception may be considered as a special type of communication, provides the framework for the semantic characterization of these words.

In these processes of communication the following constituents may be found:

	Addresser	Coding	Message	Decoding	Receiver
1.		emits light	light	sees the light	
2.	sy	emits a sound	sound	hears the sound	
	sg				
3.		emits a scent	scent	smells the scent	
4.				tastes the taste of sg	
5/1	sy	emits	heat	perceives heat	sy
5/2	sg			perceives the physical state of the surface of the shape of the temperature of something	(sg)
				perceives the weight of something	

To each word I feel it necessary to give as primary such characteristics that identify two things: what perception field does it belong to and what component of the communication does it refer to. (Incompatibilities, such as *blind light* or *mute song*, etc. may only be identified with the help of these.)

The primary characteristics are the following:

the marks of perception fields:		*the marks of communication:*	
sight	*si*	Addresser	*A*
hearing	*h*	coding	*c*

the sense of smell	*sm*	Message	*M*
the sense of taste	*ta*	decoding	*d*
sensing with		Receiver	*R*
receptors in			
the skin	*sk*		
temperature	*sk.t*		
physical state	*sk.ph*		
surface	*sk.s*		
pain	*sk.p*		
weight	*w*		

Apart from these we have associated the following elements of the characteristic classes with each word:

as syntactic markers:
N: noun,   *V*: verb,   *A*: adjective;
the additional markers of verbs: $+$*transitive*
$-$*transitive*;

the additional markers of verbs and nouns:

$+$*starting,* $+$*continuous,* $+$*completing,*
$+$*momentary,* $+$*repeated*;
as special semantic characteristics:
$+$*general*: to designate general notions of perception fields,

the counterpart of $+$*gen* is $+$*special* on the one hand, on the other hand it may be given as the following tree structure according to other points of consideration

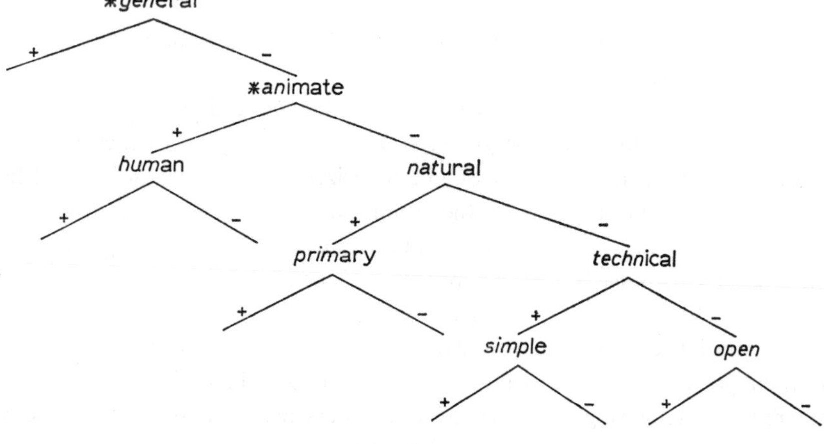

*−abstr*act: to designate all that is of "material reality",
*+grad*ient ⎫   to designate all kinds of opposing quality pairs
*−grad*ient ⎭:   wherever the presence of something (the positive
                pole of the scale) is contrasted with the lack of
                something (the negative pole of the scale), for
                example:
                +grad: light   warm   thick   solid
                −grad: dark   cold   thin   empty,

− intensive ⎫
0*intensive* ⎬: to designate the different grades,
+ intensive ⎭

− direct ⎫
0*direct* ⎬:
+ direct ⎭   to designate direct or indirect action,

in connection with sound perception:

*+ ver*bal
*− ver*bal
2 × *art*   :   with twofold articulation (spoken and sung)
1 × *art*   :   with single articulation (spoken only)
− art   :   without articulation,

to designate the condition of the addressers and receivers

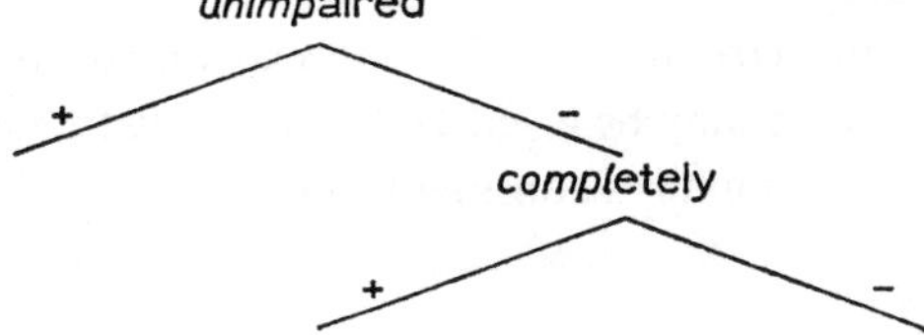

Any other characteristics are given in full (without abbreviation) every
time they occur.

Apart from these characteristics the contextual conditions of verbs and of
some adjectives must also be given. In the case of adjectives they refer to
the type of the word that may be characterized by the given adjective (the
type is determined primarily by the communicational component the adjective in question belongs to) while in the case of verbs they refer to the subject
and the object. In each case the context is given in parentheses, in the latter
case in the form: (*subject ___ object*).

The special semantic characteristics are not regarded as semantic markers
in their present form but as indicators of various points of view to be considered at a later stage. The semantic markers proper and their hierarchy

must be determined later by the characterization of the corresponding word classes related to the entire language (in other words, not to the perception field only).

When listing the examples I did not strive for completeness even with respect to the perception fields. I only aimed at outlining the classes to be created. To discover these I relied on approximately 1700 words, taken from The Defining Dictionary of Hungarian (A Magyar nyelv Értelmező Szótára) (the field of sight contains 600, the field of hearing 500, the field of taste and smell 50–50, and the field of perception by the skin contains 500 related words approximately).

When giving the final characterization, the role of word-formation must also be kept in mind. As it happens, the derived words refer to a component of the communication that is different from the one the basic word refers to. Of the elements that belong to the same paradigm class as far as the derivation of words is concerned, I have shown but one as a rule.

After all this let me now show the lexical classes of the individual perception fields.[10]

3.1.1. *Words that belong to the perception field of vision*

1. THE WORDS OF THE ADDRESSER

N si; A	+grad	+gen			source of light
		+nat	+prim		the sun
			−prim		the moon, the stars
		+an	−hum		luminous fishes, star-beetle
		−nat	−techn	+open	candle, torch, wick
				−open	lamp
			+techn		electricity, neon

2. THE WORDS OF THE MESSAGE I

(Here the words of the message precede the words of the coding because the words of the coding may refer to the message as well.)

N si; M	+grad	+gen			light, ray, ray of light
		+nat	+prim		sunlight, ray of the sun
			−prim		moonlight, ray of the moon, starlight, ray of a star
		−nat	−techn	+open	candle light, ...
				−open	lamp light,
			+techn	−	electric light, neon light
	−grad	+gen		−	darkness, dimness

3. THE WORDS OF CODING

```
V  +tr  +start   si; c  +grad   −dir (+hum___ −nat)    lights
        +compl                                          puts out
   −tr  +start                   +dir (−nat___)         lights
        +compl                                          goes out
                                     ( { A }    )
        +cont                        ( { M } — )        lights
                                     (          )
        +mom                         (−term___)         flashes
                                     ( [ +gen ]    )    vibrates,
        +rep                         ( [ −nat ] — )     glimmers
                                     ( { A }    )
   +tr  +cont                        ( { M } — )        lights up
                                     (          )
        +mom                         (−term___)         flashes
        +rep                                            flickers
        +cont            −grad   (−abstr___ −abstr)     shadows,
                                                        darkens
```

4. THE WORDS OF THE MESSAGE II

(In connection with the perception field of vision the words of *colour, form and shape vision* play an important role)

```
N    si; M  +colour  +gen   +grad   colour, shade of colour
A            +saturation    +grad   colourful, manycoloured
                            −grad   pastel
             +lightness     +grad   light
                            −grad   dark

N/A  si; M  +colourfulness          red, yellowish red, orange,
                                    yellow, yellowish green, green,
                                    blue turning green, violet
                                    coloured, pink, purple, white,
                                    gray, black, brown
                    +spec   X+colour,  X+coloured
                            X+(concrete colour)
```

In these relationships the members X must be endowed with an additional semantic characteristic that expresses a colour in order that the possible semantic incompatibility (e.g. *swan-red*) could be shown.

The various classes of the more frequently used X-members:

the body and its parts	bone, body, blood, flesh
human hair	blond, grey
animal	raven, beetle, canary, swan
plant	grass, flax, tobacco
fruit	orange, chestnut, walnut
flower	gilly flower, rose, hollyhock, violet

food	honey, coffee, milk, butter, whey
special material	brick, china, parchment
nature	water, sea, rainbow, sand,
metals	silver, gold, bronze, lead, steel
minerals	oil, coal
precious stones	opal, agate, emerald
fire	fire, ashes, smoke, soot

The connections of these first members to a specific colour is not always unambiguous. People say "oil-brown" and "oil-green" or "lead white" and "gray as lead" etc. At the same time one particular colour may have many different first members, like chalk-, frost-, milk-, wall-, swan-, silver-white.

A part of the words of *shape and form* vision are linked with the perception by the skin. (At the final characterization of these words this must be taken into consideration by all means.)

N	si/sk;	+shape	+gen	1 inherent dim	line
				2	open surface
				3	closed surface
					(=body)
			+spec	plant	clasper, tendril
				tree	crown, trunk, branch
				building	pillar, column, dome
				others	sheaf, bundle, heap
				partial	rim, milling, bump
		+line	+gen	1dim	straight line
			+spec		section of a line
			+gen	2dim	curve in a plan
			+spec		loop, wavy line
			+gen	3dim	curve in space
			+spec		spiral, helix
A	si/sk;	+line	(one)	+grad	long
				−grad	short
			(several)	−	parallel, intersecting
			+spec		entangled, winding
N		+surface	+gen	2dim	plane surface
			+spec		the various plane surface
			+gen	3dim	curved surface
			+spec		band, shell
			+partial		the right side, the back side (of a piece

				of cloth)
A		(one)	+grad	big, wide
			−grad	small, narrow
		(several)	−	parallel, intersecting
		+spec	2dim	round, oval, angular
			3dim	concave, convex
N	+body	+gen	3dim	solid body,
			+partial	the inside of various bodies
				the outside of various bodies
A		−	+grad	large, big
			−grad	small
	+layer		+grad	thick
			−grad	thin
	+density		+grad	solid
			−grad	hollow
	+spec	+an	+grad	fat
			−grad	thin
		+hum	−	lean, tall and slim, buxom

5. THE WORDS OF CODING II

V +tr +cont si;c +colour +grad ($\Box$__ −abstr) colours, paints
        −grad   makes it lose its colour, fades
        +spec   reddens, makes it yellow,…

($\Box$: a human being with some kind of a material, some colouring process)

   −tr   +grad (−abstr__)   is becoming coloured
        −grad   is losing its colour
        +spec   is reddening,…

The verbs related to the vision of shape and form could with all probability be also collected but I shall not go into this question here.

6. THE FOLLOWING WORDS REFER TO A SPECIAL COMPLETE COMMUNICATION PROCESS

V −tr +start   si; comm (nat) +grad   is dawning
    +compl   is growing dusk, night is falling
    +mom   is lightning

N	si; comm (nat)	+grad	+start	dawn, morning
			+cont	daylight
			+compl	twilight, night fall
		−grad	+cont	evening, night
		+grad	+mom	lightning
			+cont	
			+colour	rainbow

7. THE WORDS OF DECODING

V +tr +cont si; d +grad +dir ($\square$___ −abstr) looks, sees
 +mom   catches sight of
  ($\square$: all +animate with unimpaired eyes)
 +rep   is blinking
 +cont   (−abstr___) seems

$$\left(\begin{bmatrix} -\text{abstr} \\ +\text{spec} \end{bmatrix} -\right)$$ shines, glitters

8. THE WORDS OF THE RECEIVER

N	si; R	+grad	+gen			$\square$: all +animate with unimpaired eyes
A			+gen	−unimp	−compl ($\square$)	squint-eyed, cross-eyed
					+compl	blind
			+spec	−unimp	−compl	colourblind
			+gen		(−abstr)	sensitive to light, transparent, light absorbing, light reflecting

The words of vision used in connection with the arrangement in place and space also belong to the perception field of vision, on these I do not want to enlarge upon either.

3.1.2. *The Words that Belong to the Perception Field of Hearing*

1. THE WORDS OF THE ADDRESSER

N	h; A	+grad	+gen		source of sound
			+an		"all +animate that are capable of giving sound"
			+nat	−prim	plants
					fire, water, air,...
			−nat	−techn	objects
				+techn +simp	whistle, horn, bell
				−simp	radioset, taperecorder, record player, musical box
				+music	"all kinds of musical

```
                                            instruments"
                             +spec    a watch
A              +gen  -unimp -compl
                             (+an)    hoarse
                             +compl   mute
```

2. THE WORDS OF CODING

```
                                  (+hum __)
V +tr/-tr +cont h;c +grad +dir +ver 1×art 0int  speaks, says
                                           -int  whispers
                                           +int  shouts
                                         -unimp  stutters
                                             -   quarrels
                                    2×art 0int  sings,
                                        -art    wails
                                -ver 2×art      doing scales
                                    -art +int   is screaming
                                         -int   heaves, sighs
                                    +gladness   is laughing
                                    +pain       cries, sobs
                                         else   hawks
                                                sneezes
                                                pants, snores
       -tr          -grad +gen-    -      -     keeps quiet
       +tr          +grad -dir (+hum__+music) plucks
                                                the strings,
                                                blows, beats,
                                                plays the
                                                violin,...
                              (+hum__ +simp)   blows
                                                the whistle,
                                                blows
                                                the horn,...
                              (+hum__ -simp)   switches it on,
                                                winds it up,...
       -tr                    +dir (+mammal__)  grunts, howls,
                                                barks, mews,
                                                bleats,
                              (+bird__)         croaks, hoots,
                                                gaggles,
                                                cackles,
                              (+reptile__)      hisses,
```

	(+insect___)	buzzes, bums, chirrs
0dir	(+plant___)	rustles, whizzes,
	(+liquid___)	spouts, splashes
	(+earth___)	rumbles,
	(+air___)	is thundering
	(+wind___)	?
−dir	(+techn___)	the … sounds (the clock ticks)
	(−abstr___)	rattles
+tr		"makes noise'

3. THE WORDS OF THE MESSAGE I

Most of the general type of nouns that refer to the message are formed
from the above verbs. These receive as characteristics the characteristics
of the corresponding verb.

Such nouns are:

> speach, sigh, song, music, the sound of piano or of violin, din,
> clatter, etc.

Special message characterizing nouns:

N	h; M	+grad	+dir	+ver	2 × art	poetic	song, choral work
					1 × art		sonnet, ode, elegy
			−dir	−ver	−	musical	fuge, symphony
		−grad	ǀ gen	−	−	−	silence

4. THE WORDS OF THE MESSAGE II

In connection with the perception field of hearing the words related
to the pitch, tone and intensity of a sound must be classified on their
own.

N	h; M	+pitch	+gen		interval, key
			+spec	+interval	second, tercet, …
					harmony, consonance, dissonance, …
					melody,
				+key	major and minor keys
		+tone	+gen		keynote, over-tone
			+an	+hum	a man's, a woman's, a child's voice
				−hum	"voices of animals"
			+techn		the sound of …

A   +intensity   +gen   +grad   resounding
                                          −grad   quiet

5. **WORDS REFERRING IN PART TO THE ADDRESSER AND IN PART TO THE MESSAGE**

V   +tr   +cont   h; A/M   +grad   +dir   can be heard
                +compl   goes down, becomes
                                                               quiet

6. **THE WORDS OF DECODING**

V   +tr   +cont   h; d   +grad   +dir   (□___)   listens to
                           □: all animates with unimpaired hearing

The intransitive pair of this verb means that "he does not say a word" i.e. does not communicate with vocal signs.

7. **THE WORDS OF THE RECEIVER**

N   h; R   +grad   +gen   "all animates with
                                           unimpaired hearing"

A   +unimp   +musical   has a good ear for music,
                                              has absolute hearing
                     −unimp   −compl   hard of hearing
                                  +compl   deaf

3.1.3. *Words that Belong to the Perception Field of Smelling*

1. **THE WORDS OF THE ADDRESSER**

N   sm; A   +grad   +gen   the source of smell
                      +nat   +prim   plants
                                          fruits
                                          spices
                                          minerals
                     −nat   −techn   foods, drinks
                                +techn   chemical products
                                              (parfumes and others)
                          else   products of decomposition

2. **THE WORDS OF CODING**

V   −tr   +cont   sm; c   +grad   +pleasant   (?___)   is fragrant
                                          0pleasant   smells
                                           −pleasant   stinks

3. **THE WORDS OF THE MESSAGE**

N   sm; M   +grad   +pleasant   scent
                                          0pleasant   smell
                                          −pleasant   stench

V   −tr   +cont   +gen   spreads

4. THE WORDS OF DECODING

    V +tr +cont sm;d +grad +gen ($\square$___ −abstr) smells, sniffs at

                               $\square$: all animates with unimpaired sense of smell

5. THE WORDS OF THE RECEIVER

    N   sm; R +grad +gen   "all animates with un-
                                                  impaired sense of smell"

The words that belong to the perception field of smelling are related in many cases to the words that belong to the perception field of taste.

3.1.4. *Words that Belong to the Perception Field of Tasting*

1. THE WORDS OF THE ADDRESSER

    N ta; A +grad +gen   the source of taste
                 +nat +prim   plants
                                fruits
                                spices
                                minerals
                                animal products
                                    (honey, milk,...)
                 −nat −techn   foods, drinks
                        +techn   chemical products (drugs)

2. THE WORDS OF THE MESSAGE

    N ta; M +grad +gen   taste
    A   +grad +gen   tasty
             −grad   tasteless
             −   +gen   sweet, salty, sour, bitter
                  +spec   acrid, hot
                          tender, fresh, rotten

Various "taste like X" compounds may stand as an adjective referring to the message, where X is the name of an "addresser"

3. THE WORDS OF DECODING

    V +tr ta; d +grad +gen ($\square$__) tastes
           $\square$: all animates with unimpaired sense of taste
                         +spec   tastes, swallows, sips,
                                        eats, drinks

4. THE WORDS OF THE RECEIVER

    N ta; R +grad +gen   "all animates with unimpaired sense
                                of taste"

3.1.5. *Words that Belong to the Field of Perception by the Skin*

The words that belong to the field of perception by the skin may be classified into various subclasses such as the perception of heat and temperature, of physical state, of surface and that of pain.

3.1.5.1. *The perception of heat and temperature.* In part it is accomplished
with the help of telereceptors (like the perception of light, sound and smell),
in part with the help of contact receptors (like the perception of taste).

1. THE WORDS OF THE ADDRESSER

N	sk.t	+gen				the source of "heat"
		+grad	+nat	+prim		sun
				−prim		lava
			−nat	−techn	+open	+int	stake
						0int	fire in the open
						−int	embers
					−open	−	stove
					+techn	+simp	−	radiator
		−grad	+nat	−prim	−	−	ice (snow, frost)
			−nat	+techn	−	−	refrigerator

The nouns given to the remains, by-products and elements of fire deserve
to be mentioned on their own.

the elements of fire	spark, flame
by-products of fire	smoke, soot
the remains of fire	cinder, ash.

2. THE WORDS OF CODING

V	−tr	+cont sk.t; c	+gen			emits "heat"
		+start	+grad	+dir	(+fire___)	catches fire
		+cont			+int	scorches
					0int	warms, burns
					−int	glimmers, smoulders
		+compl			−	goes out, dies down
		+cont	−grad	−	−	(+techn___)	cools
	+tr	+start	+grad	+dir	(+hum___ +fire)	lits
		+rep				strikes fire
		+compl				puts out
		+start			(+hum___ +techn)	switches on
		+compl				switches off

3. THE WORDS OF THE MESSAGE

N	sk.t; M	+gen	+grad	+int	heat
				0int	warm
			−grad		cold

The following words designate special cases referring to a full communicational process:

N   sk.t; comm (+nat)   +grad   +start   spring
                                +cont   summer
                                +compl   autumn
                        −grad   +cont   winter

4. THE WORDS OF DECODING

V   −tr sk.t; d +grad   +int   (+hum__)   sweats
                          0int   is hot
                  −grad   is cold
                  +grad   +int   (+flammable__)   gets baked,
                                                      burns
                                 (+freezable__)   gets frozen

5. THE WORDS OF THE RECEIVER

N   sk.t; R   +an   all animates able to perceive heat
              −abstr   all substances that may be put on fire, warmed,
                         cooled, or frozen

3.1.5.2. *The perception of physical state.* The perception of physical state, of surface and pain is done with contact receptors. The components of the communication of these are not distinguished from each other.

A   sk.ph +gen   +grad   solid
                              0grad   liquid, fluid
                              −grad   gas
A   sk.ph (+solid)   +grad   hard
                              −grad   soft
                (+liquid)   +grad   thick
                              −grad   thin, dilute
                (+gas)   +grad   saturated
                              −grad   of low
                                                  concentration
N   +solid   +gen   −
                +liquid   liquid, water
                              +spec   solution
                +gas   +gen   gas, steam

V +tr +cont +gen sk.ph $\left(+\text{hum}\underline{\quad} \begin{bmatrix} +\text{liquid} \\ -\text{grad} \end{bmatrix} \right)$ pours

                           $\left(+\text{hum}\underline{\quad} \begin{bmatrix} +\text{liquid} \\ +\text{grad} \end{bmatrix} \right)$ smears

                           $\left(+\text{hum}\underline{\quad} \begin{bmatrix} +\text{solid} \\ -\text{grad} \end{bmatrix} \right)$ kneads, pugs

   −tr $\left(\begin{bmatrix} +\text{solid} \\ +\text{grad} \end{bmatrix}\underline{\quad} \right)$ breaks

$$\left(\begin{bmatrix} +\text{solid} \\ -\text{grad} \end{bmatrix} \text{---} \right)$$ softens

           (+liquid__)   gushes, pours, trickles

+change of physical state

           (+solid__)   hardens, softens, melts

           (+liquid__)   evaporates, sets

           (+gas__)   condensed

N sk.ph +spec (+nat) +solid   ice

           +liquid   rain, shower, dew

           +gas   wind, breeze

           else   frost, rime, snow

3.1.5.3. *The perception of surface.*

A sk.s +gen +plane-like +grad rough, cloddy, wavy

            −grad smooth

       −plane-like +grad sharp

                pointed

            −grad dull

       +solid   +grad wet

                adhesive, sticky, filthy

            −grad dry "clean"

3.1.5.4. *The perception of pain.*

V +tr sk.p (+rough__ +an)   grazes, bruises

      (+sharp__ +an)   splits, cuts

      (+pointed__ +an)   stabs

      (+dull__ +an)   presses, smashes

$$\left(\begin{bmatrix} -\text{liquid} \\ +\text{gas} \end{bmatrix} \text{---} +\text{an} \right)$$ burns

V +tr sk.p (+an__ +an)   pinches, bites, claws

      (+hum__ +an)   suffocates, beats, whips

The verbs expressing interactions between objects could be systematized in analogy to the perception of pain.

3.1.6. *The Perception of Weight*

The perception of weight belongs to the class of the so-called cynesthetic perceptions.

A w; +gen +grad weighty, heavy

      −grad weightless, light

I am not concerned here with the words the perception of equilibrium and time.

3.2. *The Syntactico-Semantic Characterization of Single Images*

I would like to illustrate the method of analysis on synaesthetic images chosen from the work of the Hungarian poet Árpád Tóth.[11]

The analysis will be carried out in two parts. First the corresponding deep structure will be set up for each image. This will be followed by the determination of the characteristics of the single images. (Here I shall aim at showing the general syntactic and semantic characteristics only.)

3.2.1. *On the Discovery of the Corresponding Deep Structure*

The chosen examples are of various complexity: image-like compound words: 24, 42; sytagms: 5, 17, 24, 25, 30, 36, 38, 39, 40, 43 (of these the images (17) and (25) contain the nominalized form of embedded sentences), sentences: all the others. The image (3) is made up of three communication units according to my terminology: *the dawn was blind, dirty, grey.* (The section 4 of this study deals with images extended over several sentences.)

The grouping of images will be carried out in the following sequence: sight, hearing, sense of taste, sense of smell, perception by the skin. Within each group I shall analyze the images formed by the words that belong to the perception field in question or to the next in line but different perception field. The examples No. 45 to 50 show images formed by words that belong to more than two perception fields at the same time.

The deep structures are rendered in a somewhat simplified form with labelled parentheses. The abbreviations and notational conventions are the following:

Syntactic conventions:
S: sentences, NP: nominal phrase, VP: verbal phrase, N: noun, V: verb, A: adjective acting as predicate, D: modifier of the noun (Da: adjective, Dg: noun in the genitive case, DnomP: modifier brought about by the nominalization of a sentence), M: modifier of the verb, AdvP: adverbial phrase; n_1, n_2... the components of compound words;

the lower indices differentiate the components of the same character from each other; upper indices indicate hierarchical relationships (subordinations);

the lexical units are joined to the appropriate symbols by colons; those lexical units which are lexically not represented in the examples are put in quotation marks.

Special semantic conventions:
Under each lexical unit there is the name of the appropriate perception field

and the name of the corresponding communication component in the following format:

$$\begin{bmatrix} \text{the name of the} \\ \text{perception field;} \end{bmatrix} : \begin{bmatrix} \text{the name of the} \\ \text{communication component} \end{bmatrix}$$

These are followed by those special semantic characteristics that are listed above.

In certain cases I have added some characteristics that follow organically from these to make the incompatibilities even more obvious. (An example for such characteristics: if something is a *message* then it is certainly $-$*animate*.) These rewriting rules must belong to the redundancy rules characterizing lexical units.

The question marks to be made use of in certain places will mean that the words in question belong somehow to an "outer circle" of the communication or perception field.

After all what has been said so far let us turn to the examples. (The numbers in parentheses indicate the source of the image.[12])

Sight

1. *megvakult a fény* (46)
   S(NP(N:*the light*) VP(*went blind*))
       si; M   si; R
                                (+an)

2. *két sóvár égő szem végigragyogja vállad* (45)
   S(NP(DP(Da:*two* DaP(Da$_1$:*eager* Da$_2$:*burning*)) N:*eyes*)
                                     si; A   si; R
                                     or sk.t; A   (part
                                     (−an)   of +an)
       VP(V:*glitter along* NP(N:*your shoulder*)))
           si; A or M

3. *vak volt a hajnal, szennyes, szürke* (25)
   S(NP(N:*the dawn*) VP(V:*was* NP(A$_1$:*blind* A$_2$:*dirty* A$_3$:*grey*)))
       si; comm   si; R   si;   si; +colour
                                                  or sk.s

Sight – hearing

4. *alkony jajja nyög* (1?)
   S(NP(N:*cry* Dg:*of twilight*) VP(V:*groans*))
       h; M   si; comm   h; c
       (+an)   (−an)   (+an)

5. *vak zaj* (18)
   NP(Da:*blind* N:*noise*)

                si; R   h; M
                (+an)   (−abstr)

6. *hársak ezüst dala fájva zizzen* (27)
    S(NP(NP^2(Da:*silver* N:*song*) Dg:*of linden trees*)
                si; +colour h; M +plant
                    (+an
                    Addr)
        VP(M:*achingly* V:*rustles*))
            (+an)   h; c
                        +plant

7. *zendíti a harangok bronzát* (15)
    S(NP(N:*"he"*) VP(V:*sounds* NP(N:*the bronze* Dg:*of the bell*)))
                h; c   si; +colour   h; A
                (__ +techn)   +techn

8. *a színek víg pacsirtái zengtek* (25)
    S(NP(NP^2(Da:*gay* N:*larks*) Dg:*of the colours*) VP(V:*resounded*))
                h; A   si; +colour   h; c
                +dir   −dir
                (+an)   (+metal__)

Sight – tasting

9. *iszom a fényt* (30)
    S(NP(N:*"I"*) VP(V:*drink* NP(N:*the light*)))
                ta; d   si; M
                (__ +liquid)

10. *minden fénynél édesebb* (14)
    S(NP(N:*"it"*) VP(V:*is* NP(A:*sweeter*) **than**
                    ta; M
            than NP^2(Dx:*every* N:*light*))))
                    si; M

Sight – smelling

11. *bús éjszaka volt a háznak* (13)
    S(NP(N:*the house*) VP(V:*had* NP(Da:*sorrowfull* N:*night-odour*)))
                                (+an)   si; comm sm; M

12. *egy sovány akác részegen szítta be a drága napfényt* (25)
    S(NP(Dx:*a* Da:*thin* N:*acacia*)
                (+an)   +plant
        VP(M:*drunken* V:*inhausted* NP(Dx:*the* Da:*dear* N:*sunlight*)))
            sm;   sm; d   si; M
            (+hum)   (+an__ +gas)

Sight – perception by the skin

13. *jégkéreggé fagy a fákon a verőfény* (40)
    S(NP(N:*sunshine*) VP(V:*freezes* NP(*to* N:*crust-of-ice*)) AdvP
        si; **M**   sk.t; d   +part of   sk.t
         +grad   −grad   plant   −grad
      AdvP(*in* N:*the trees*))
        +plant

14. *lemálltak testemről az üde szinek* (1)
    S(NP(Dx:*the* Da:*fresh* N:*colours*) VP
              +unimp   si; +colour
      VP(V:*parted* NP(*from* N:*my body*)))
        −unimp   +part
       (−abstr__)   of +an

15. *árnyam az égi útra kentet elnézem merőn* (26)
    S(NP(N:"*I*") VP(M:*fixedly* V:*stare* NP(*at* N:*my shadow* DnomP
                        si; d   si; M
     DnomP(S NP(N:"*my shadow*") VP(V:*is smeard* NP
         si; M   sk.s
                      (+hum__ +liquid)
       NP(*on* N:*the sky-road*))))))
          +abstr −abstr

16. *a vén nap a hervadt kerteken pompás aranyszint fen szét* (38)
    S(NP(Dx:*the* Da:*old* N:*sun*) VP(V:*smears* NP(Da^2:*sumptuous* Da:
              si; A   sk.ph;
                    (+hum__ +liquid)
      Da:*golden*   N:*colour*)) AdvP(NP(*over* Da:*the* Da:
      si; +colour   si; +colour
      +spec   +gen
      Da:*faded* N:*gardens*)))
      ?

17. *arany sugárral ázó langy homok* (33)
    NP(Da:*lukewarm* N:*sand* DnomP
      sk.t;
    DnomP(S(NP(N:"*the sand*") VP(V:*soaks* NP
                    sk.ph;
                    (+liquid)
        NP(*with* Da:*golden*   N:*ray*))))
             si; +colour   si; M
             +spec   or sk.t; M

Hearing

18. *e síró szavak zengő és furcsa bilincsek* (3)
   S (NP(Dx:*the* Da:*weeping* N:*words*) VP(V:*are* NP
        h; A   h; M
        −ver   +ver
    NP(DaP(Da_1:*sounding* **and** Da_2:*strange*) N:*shackles:*))
        h; A or M   +metal

19. *csend csobog körülünk halk patak* (16)
   S(NP(N:*silence*) VP(V:*splashes*) AdvP(*around* N:*us*))
        h; M   h; c
        −grad   +grad
                     (+liquid__)
   S(NP(N:*"the silence"*) VP(V:*"is"* NP(Da:*low-voiced* N:*brook*)))
        h; M   h; A or M   h; A
        −grad   +grad   (+liquid)
                            −int

20. *vén kastély süket csendben borong* (23)
   S(NP(Da:*old* N:*castle*) VP(V:*broods*) AdvP
   AdvP(NP(*in* Dx:*a* Da:*deaf* N:*silence*)))
                h; R   h; M
                −unimp −grad
                +compl

21. *rekedt kürt hurrog* (29)
   S(NP(Da:*hoarse* N:*horn*) VP(V:*shouts*))
        h; A   h; A   h; c
        +an   +techn   −musical
        −unimp +musical
        −compl

22. *mondogat ajkam enyhe zenét* (39)
   S(NP(N:*my lips*) VP(V:*tell* NP(Da:*mild* N:*music*)))
        h; A   h; c   h; M
        (part   (+hum__)   −ver
        of +an)   +ver   2 × art
                  1 × art

23. *dadog a dal* (34)
   S(NP(N:*the song*) VP(V:*stammers*))
        h; M   h; c
        M of +an   (+hum__)
        2 × art   1 × art
                  −unimp

24. *csermelyhangu csízek* (11)
    NP(Da:*brooklet-voiced* N:*siskins*)
        h; A   h; M   h; A
        −prim   +gen   +an
        +liquid   +bird

Hearing – tasting

25. *litániák cukros hullámát untan szürcsölő egek* (9)
    NP(N:*skies* DnomP(S(NP(N:"*the skies*") VP(M:*ennoyedly* V:
        +abstr   +abstr   (+hum)
        V:*sip* NP(NP² (Da:*sugared* N:*waves*) Dg:*of litanies*))))
        ta; d   ta; M   ?   h; M
        (+hum− +liquid)   2×art
                                                        +poetic

26. *az emberek zsivaja édes zenévé fátylasult* (7)
    S(NP(N:*noise* Dg:*of people*) VP(V:*veiles* NP
        h; M   h; A   ?
        +an   +hum
        −ver
        −art
    NP(*into* Da:*sweet* N:*music*)))
            ta; M   h; M
                       −ver
                       +musical

27. *az ajkak édesebb zengését formálják a jajnak* (24)
    S(NP(*lips*) VP(V:*form* NP(NP²(Dx: a Da:*sweeter* N:*sounding*) Dg
        h; A   ?   ta; M   h; M
        (part)   +musical
    Dg:*of a cry*)))
    h; M
    M of +an
    −art

Hearing – smelling

28. *a tubarózsák túlvilági illata énekelt* (31)
    S(NP(NP²(Da·*afterlife* N:*scent*) Dg:*of the tuberoses*) V(*sang*))
            +abstr   sm; M   sm; A   h; c
                      +gen   +prim   +ver
                                                  2×art

29. *valami kancatej-szagú dal lelkem ős pusztáiból följön* (19)
    S(NP(Dx:*some* Da:*mare's milk-smelled* N:*song*) VP(V:*rises*) AdvP

$$sm; M \quad h; M \qquad ?$$
$$+gen \quad 2 \times art$$

AdvP(Np(NP^2(*from* Dx:*the* Da:*ancient* N:*prairies*) Dg:
$$-abstr$$

Dg:*of my soul*)))
$$+abstr$$

30. *néma illat* (17)

NP(Da:*mute*   N:*scent*)

h; A	sm; M
(+an)	+gen
−unimp	+grad
+compl	

Hearing – perception by the skin

31. *dúdolni kezd titokban a venyigetűz* (6)

S(NP(N:*the vine-shoot-fire*) VP(M:*in secret* V:*croons*))

sk.t; A	?	h; c
−techn		(+hum__)
(−an)		

32. *lágy nyári dalt dalol* (2)

S(NP(N:*"somebody"*) VP(V:*sings* NP(Dx:*a* Da$_1$:*soft* Da$_2$:

	h; c	sk.ph;
	(+an__)	+solid
	2 × art	−grad

Da$_2$:*summer* N:*song*)))

sk.t; comm	h; M
+grad	M of +an
+cont	2 × art

33. *szúró zaj sír a légben* (44)

S(NP(Da:*piercing* N:*noise*) VP(V:*weeps*) AdvP(NP(*in* N:*the air*)))

sk.p;	h; M	h; c
+pointed	+gen	−ver
	+grad	−art
		(+hum__)

34. *nehéz hang érdesíti a futamot* (21)

S(NP(Da:*heavy* N:*voice*) VP(V:*roughs* NP(N:*the roulade*)))

w;	h; M	sk.s;	h; M
+grad	+grad	+plane	−ver
			2 × art

35. *ketyegésében rekedt tompa dal van* (8)

S(NP(Da$_1$:*hoarse* Da$_2$:*blunt* N:*song*) VP(V:*is*) AdvP

```
        h; A          sk.s;      h; M
        (+hum)        −plane     M of +an
        −unimp        −grad      +musical
                                 2 × art
    AdvP(in N:its ticking))
            h; M
            +spec
            (clack)
```

36. *pelyhes csend* (42)
```
    NP( Da:fluffy N:silence )
        sk.s;      h; M
        +spec      −grad
        (+bird)
```

37. *izzék a dal duhajjá* (41)
```
    S( NP(N:the song) VP(V:should glow NP(to N:debauchee)) )
        h; M              sk.t; c
        M of +an          +grad
                          +int
```

Tasting − perception by the skin

38. *a vad vágy édes szennyei* (43)
```
    NP( NP²(Da:sweet N:dirts) DgP(of Dx:the Da:wild N:desire) )
            ta; M     ?                                  +abstr
```

39. *keserű zimankó* (4)
```
    NP( Da:bitter N:cold )
        ta; M     sk.t; M
                  −grad
```

40. *fanyar parázs és keserű korom* (43)
```
    NP( Da:acrid N:embers) and NP( Da:bitter N:soot)
        ta; M     sk.t; A          ta; M     sk.t;
     or sm; M     +grad         or si; +colour
                  +element                 −grad
                  of fire                  +element of fire
```

Smelling

41. *illatjuk omlik mint a vér* (28)
```
    S( NP(N:their scent) VP(V:crumbles like NP(N:the blood)) )
        sm; M           (+solid__)           sk.ph;
        +grad           ?                    +liquid
                                             +part of +an
```

42. *omlanak a nyári illatlavinák* (22)

S(NP(Da:*summer* N:*odour*+*avalanches*) VP(V:*crumble*))
   sk.t; comm sm; M   sk.t;   (+solid___)
   +grad   −grad   ?
   +nat   +solid
                    +nat

Perception by skin

43. *a nyúlós állott és nehéz lég* (36)
   NP(Dx:*the* DaP(Da$_1$:*viscid* Da$_2$:*stale* **and** Da$_3$:*heavy*) N:*air*)
           sk.ph;   w;   sk.ph;
           +solid   +grad   +gas
           −grad

44. *poharak alján tompa tűz* (32)
   S(NP(Da:*blunt*   N:*fire*) VP(V:*is*) AdvP
      sk.s   sk.t
      +pointed +grad
      −grad
   AdvP(*in* N:*the bottom* Dg:*of glasses*))

45. *tavaszban, amikor a hősugár se karmol* (37)
   AdvP(NP(N:*in springtime* **when** S
         sk.t; comm
         +grad
         +start
    S(NP(N:*the heat-ray*) VP(M:*not even* V:*crobbles*)))
      sk.t; M   sk.p;
      +grad   (+an___ +an)

Images belonging to more than two perception fields

46. *a sötétség lebomlik a fák törzsén nesztelen* (20)
   S(NP(N:*the darkness*) VP(M:*noiselessly* V:*slips down*) AdvP
      si; M   h; ?   ?
      −grad   −grad
   AdvP(NP(*on* N:*the trunk* Dg:*of the trees*)))

47. *torkomból hurrák skárlát szökőkútja bugyogna* (46)
   S(NP(NP^2(Da:*crimson*   N:*fountains*) Dg:*of hoorays*) VP
         si; +colour ?   h; M
         +spec   +liquid   +grad
                 +spec   +ver
                         +int
   VP (V:*would bubble*) AdvP(NP(*from* N:*my throat*))
     ?   h; A

$$(+\text{liquid}\underline{\quad}) \qquad\qquad +\text{part of} +\text{an}$$

48. *az orgona csövén ömölve zuhog a sötét zene* (35)

S(NP(Da:*dark* N:*music*) VP(M:*pouringly* V:*showers*) AdvP

    si; M   h; M   ?   ?

    −grad   −ver   (+liquid) (+liquid__)

          +musical +int   +int

AdvP(NP(*in* N:*the tube* Dg:*of the organ*)))

        ?   h; A

                  +techn

                  +music

49. *csöndem éjén milyen jajok égnek* (10)

S(NP(Dx:*what* N:*cries*) VP(V:*burn*) AdvP(NP(*in* N:*the night* Dg

    h; M   sk.t; c   si; comm

    M of +an +grad   −grad

    −art   0int

Dg:*of my silence*)))

  h; M

  −grad

50. *nézésed mint a tiszta méz csordul alá* (5)

S(NP(N:*your looking*) VP(V:*spills down **like***

  si; d   ?

  (+an)   +liquid

like NP(Da:*pure* N:*honey*)))

    ?   +solid

        −grad

3.2.2. *On the Determination of the Characteristics of Single Images*

In determining the semantic incompatibilities I shall follow the method of semantic interpretation propounded by J. A. Fodor, J. J. Katz and U. Weinreich.[13]

The first task is the determination of those "pairs of elements" whose sets of semantic characteristics are to be compared. These pairs of elements are the following:

component of compound words;

nouns and their determinants (article, attribute, possessive attribute,...);

the heads of the subjective and predicative phrases of a sentence;

the head of the predicative phrase and the head of the phrase of comparison;

the modifier and the head of the predicative phrase;

the modifier of the predicative phrase and the head of the subjective phrase;

the head of the predicative phrase and its compulsory governments.

Special attention must be given to the question of how and in what manner the free complements – the various adverbial phrases – should be compared to each other and to other parts of the sentence.

The characterizations to be given are far from being complete – as this would need a full semantic characterization of all the lexical units of the images. I believe, however, that they will suffice to illustrate what I am after.

The method of characterization and the notational conventions applied are as follows:

The above listed pairs of elements are taken one by one and the incompatibilities are written down in the following form.

The role of the element in question within the hierarchy of the sentence is given by categories separated by full stops; the head of the subject phrase of a sentence is, for example, rendered as S. NP.N;

following the categories that designate incompatible lexical elements, those elements of the set of semantic characteristics that are incompatibles, are given after colons;

$\neq$ shows the fact of incompatibility;

$n\neq$ following the end parenthesis of an incompatibility characteristic is meant to show the degree of incompatibility of the element in question and $n\neq_k$ identifies which of these is given by the characteristics in question;

apart from the incompatibilities there may be compatibilities between the indirectly interrelated elements of the structure unit that contains the incompatibilities, these are also given, and the sign of compatibility is $=$;

following the identifier of the analyzed image (such as the serial number, for example) all the elements, that contain incompatibilities are listed; these are separated by $+$ signs and the class of the incompatible characteristics of each of them is given, such as: perception, communicational, ontological, etc.

Thus the format of the characteristics is the following (the numbers refer to the serial numbers of the sample images in Section 3.2.1.):

10. – S.VP.NP(perception)

    10. – S.VP.NP(A:ta$\neq$*than* .NP^2.N:si)

 5. – NP(perception; communication); $2\neq$

    5. – NP(Da:si$\neq$N:h); $2\neq_1$

    5. – NP(Da:R$\neq$N:M); $2\neq_2$

49. – S(perception) $+$AdvP.NP(perception)

    49. – S(NP.N:h$\neq$VP.V:sk.t)

    49. – AdvP.NP(Dg:h$\neq$N:si)

42. – S.NP.N(perception; physical state); $2\neq$ $+$S.NP(grad)$+$S(phys. st)

    42. – S.NP.N(n$_1$:sm$\neq$n$_2$:sk.t); $2\neq_1$

42. – $S.NP.N(n_1:+gas \neq n_2:+solid)$; $2 \neq_2$
42. – $S.NP(Da:sk.t.+grad \neq N.n_2:sk.t.-grad)$
42. – $S(NP.N:-solid \neq VP.V:+solid)$
 6. – $NP^2(perception) + NP(communication) + S(ontological)$; $2 \neq$; $1 =$
 6. – $NP^2(Da:si \neq N:h)$
 6. – $NP(Dg:plant \neq NP^2.N:M$ of $+an)$
 6. – $S(NP.NP^2.N:+abstr \neq VP.V:+plant)$; $2 \neq_1$
 6. – $S(NP.NP^2.N:+abstr \neq VP.M.+an \neq VP.V:+plant)$; $2 \neq_2$
 6. – $S(NP.Dg:+plant = VP.V:+plant)$; $1 =$

This enables us to give the individual images such intensional characterization that allows for a typology that is not determined beforehand.

4. THE LINGUISTIC ANALYSIS OF THE "IMAGE FIELD" OF A WORK

The "individual" characteristics of each image are determined by the text
analysis of the complete work that contains the image.

In order to elaborate the methods of the analysis of grammatical structure
it is essential to extend the sentence-centered grammar into a text grammar.

It is evident that a grammar of texts must be made up of co-textual-
syntactic, co-textual-semantic and co-textual-phonological components in
analogy of the sentence-centered grammar. – Only within these frames could
the requirements of Weinrich to create a text-semantics be satisfied. – A
detailed elaboration of all components necessitates the solution of some
rather complicated problems. This will be, with all probability, one of the
most important tasks of linguistic research in the next decades.

Owing to the lack of a co-textual grammar we are not yet in the position
to give a full text analysis of the poems shown below. We could, however,
make an attempt to discover the relationships between their synaesthetic
images. (The poems are written by the Hungarian poet Árpád Tóth.)

1. *Köszönöm hegedűd...*

(1)   Köszönöm hegedűd hangjait, zenész,
(2)   Barnák és búsak vannak köztük,
        Mint őszi lomb, mint rozsdás venyigék,
(3)   És simák, édesek és hűvösek,
        Mint női testek a fürdő után.
(4)   És könnyedek és fölényesek,
        Mint a táncosok őrjitő mozdulatai,
        Mint egy szőke főhercegnő mosolya,
        Amelyről diákkoromban egy hétig álmodtam,
(5)   S feketék, mint a szénbányász köhögése,

Amely miatt diákkoromban egy hétig nem aludtam.

(6)   Most már higgadt vagyok...

Thanks for your violin's...

(1)   Thanks for your violin's sounds, musician,
(2)   Brown and sad they are,
      Like autumn leaves, like rosty vine-shoots,
(3)   And smooth, sweet and cool,
      Like the bodies of women after bath,
(4)   And light and sure,
      Like maddening movements of dancers,
      Like the smile of a blond princess,
      I dreamt of as a student for a week,
(5)   And black like the cough of the miner,
      That kept me awake as a student for a week.

(6)   Now I am calm and wise...

If we disregard the communication unit (6) the whole poem is a complex synaesthetic image. The sound sensations are referred to by the nominal predicates which belong to other sensation fields and which are made complete by the addition of a simile pointing to details or by summing up.

Let us rewrite the poem into the form that expresses the structure more clearly.

(1)   Thanks for your violin's sound, musician.

Among the sounds there are

(2)   *brown* and *sad* ones,
        like autumn leaves, like rosty vine shoots,
(3)   and *smooth, sweet* and *cool* ones,
        like the bodies of women after bath,
(4)   and *light* and *sure* ones,
        like maddening movement of dancers,
        like the smile of a blond princess,
          I dreamt of as a student for a week,
(5)   and *black* ones,
        like the cough of the miner
          that kept me awake as a student for a week.

The enumeration of the predicates starts by naming a visual sensation, a spiritual quality, then a sensation of surface, followed by a taste. Later a return is made to the visual sensation by naming another spiritual quality.

The names of the two spiritual qualities divides the six predicates symmetrically:

brown/sad/smooth, sweet, cool, light/sure/black ones.

The distribution of the predicates into communication units is, however, asymmetrical:

brown/sad/smooth, sweet, cool/light, sure/black ones.

Apart from the asymmetrical distribution, the surface structure of the communication units shows the relationships of the predicates and the comparers in various ways.

Each of the two predicates of the communication units (2) and (4) forms a single unit that is related to the two comparers which in turn may be regarded as a single unit (a and b) — (as A, as B). On the other hand, in this relationship the hidden possibility of the correspondence of a as A, b as B as the decomposition of the structure (a and b) — (as A, as B), plays an important role.

Apart from this, the structure of the comparers in the communication units (2), (3) and (4) gradually become more and more complicated in their form as well. In the communication unit (5) – unlike all the others – the number of both the predicates and that of comparers is reduced to *one*. At the same time, the communication units (4) and (5) are joined together by the identical syntactic structure of the comparers extended by the relative clause and the semantic proximity of the relative clauses.

These comparers color the semantic interrelation of sound sensation and non-sonic sensation differently in every case.

In the first case the predicate *sad* personifies both the comparer and the compared. In the second the passive human being appears (*bodies of women*), in the next case the human "motion" (*maddening movements of dancers, the smile of the blond princess*) and, finally, in the last case the human "voice" (*the cough of the miner*). It is interesting to note the position of the adjectives within these structures with possessive attributes.

In the last communication unit, in order to complete the interrelationship network of the elements that belong to different perception fields, sound sensations are compared to sound sensations: *the sound of the violin is as black as the cough of the miner*. In this communication unit the *violin-sound – cough* opposition stands also against the *black – miner* association. In its relationship to the other communication units *coalminer* is contrasted with *blond princess*, *cough* with *smile*, *being awake* with *dream*.

The incompatibility of the words that belong to different perception fields, felt throughout the poem, form a series of concrete images elicited in the memory by the personifying similes.

2. *Orgona*

K_1 K_{11} (1)   Bár holtra metszé kertész görbe kése,
                          Még édesíti a fanyar szobát,
              (1′)   S a hűs homályon úgy remeg tovább
                          Illatja, mint halk húrok reszketése.

K_{12} (2)   Ám olykor egy-egy függöny rezge rése
                          A lila fürtön arany fényt dob át,
              (3)   S felgyújtja, mint egy nagy, kevély opált,
                          Melynek szikrázva szédít színverése.

K_2 (4)   Ó, én szerelmem, kit sok ferde kés
                          Már halni vágott: bú és szenvedés,
                          Ó, édes emlék, te is így jelensz meg:

              (5)   Olykor: sóhajtó illat, hűs zene,
              (6)   Olykor: tágranyílt opál szeme
                          Egy-egy felfénylő, drága, ritka percnek…

Lilac

K_1 K_{11} (1)   Though cut dead by the bent knife of the gardener
                          The acrid room is sweetened still by it
              (1′)   In cool shadow, keeps trembling on
                          The scent, like trembling muted cords.

K_{12} (2)   At times some curtain's rippling rift
                          Throws golden light across the lilac branch,
              (3)   It is lit like a huge and haughty opal,
                          Whose whilring colours spin me sparkling.

K_2 (4)   Oh, my love, whom many slanting blade
                          Already cut to die: sorrow and suffering,
                          Oh, sweet memory you, too, appear thus:

              (5)   At times: sighing scent, cool music,
              (6)   At times: wide-open opal eyes
                          Of rare, precious minutes shining forth.

The sonnet is a single simile in which various perception fields are blended. The six communication units are organized into composition units and make up the whole work itself in part by the syntactic relationships (including the simile itself), and in part by paraphrase-type references.

The verbal structure of the sonnet is the following:

	octet		*sextet*
K_1:	Lilac	K_2:	my love
	cut dead	***thus***	cut to die

lilac branch	sweet memory
K_{11}: scent (music)	(5): scent (music)
K_{12}: light	(6): light

In addition to the obvious parallelism of the above structure I would like to draw the reader's attention to the correspondence of the elements in paraphrase-like relationships:

K_{11} (1) the acrid room is *sweet*ened K_2 (4) *sweet* memory you, too, appear thus:

(1') ***trembling on*** its *scent* (5) ***sighing*** *scent*
in the *cool* shadow *cool*
like *muted **trembling*** cords *music*

K_{12} (2) but ***at times***
it is lit like a *huge* (6) *wide*-open
haughty *opal* *opal* eye
whose whirling colours spin ***shining forth***
me sparkling of ***rare*** precious
moments

The composition unit K_{11} lends itself to two possible articulations. If the title is regarded as an organic part of the beginning of the poem, (1) and (1') are independent communication units. If treated as a separate phenomena, then the whole K_{11} forms a single communication unit whose subject is *scent* which indirectly refers to *lilac*. At the same time, the word *scent* is in a possession-possessor relationship with the *lilac branch* of the communication unit (2).

In the $K_{11} - (4) + (5)$ correspondence the parallelism is stronger, while in the $K_{12} - (6)$ correspondence it is weaker. To be able to show the correspondence in the case of individual words, internal characteristics are needed with the help of which the relationships of the words *sighs* – *trembles* (trembles on), *huge* – *wide* (wide open) may be grasped.

The images taken from the perception field return in both cases in a transformed form showing new characteristics (personification): *sighing, eye* (of the minute). This is the natural counterpart of the parallel *lilac branch – love*.

3. *Bús bérház-udvar ez...*

K_1 (1) Bús bérház-udvar ez, (2) magasba tolt
Négy fal között hideg rés, (3) vaksi, (4) holt,
(5) És fönt az ég is ócska, szürke folt.

K_2 (6) De most e messzi, négyszögű égen,
Mint szétfeszülő, kékszín szőnyegen,
Víg, lenge tánccal egy tündér megyen.

(7) És felragyog, amerre lép, az ég,
(8) Szikrás örvénnyé háborul a lég,
(9) S március édes jószagával ég.

(10) Már a tetőt is felgyujtotta, (11) lám,
Kék szikra izzik a hideg palán,
(12) S bíbor téglák a tűzfal oldalán.

(13) Egy felső ablak, mint arany edény,
Mint egy fény-tepsi, fordul tengelyén,
(14) S csúszós lapjáról lecsurog a fény.

(15) Rá felragyog az udvar-mélyi kő, –
(16) Vagy tán a táncos, drága, légi nő
Lábáról hullt le az arany cipő?...

This is a sad Apartmenthouse-courtyard

K₁ (1) This is a sad Apartmenthouse-courtyard, (2) pushed up high
(2) Cold gap surrounded by four Walls, (3) blind, (4) dead,
(3) And the sky above is trashy grey patch.

K₂ (6) But now on this distant rectangular sky,
Like on a stretching blue carpet
A fairy goes with happy light dance.

(7) In her steps the sky brightens
(8) Air is whirled to sparky whirl pool
(9) And it burns with the sweet good scent of March.

(10) The roof is on fire, too, (11) look,
Blue spark burns on the cold slate
(12) And purple bricks on the side of the partition wall.

(13) An upper window, like a gold vessel,
Like a frying pan of light, turns on its hinge,
(14) And on its slippery plane trickles down the light.

(15) To it shines up the stone of the deep yard, –
(16) Or perhaps the dancing precious airy woman
Let the golden shoe drop from her foot?...

The first composition unit of the poem is a static image drawn with the help of purely nominal predicates. The dynamic change is given by (K₂):

K₁: This is a sad apartmenthouse-courtyard
And the sky above is trashy grey patch

But

K₂: But now on this distant rectangular sky

A fairy goes with happy light dance
In her steps the sky brightens
To it shines up the stone of the deep yard.

While classifying the words according to the perception fields they belong to, I did not deal with the words and characteristics of place and spatial arrangement. These play an important role in the compositional structure of this poem.

The representation is set off with the image of *a sad apartmenthouse court-yard* and returns to *the stone of the deep yard*. The words that depict the arrangement *yard – sky – yard* are listed below:

(2)   four walls *pushed up high*
(5)   the *sky above*
(6)   on this *distant sky*
(7)   the *sky* brightens
(10)   the *roof* is on fire
(12)   purple bricks on the side of the *partition wall*
(13)   an *upper* window
(14)   on its slippery plane trickles *down* the light
(15)   to it shines *up* the stone of the *deep* yard.

The communication units that contain references to spatial arrangements are attached to others or bind others to themselves by various (mostly explicite grammatic) relationships.

The composition unit K_1, apart from other characteristics, differs from K_2 in its adjectives: *sad, cold, blind, dead, trashy, grey*.

K_2 is a paraphrase, represented by a series of sensual images, of the following statement: "it is becoming light and full of sunshine". The paraphrase is started and concluded with the image of "fairy". These two images are the two poles of "path of light":

(6)   on this distant rectangular sky
         a fairy goes with happy light dance
         (– (14) *trickles down the light* –)
(16)   or perhaps the dancing precious airy woman
         let the golden shoe drop from her foot?...

Both of the communication units (8) and (12) refer to the "fire"-like quality of light: (8) sparky whirlpool, (9) burns, (10) put on fire, (11) burns. This row of images are closed with the already quoted synaesthetic image of the perception field of vision and perception by the skin: *On the slippery plane of the window* (gold vessel, frying pan of light) *trickles down the light*.

The prefix *down* is the response to the inner quality "up" of the *pushed up high* element of the communication unit (2).

As a result of the "up" (2) – "above" (5–9) – "down" (10–14) context the verb *shines up* of the communication unit (15) carries not only the meaning "becoming shiny" like the verb *brightens* of the communication unit (7), but the meaning of being directed "upwards from down below".

Though in these rough analyses I have tried to point out the relationships between the various structure units of these poems I feel that these examples are insufficient to draw any general conclusions upon the structure of the "individual" characteristics. I believe, however, that the progressing research into text grammar will soon enable us to do so.

5. SUMMARY

As I have tried to express it in the title of my study, I did not wish to undertake more than examining the problems of poetic images in the light of the results of recent linguistic research.

Both in the characterization of the words that belong to the perception fields and in the determination of the general and individual characteristics of images there are many yet unsolved questions – as I have repeatedly pointed out. The method of analysis itself, however, is suitable, I strongly feel, to answer those questions that were raised in the studies and discussions described in the first chapter. I do not regard my work but as a first step taken in this direction.

Hungarian Academy of Sciences, Budapest

REFERENCES

[1] Petőfi, S. J., 'On the Comparative Structural Analysis of Different Types of "Works of Art"', *Social Science Information*, forthcoming (1969).

[2] Guiraud, P., *La stylistique*, Paris 1954, p. 118.

[3] Brooke-Rose, Chr., *A Grammar of Metaphor*, London 1958, p. 343.

[4] Vinogradov, V., 'K sporom o slove i obraze', *Voprosi Literaturi*, No. 5, 1960.

[5] Ullmann, St., 'L'image littéraire. Quelques questions de méthode', in *Langue et littérature*, Actes du VIIIe Congrès de la Fédération Internationale des Langues et Littératures Modernes, Paris 1961, pp. 41–59. (English version: 'The Nature of Imagery', in Ullmann, St.: *Language and Style*, Oxford 1964, pp. 174–201.)

[6] 'Die Metapher (Bochumer Discussion)', *Poetica* 2, 1 (1968) 100–130.

[7] Weinrich, H., 'Semantik der kühnen Metapher', *Deutsche Vierteljahrsschrift für Literaturwissenschaft und Geistesgeschichte* 37 (1963) 325–44.

[8] Kristeva, J., 'Pour une sémiologie des paragrammes', *Tel Quel* 29 (1967).

[9] Petőfi, S. J., 'On the Structural Linguistic Analysis of Poetic Works of Art', *Computational Linguistics*, Vol. VI, Budapest 1967, pp. 55–82. – 'Notes on the Semantic Interpre-

tation of Verbal Works of Art', *Computational Linguistics*, Vol. VII, Budapest 1968, pp. 91–123.

[10] The characteristics given are valid until another characteristic or the sign – appears in the column in question.

[11] Cf. Whitney, A. H., 'Synaesthesia in Twentieth-Century Hungarian Poetry', *The Slavonic and East-European Review* XXX (1951–52) 444–64.

[12] *Tóth Árpád összes versei*, Budapest 1962.

The titles of poems in which the analyzed synaesthetic images can be found:

1. A herceg (1908)	24. Költő könnye (1923)
2. Akár egy bús kamasz (1908)	25. Körúti hajnal (1923)
3. A rabról aki király volt (1911)	26. Légyott (1909)
4. Arany János ünnepére (1917)	27. Lomha gályán (1914)
5. A tympanon istennőjéhez (1919)	28. Május éjén a régi bor (1925)
6. A vén magyar hegy (1919)	29. Óda az ifju Caesárhoz (1916)
7. Az árnyból szőtt lélek (1919)	30. Ó, édes napsütés (1912)
8. Az órainga (1923)	31. Ó, én nem a halált (1924)
9. Az új isten (1919)	32. Október (1916)
10. Álarcosan (1926)	33. Ó, lankadó bűbájú (1913)
11. Áprilisi capriccio (1926)	34. Ó, napsugár (1923)
12. Boldog csönd (1913)	35. Ó, örök Isten (1915)
13. Bús éjszaka volt (1914)	36. Ó, tudsz e szállni (1916)
14. Elejtetted a napot (1926)	37. Örök tavaszban járnék (1917)
15. Elégia egy elesett ifju emlékére (1916)	38. Őszi alkonyat (1909)
16. Esti kertben (1913)	39. Próbálom, hátha (1921)
17. Ez a nap is (1926)	40. Régi dallamok (1907)
18. Éjféli eső (1913)	41. Rímes furcsa játék (1916)
19. Fénylő búzaföldek között (1925)	42. Rozskenyér (1924)
20. Hajnali szerenád (1912)	43. Száz év után (1926)
21. Hegyi beszédek felé (1923)	44. Szeptember (1917)
22. Illatlavinák alatt (1926)	45. Tárcámban egy kép (1912)
23. Kastély és temető (1915)	46. Téli verőfény (1912)

[13] Fodor, J. A. and Katz, J. J., 'The Structure of a Semantic Theory',' *Language* 39 (1963) 170–211. – Weinreich, U., 'Explorations in Semantic Theory', in *Trends in Linguistics*, Vol. III (ed. by Th. Sebeok), The Hague 1966, pp. 395–478.

PETR SGALL

L'ORDRE DES MOTS ET LA SÉMANTIQUE

1.1 Il y a au moins deux manières d'envisager le problème de l'ordre des mots; car il n'est pas précis de parler de l'ordre des *mots*, et il faut tout d'abord se demander quelles sont les unités dont on examine l'ordre, ou en d'autres termes, quelle classification de mots est à la base de l'étude donnée. Deux classifications sont plus ou moins usuelles.

Avec la première, on étudie l'ordre des unités syntaxiques de la phrase (des membres de la phrase, des syntagmes, des constituants, etc.). On peut trouver cette conception avant tout dans des travaux concernant les langues de l'Europe occidentale; Chomsky et les autres transformationalistes s'en servent, ainsi que la grammaire traditionnelle.

La seconde conception peut être illustrée de la manière suivante: si le locuteur veut parler, en russe, de l'arrivée du père, alors la variante non-marquée sera la phrase *Otec prišel*. Mais s'il s'agit du début du printemps, la variante non-marquée sera *Nastupila vesna*. (Pour pouvoir détacher les fonctions de l'ordre des mots de celles de l'intonation nous ne parlerons dans l'article présent que de phrases à intonation "normale".) Daneš (1967) et Worth (1964) ont montré clairement, que pour l'analyse de phénomènes de ce genre il n'est pas suffisant d'employer une classification comprenant les parties du discours et les membres de la phrase; il faut travailler avec des sous-classes de verbes (pour l'exemple donné, en russe *prijti* appartient à une sous-classe, *nastupit'* à une autre, dont la première contient des verbes succédant dans le cas non-marqué à leur sujet, ou premier actant, tandis que les verbes appartenant à la seconde sous-classe le précèdent). Une telle classification sera utile aussi pour des types de compléments adverbiaux, comme cela a été présenté par Firbas.

On peut voir que cette seconde conception nous amène à travailler, pour une description des phénomènes principaux de l'ordre des mots, non seulement avec la structure grammaticale de la phrase, mais aussi avec sa structure sémantique (si l'on emploie p.ex. la terminologie de Dokulil et Daneš 1958); car les sous-classes mentionnées ci-dessus ont de toute évidence un caractère sémantique. Il est clair aussi que cette conception est liée à l'articulation de la phrase en thème et propos, analysée, selon le point de vue de l'École de la linguistique structurale de Prague, par Mathesius (1929), Daneš (1964a, 1967, 1968), Firbas (1961, 1964a, 1964b, 1965, 1968) et d'autres. On peut considérer comme bien établi aujourd'hui la nécessité de rendre compte

F. Kiefer (ed.), Studies in Syntax and Semantics, 231–240. © *D. Reidel, Dordrecht - Holland*

de cet articulation dans chaque description complète du système d'une langue naturelle (v. p.ex. Staal 1967; Halliday 1967; aussi Uhlířová 1966). Il a été démontré qu'il ne s'agit pas seulement d'une articulation de la phrase elle-même, mais aussi des divers groupes syntagmatiques (le dernier article, analysant en détail certaines questions de cette hiérarchie, est celui de Svoboda, 1967); cette articulation de la phrase et de ses parties, de même que son articulation syntagmatique, est caractérisée par les qualités de récursivité.

La seconde conception est employée assez fréquemment dans l'analyse des langues slaves (pour le tchèque, v. Pala 1966, 1967), où l'ordre des mots est "libre". Cet ordre est libre du point de vue des parties du discours, ou des types de groupes syntagmatiques; autrement dit, il n'y a pas, dans ces langues, des règles strictes du point de vue de la première conception (ou, au moins, ces règles sont peu nombreuses). Cependant, il y a là des règles strictes du point de vue de la seconde conception; l'ordre des mots est lié directement à l'articulation en thème et propos, tandis qu'en anglais, français, etc. il est lié à cette articulation d'une manière indirecte seulement (v. plus bas).

1.2 Pendant ces dernières années, Isačenko (1966), et d'autres ont examiné la possibilité d'appliquer la première conception, en combinaison avec les notions de la grammaire transformationnelle, aux langues slaves, en déterminant un seul ordre des éléments de la structure profonde, dont on peut obtenir, en appliquant des règles transformationnelles, plusieurs variantes de l'ordre de surface. Il est possible aussi avec la première conception de rendre compte des rapports entre l'ordre des mots et l'articulation en thème et propos; on parle souvent de la "thématisation" (angl. *topicalization*) et on cherche à l'incorporer dans la grammaire transformationnelle (p.ex. Kiparsky 1965). Il faut distinguer plusieurs types de la thématisation – deux d'après Fillmore (1968), au moins trois d'après ce qui suit ici dans l'alinéa 3.1. Il y a cependant un obstacle plus profond: si les variantes de l'ordre des mots sont obtenues seulement avec l'application des règles transformationnelles, cela présuppose que toutes les variantes ont la même interprétation sémantique.

Considérant cette supposition comme douteuse, je voudrais poser tout d'abord l'autre question: Est-il possible – ou utile – d'appliquer la seconde conception à l'étude de l'anglais, du français et d'autres langues à ordre "fixe" (et non seulement à l'étude des langues à ordre "libre")? Avec cette seconde conception il y a certaines variantes où l'ordre des éléments est différent (p.ex. $NP-VP$, et aussi $VP-NP$; ou $V-NP$, aussi $NP-V$) déjà dans la représentation de la phrase au niveau de la structure profonde (ou, avec une autre terminologie, au niveau sémantique, cf. Sgall 1964).

En anglais, cette articulation est liée à l'ordre de surface par des règles de grammaire; on sait déjà depuis Mathesius qu'une des fonctions du passif anglais consiste à permettre l'ordre objet (profond) – verbe – acteur dans des cas où cet ordre correspond à l'ordre non-marqué thème – propos (v. aussi Svoboda 1968). Certainement, il y a là aussi d'autres moyens, qui représentent (réalisent) l'articulation en thème et propos, comme par exemple l'article; il y a aussi des cas où l'ordre de surface ne correspond pas à cette articulation (v. p. ex. Firbas, 1966). On peut trouver de tels cas non seulement en anglais, mais aussi en russe (Adamec, 1966). En tout cas, il y a un lien assez étroit entre l'ordre thème – propos et entre l'ordre de surface (sa variante non-marquée) même dans les langues à ordre "fixe".

2.1 Pour pouvoir analyser la seconde conception de l'ordre des mots, il est nécessaire de caractériser d'une manière plus systématique ladite articulation, car il y a beaucoup de lacunes dans la connaissance empirique que nous en avons, et d'incertitudes quant à sa place dans le système du langage. D'après quelques formulations (p.ex. celle de Daneš 1958, p. 127) on pourrait spécifier l'articulation en thème et propos à la base des différences, qui existent entre des phrases à ordre des mots différent (ou à intonations diverses), mais à structure grammaticale (et lexicale) identique.

En spécifiant l'articulation d'une telle manière, on doit reconnaître, qu'elle est, dans le cas général, décisive pour l'interprétation sémantique. Il est possible de citer des exemples ayant une différence du thème et du propos liée à la signification cognitive des phrases, sans aucune différence grammaticale ou lexicale:

(1)   *Each of these types of description is adequate for some language.*
        Chacun de ces types de description est adéquat pour quelque langue.
        Každyj iz etich tipov opisanija javljajetsja adekvatnym dlja nekotorogo jazyka.

(2)   *For some language each of these types of description is adequate.*
        Pour quelque langue chacun de ces types de description est adéquat.
        Dlja nekotorogo jazyka javljajetsja adekvatnym každyj iz etich tipov opisanija.

Certainement, cette différence de l'ordre peut être liée à la différence entre actif et passif, comme c'est le cas dans l'exemple discuté par Chomsky et d'autres:

(3)   *Everybody in this room knows at least two languages.*
(4)   *At least two languages are known by everybody in this room.*

Mais c'est seulement un cas spécifique, où l'articulation en thème et propos est liée directement à l'objet et l'acteur, et où il est alors nécessaire, en anglais, d'employer le passif pour permettre à l'objet de précéder le verbe (pour une analyse de tels cas, v. Sgall 1967, 1968).

2.2 Si on spécifie l'articulation de la phrase en thème et propos à la base du contexte (en employant, p.ex., dans la définition du thème des notions comme "connu du contexte précédant"), il faut exclure des cas comme nos exemples (1)–(2) du domaine de cette articulation, car une différence dans l'articulation ne peut pas, dans ce cas, être liée elle même à une différence dans l'interprétation sémantique. Deux énoncés différant seulement dans l'articulation en thème et propos seraient deux variantes combinatoires d'une seule phrase. Une telle attitude est adoptée par Savický (sous presse), qui voit dans l'ordre des mots dans des cas comme (1)–(2) un moyen d'expression de la quantification, et non de l'articulation de la phrase; il rappelle justement, que des exemples avec des noms propres, avec lesquels on opère souvent dans ce domaine, sont trop spécifiques.

Nous avons deux remarques à faire sur ce point:

(a) Il ne suffit pas de distinguer, s'il y a une quantification dans la phrase (ou sa partie) donnée, ou non; il faut distinguer tout d'abord divers types de quantification (ou de quantificateurs), et – leur ordre: on pourrait rendre (1) et (2) par exemple au moyen d'une formule comme

(5)   *Adeq* (*descr, lang*)

où *Adeq* est un prédicat binaire; mais cette formule devrait être précédée par deux quantificateurs correspondant aux deux variables présentes, dont l'ordre correspond (du point de vue sémantique) à l'ordre des mots (v. Sgall 1967). Une telle représentation du sens des phrases est simplifiée, mais elle peut montrer que la valeur distinctive de l'ordre des mots devrait être étudiée en rapport avec la valeur distinctive de l'ordre des quantificateurs dans le calcul des prédicats (où cette valeur est déduite de la langue naturelle).

(b) Il y a aussi d'autres exemples, où l'ordre des mots a une valeur sémantique, sans que la présence d'une quantification soit apparente: Si on dit, en russe, avec une intonation normale, *Kušajte za stolom* (*Mangez à table*) ou *Za stolom kušajte* (*A la table, mangez*), le sens n'est pas identique; de même avec *Kurite tabak* (*Fumez du tabac*) et *Tabak kurite* (*Le tabac, il faut le fumer*). On peut chercher ici une quantification implicite (mais on devrait l'associer au verbe, donc à une relation), ou une transformation dont la seconde variante de ces exemples est le résultat (en dérivant la phrase simple d'une structure profonde complexe du type "*Si vous…, il faut…*").

Les difficultés, qui sont liées à chacune de ces deux possibilités, peuvent nous aider à rappeler qu'il y en a encore une troisième, dont nous avons parlé dans l'alinéa 2.1.

Avec cette troisième possibilité[1], deux phrases dont l'unique différence consiste à avoir des différentes articulations doivent correspondre à deux structures profondes et à deux interprétations sémantiques différentes. Il s'agit ici d'une question empirique, et on peut contester cette nécessité, car dans beaucoup de cas la valeur cognitive de telles phrases est la même. Cependant, la valeur cognitive est un phénomène ontologique, qui doit être distingué de la valeur sémantique propre (élément linguistique). Si l'interprétation sémantique d'une phrase doit être suffisante pour déterminer une traduction acceptable de cette phrase dans une autre langue, il semble incontestable que son articulation aussi doit y être représentée, même dans les cas où elle n'est pas décisive pour la valeur cognitive.

2.3   La différence entre une proposition (le sens d'une phrase) et une formule du calcul des prédicats réside entre autre dans le fait que les parties de la formule sont au même niveau, tandis que dans la proposition il y a divers niveaux d'actualisation. Nous appelons ainsi – provisoirement – les niveaux ou degrés du rapport entre ce qui est énoncé par cette proposition même (A) et ce qui est contenu ici comme déjà connu (B). Fillmore (1969) parle des présuppositions, appartenant à (B) et données dans le dictionnaire, mais distinctes du sens propre des unités lexicales (le verbe anglais *accuse x of y* présuppose qu'on pense que *y* soit "mauvais" et son propre sens consiste à indiquer que *x* a causé *y*, tandis que la présupposition du verbe *criticize x for y* est identique au sens du verbe précédant, et son propre sens est identique à la présupposition de celui). On peut comparer ce rapport, qui appartient au dictionnaire, avec des rapports pareils entre le dictionnaire et la syntaxe, et dans la syntaxe elle-même (v. McCawley 1967; aussi Kiefer, sous presse): par exemple un group nominal désigne des propriétés dont le locuteur suppose qu'elles appartiennent aux entités conceptuelles contenues dans le discours. Pour d'autres attitudes concernant questions de ce domaine, v. Vachek 1955; Jelinek 1965, 1966.

En employant le terme de Fillmore pour tous ces niveaux, on pourrait dire, que les présuppositions sont spécifiées d'une part dans le dictionnaire, d'autre part par des règles de grammaire. Pour pouvoir déterminer, par quelles règles une telle spécification est donnée, il faut examiner le rapport entre les présuppositions et les relations syntaxiques (prédication–determination), én distinguant, (i) si la présupposition est spécifiée dans le dictionnaire ou par une règle de syntaxe, (ii) si une présupposition est niée ou non par la négation de la phrase concernée (v. McCawley 1967), (iii) si une proposition est présupposée (comme chez Fillmore 1969), ou seulement le fait que l'objet dénoté par un mot est déjà connu du contexte, etc. (ces présuppositions sont typiques aussi pour les conditions de l'emploi des pronoms anaphoriques,

v. Palek 1967; ce sont elles qui jouent un grand rôle dans la théorie de Daneš et de Firbas).

La diversité des niveaux d'actualisation est liée à la distinction entre "ce dont on parle" et "ce qu'on dit" en une proposition. Cette distinction se situe certainement à un niveau intuitif, mais on sait que dans diverses langues les verbes du groupe sémantique de "dire quelque chose sur quelque chose", "penser quelque chose de quelqu'un" etc. distinguent assez strictement ces deux parties de l'énoncé. McCawley, dans son article cité, examine des phrases comme

(6)   *John says that he didn't kiss the girl who he kissed.*

(7)   *John admits that he kissed the girl who he kissed.*

et il montre qu'il y a là une ambiguïté intéressante: p.ex. la phrase (6) peut être comprise soit comme une assertion que John renie un fait connu, soit comme une affirmation qu'il énonce une contradiction. D'après McCawley on peut rendre compte de cette ambiguïté en distinguant, dans la représentation sémantique, deux types de lien entre le verbe et un de ses actants. On peut trouver des exemples où de tels types de lien plus étroit et plus libre sont distingués, à un certain degré, même dans la structure de surface. Si l'on confronte les exemples (6) et (7) avec les deux phrases suivantes

(8)   *John told me about the girl he kissed, that he didn't kiss her.*

(9)   *As for the girl he kissed, he admits that he kissed her.*

on voit que les phrases (8), (9) correspondent seulement au lien plus libre entre le verbe et l'actant donné, donc p.ex. (8) ne nous informe pas d'une contradiction énoncée par John, mais seulement du fait qu'il renie avoir embrassé la jeune fille.

Alors, avec des verbes de ce groupe sémantique, on trouve clairement deux actants "d'objet" – l'un correspond à ce "dont on parle", l'autre à "ce qu'on en dit". (Il y a ici, p.ex., le problème d'une coincidence référentielle entre le premier de ces deux actants et un des éléments de la phrase subordonnée, qui peut être comparé au rapport entre un substantif et un élément d'une phrase relative subordonnée à ce substantif; v., pour le tchèque, Konečná 1966). Si le sujet parlant, en reprenant un discours, doit distinguer de tels actants, l'analyse linguistique aussi doit rendre compte d'une telle distinction.

3.1 Pour pouvoir rendre compte de l'articulation en thème et propos, une description linguistique doit, d'après ce qui precède, respecter au moins les points suivants:

(i) l'articulation est décisive pour l'interprétation sémantique, qui devrait être distinguée de la valeur cognitive d'une phrase (v. l'alinéa 2);

(ii) l'articulation en thème et propos n'est pas identique à une répartition de l'information "déja connue" et "nouvelle" dans la phrase (v. 2.1 et 2.2);

(iii) l'articulation ne consiste pas en une dichotomie (thème et propos de la phrase), mais en une échelle du dynamisme communicatif de toutes les unités lexicales (ou même morphologiques) de la phrase (v. 1.1 et les travaux de Firbas et Svoboda);

(iv) c'est la structure sémantique de la phrase qui détermine la variante de base (non-marquée) de son articulation (v. 1.1);

(v) un lien entre l'articulation en thème et propos et entre l'ordre des mots peut être trouvé non seulement dans des langues à ordre "libre", mais aussi dans celles à ordre "fixe" (v. 1.2).

Il faut ajouter encore que, d'après Firbas et Daneš, la variante non-marquée de l'ordre des mots est, dans la plupart des cas, déterminée seulement par la structure sémantique de la phrase (et elle coïncide avec l'échelle du dynamisme communicatif)[2]; si la phrase est "integrée dans un contexte", cette échelle (et avec elle aussi la variante non-marquée de l'ordre des mots) peut avoir une autre forme (un autre ordre). En d'autres mots, l'ordre des mots non-marqué n'exige aucune présupposition disant qu'un objet soit considéré comme "déjà connu" (v. Kiefer, sous presse).

On peut proposer de rendre compte de l'articulation en interprétant l'ordre des symboles du niveau sémantique comme l'échelle du dynamisme communicatif.

Si l'on travaille avec une grammaire de dépendence, en donnant une règle pour chaque syntagme binaire (v. Sgall 1967)[3], l'ordre des éléments de ce syntagme dans la règle peut correspondre à la variante non-marquée de l'échelle, et dans le cas où le second élément est caractérisé comme déjà connu, leur ordre est changé. Par exemple, si le verbe russe *prijti* appartient à la classe V_1, et *nastupit'* à la classe V_2, on peut avoir des règles comme (N, V_1) et (V_2, N), avec une règle de la théorie générale, disant, que

(I) l'ordre des symboles dans la chaîne engendrée correspond à l'ordre des symboles dans la règle de grammaire, si aucune présupposition du type mentionné n'est présente (c.à.d., si la phrase n'est pas "integrée dans un contexte", selon la terminologie de Mathesius, Daneš, Firbas);

(II) si un des éléments du syntagme est caractérisé comme déjà connu, cet élément précède l'autre dans la chaîne obtenue après l'application d'une telle règle.[4]

Il faut alors distinguer deux types de thèmes, car V_2, p.ex., peut être un thème ("thématisé", *topicalized*) soit d'après (I), soit d'après (II). En outre,

il y a au moins un troisième type de thèmes (avec contraste, emphase, etc.,
v. surtout Firbas 1966, et la littérature donnée par lui); la description des
thèmes de ce dernier type doit respecter, entre autres, les exigences rappelées
par Kiefer (sous presse); pour le tchèque, v. aussi Benešová, sous presse.

L'appareil des composantes transductives de la description doit rendre
compte du rapport entre l'ordre "profond" et entre l'ordre des mots de la
surface, qui n'est pas toujours un rapport d'identité (p.ex. l'ordre profond
Objet–Verbe–Acteur peut entraîner, en anglais, soit la "passivisation", soit
un changement de l'ordre accompagné d'un changement de l'intonation de
la phrase).

3.2 Si c'est au niveau sémantique (ou tectogrammatique, de la structure
profonde), où l'articulation en thème et propos est décrite, il n'est pas possible
de donner sa description complète en prenant seulement la phrase comme
unité décrite. Car au niveau sémantique il faut tenir compte aussi de la
synonymie entre une phrase et une suite de phrases. La proposition (l'unité
du niveau sémantique) peut être représentée à d'autres niveaux soit par une
phrase, soit par une suite des phrases (qui est synonyme à une seule phrase;
mais v. Sgall 1967, p. 213, pour une classe d'exceptions).

Une classification systématique de telles suites de phrases, du point de vue
de leur articulation, est présentée pour la première fois par Daneš (1968). Il
considère cette suite comme une chaîne dont les éléments (c.à.d. les paires
individuelles d'un thème et un propos) sont liés entre eux par des rapports
différents (le thème d'un élément peut être identique, quant à sa référence,
au propos ou au thème de l'élément précédent, ou à une partie d'un complexe
thématique supérieur, etc.). Comme critère pour déterminer le thème de
chaque élément il emploie une question qui pourrait intervenir dans la suite
immédiatement avant l'élément examiné. Certainement, une telle classification est nécessaire pour l'investigation des liens entre l'articulation en thème
et propos et les types différents de déprédication, de "l'accent logique",
soulignement, etc., ou, en d'autres mots, entre tous les types des présuppositions grammaticales (non-lexicales).

La question se pose, si l'unité du niveau sémantique (la proposition) n'est
pas identique à la chaîne caractérisée par Daneš, et si le deuxième type de
thèmes, dont nous avons parlé (3.1), n'appartient pas seulement à un élément
de cette chaîne précédé déjà par un ou plusieurs autres éléments

Nous avons présenté seulement des hypothèses intuitives; mais il est clair,
que l'analyse de l'articulation en thème et propos (et d'autres phénomènes
liés aux présuppositions grammaticales) deviendra un des plus importants
domaines de la linguistique. Comme Garvin (1963) l'a remarqué, cette analyse
est de la plus grande importance pour les applications techniques de la

linguistique, pour lesquelles il sera nécessaire de décrire non seulement la syntaxe de la phrase, mais aussi "l'hypersyntaxe" du discours et la sémantique.

Charles University, Prague and C.E.T.A. Grenoble

BIBLIOGRAPHIE

Adamec, P. (1966), 'Porjadok slov v sovremennom russkom jazyke', Rozpravy ČSAV-ŘSP 76/15, Praha.

Benešová, E. (sous presse), 'Modal'nyje konstrukcii i porjadok slov v poroždajuščem opisanii češskogo j' (prép. pour le *Prague Bulletin of Mathematical Linguistics*).

Daneš, F. (1964a), 'A Three-Level Approach to Syntax', *Travaux linguistiques de Prague* 1, 225–40.

– (1964b), 'Téma ‖základ‖ východisko výpovědi', *Slovo a slovesnost* 25, 148s.

– (1967), 'Order of Sentence Elements and Sentence Intonation', *To Honor Roman Jakobson*, La Haye, pp. 499–512.

– (1968), 'Typy tematických posloupností v textu', *Slovo a slovesnost* 29, 125–41 (avec un résumé en anglais).

Dokulil, M. et Daneš, F. (1958), *K tzv. významové a mluvnické stavbě věty, O vědeckém poznání soudobých jazyků*, Prague, pp. 231–46.

Fillmore, C. J. (1968), 'The Case for Case', in *Universals in Linguistic Theory* (réd. par Bach et Harms), New York, pp. 1–88.

– (1969), 'Types of Lexical Information', dans le présent volume, pp. 109–137.

Firbas, J. (1961), 'On the Communicative Value of the Modern English Finite Verb', *Brno Studies in English* 3, 79–104.

– (1964a), 'On Defining the Theme in Functional Sentence Analysis', *Travaux linguistiques de Prague* 1, 267–80.

– (1964b), 'From Comparative Word-Order Studies', *Brno Studies in English* 4, 111–28.

– (1965), 'A Note on Transition Proper in Functional Sentence Analysis, *Philologica Pragensia* 3, 170–76.

– (1966), 'Non-Thematic Subject in Contemporary English', *Travaux linguistiques de Prague* 2, 239–256.

– (1968), 'On the Prosodic Features of the Modern English Finite Verb as Means of Functional Sentence Perspective', *Brno Studies in English* 7, 11–48.

Garvin, P. L. (1963), 'Fulcrum Techniques to Semantic Analysis', Final Report, Thompson Ramo Wooldridge Inc., Canoga Park, Calif.

Halliday, M. A. K. (1967), 'Notes on Transitivity and Theme in English', Part 2, *Journal of Linguistics* 8, No. 2.

– (1968), *ibid.*, Part 3, *Journal of Linguistics* 4, 179–215.

Isačenko, A. S. (1966), 'O grammatičeskom porjadke slov', *Voprosy jazykoznanija* No. 6, 27–34.

Jelínek, J. (1965), 'A Linguistic Aspect of Transformation Rules', *Acta Universitatis Carolinae – Slavica Pragensia* VII, 81–6.

– (1966), 'Construct Classes', *Prague Studies in Mathematical Linguistics* 1, 167–182.

Kiefer, F. (sous presse), 'On the Problem of Word Order' (prép. pour *Progress in Linguistics*, réd. par Bierwisch et Heidolph, La Haye).

Kiparsky, P. (1965), 'On Accent, Intonation and Anticipatory *es* in German Complement Constructions', Berlin – AFSG So 137 (multiplié).

Konečná, D. (1966), 'K otázce druhů objektu podle významu', *Acta Universitatis Carolinae – Slavica Pragensia* 8, 311–16.

240 PETR SGALL

Mathesius, V. (1929), 'Zur Satzperspektive im modernen Englisch', *Archiv für das Studium d. neueren Spr. u. Litter.* **155**, 202–10.
McCawley, J. D. (1967), 'Where Do Noun Phrases Come From' (multiplié), (prép. pour *Readings in English Transform. Grammar*, réd. par Jacobs et Rosenbaum).
Pala, K. (1966), 'O nekotorych problemach aktual'nogo členenija', *Prague Studies in Mathematical Linguistics* **1**, 81–92.
– (1967), 'Otnošenije meždu porjadkom slov i aktual'nym členenijem v češskom jazyke', *Prague Studies in Mathematical Linguistics* **2**, 51–64.
Palek, B. (1967), *Odkazování jako prostředek nadvětné syntaxe*, dissertation, Université Charles, Prague.
Robinson, Jane (1968), 'Dependency Structures and Transformational Rules' (2e section de W. J. Plath, *Specification and Utilization of a Transformational Grammar*, IBM, AF 19(628)-5127, No. 3, Yorktown Heights, N.Y.).
Savický, N. (sous presse), 'Smyslorazličitel'nyje funkcii porjadka slov i poroždajuščije modeli jazyka' (prép. pour *Prague Studies in Mathematical Linguistics* **3**).
Sgall, P. (1964), 'Zur Frage der Ebenen im Sprachsystem', *Travaux linguistiques de Prague* **1**, 95–106.
– (1967), 'Functional Sentence Perspective in a Generative Description', *Prague Studies in Mathematical Linguistics* **2**, 203–25.
– (1968), 'Porjadok slov i aktual'noje členenije predloženija v generativnom opisanii slavjanskich jazykov', *Čs. přednášky pro VI. mezin.sjezd slavistů*, Praha, pp. 61–5.
Staal, J. F. (1967), 'Some Semantic Relations between Sentoids', *Foundations of Language* **3**, 66–88.
Svoboda, A. (1968), 'The Hierarchy of Communicative Units and Fields as Illustrated by English Attributive Constructions', *Brno Studies in English* **7**, 49–101.
Uhlířová, L. (1966), 'Some Aspects of Word Order in Categorial and Transformationa Grammars', *Prague Studies in Mathematical Linguistics* **1**, 159–66.
Vachek, J. (1955), 'Some Thoughts on the So-Called Complex Condensation in Modern English', Sborník prací filosof. fakulty brněnské university A3, pp. 63–77.
Worth, D. S. (1964), 'Ob otobraženii linejnych otnošenij v poroždajuščich modeljach jazyka', *Voprosy jazykoznanija*, No. 5, 47–58.

RÉFÉRENCES

[1] Pour d'autres différences entre une spécification contextuelle (information déjà connue – information nouvelle) et entre une spécification du type caractérisé en 2.1, ou encore en 2.3, v. Daneš 1964b; Halliday 1967; il y a des cas, où une ou plusieurs parties du propos sont connues du contexte précédant.

[2] Il est vrai, qu'en anglais le parallélisme entre le dynamisme communicatif et l'ordre des mots n'est pas si prononcé comme dans des langues slaves (notamment en tchèque); il y a ici d'autres moyens de surface, exprimant la thématisation (p.ex. les articles); v. Firbas 1966.

[3] Il est possible de généraliser ce procédé aussi pour des groupes à un plus grand nombre d'éléments. Pour obtenir une description adéquate d'une langue naturelle, il faut combiner la grammaire de dépendence avec d'autres composantes (pour une possibilité de sa combinaison avec la composante transformationnelle, v. Robinson 1968).

[4] Il faut chercher une forme explicite pour la description de telles caractéristiques des éléments connus du contexte précédant ou de la situation; le fonctionnement de ces caractéristiques est contrôlé, lui aussi, par la compétence linguistique du sujet parlant; v. Palek 1967.

INDEX OF NAMES

FOUNDATIONS OF LANGUAGE
SUPPLEMENTARY SERIES

Edited by Morris Halle, Peter Hartmann,
K. Kunjunni Raja, Benson Mates, J. F. Staal,
Pieter A. Verburg, and John W. M. Verhaar

Sole Distributors in the U.S.A. and Canada:
HUMANITIES PRESS / NEW YORK